International Stability:
military, economic and
political dimensions

Edited by

DALE J. HEKHUIS
Tempo, General Electric Company

CHARLES G. McCLINTOCK
Department of Psychology, University of California, Santa Barbara

ARTHUR L. BURNS
Department of Political Science, Australian National University

International Stability: military, economic and political dimensions

JOHN WILEY & SONS, INC., NEW YORK · LONDON · SYDNEY

To the memory of John F. Youngblood

Contributors

Ernst B. Haas
Department of Political Science, University of California, Berkeley
Nina Heathcote
Department of Political Science, Australian National University
Thomas W. Milburn
Project Michelson, Naval Ordnance Test Station, China Lake, California
Robert E. Osgood
Center for the Study of American Foreign and Military Policy, University of California
Lucian W. Pye
Center for International Studies, Massachusetts Institute of Technology
Paul N. Rosenstein-Rodan
Center for International Studies, Massachusetts Institute of Technology
Thomas C. Schelling
Center for International Affairs, Harvard University
Robert C. Tucker
Department of Government, Indiana University
The late John F. Youngblood
Physicist, Tempo, General Electric Company

Preface

This book is an outgrowth of a study project undertaken by the Technical Military Planning Operation (Tempo) of the General Electric Company for the purpose of exploring the military, economic, and political nature of the future international environment and identifying possible alternative strategies for coping with various environmental contingencies.

Our belief that the future international system would probably continue to be influenced by the vagaries of thermonuclear deterrence and the social revolutions in newly emerging countries led us to concern ourselves with the "stability" of the system. We began with the difficult problem of defining stability, proceeded to an analysis of threats to stability and a study of the means for alleviating instability.

In order to carry out this analysis systematically a series of papers was commissioned. Seven of these are included in this volume along with five previously published papers by Arthur L. Burns and Nina Heathcote, Ernst B. Haas, Thomas W. Milburn, Robert E. Osgood, and Thomas C. Schelling. For the use of previously published material we are grateful to the following: John A. Praeger, Inc.; the *Journal of Conflict*

Resolution; the Melbourne University Australian Labor Party Club; *American Political Science Review; World Politics;* and *International Organization.* We are also grateful to Professor Lucian Pye and *Orbis* for permission to publish certain material in Chapter 4.

Since a book of this type contains an element of audacity, it is especially important to acknowledge the hazards inherent in projections and prescriptions. There are a variety of logics for projecting and prescribing, but decision-making is seldom based wholly on rational considerations. As Harold Nicolson has stated in the *Congress of Vienna:*

Nobody who has watched "policy" expressing itself in day-to-day action can realize how seldom is the course of events determined by deliberately planned purpose, or how often what in retrospect appears to have been a fully conscious intention was at the time governed and directed by the most potent of all factors—"the chain of circumstance." Few indeed are the occasions on which any statesman sees his objective clearly before him and marches towards it with undeviating strides; numerous indeed are the occasions when a decision or event which at the time seemed wholly unimportant leads but fortuitously to another decision which is no less incidental, until, link by link, the chain of circumstance is forged.

Nevertheless, imaginative assessments of the future may be of significance for the policy formulator, the decision maker, and the student of international affairs, if only by enlarging the domain of reasoned alternatives for viewing and coping with the international environment.

This book itself would not have been written without the unflagging support of Richard C. Raymond and the patient counsel of the late John F. Youngblood. We have greatly benefited from Richard Snyder's insightful criticisms of Chapter 1, although the views expressed in this and the remaining chapters are solely those of the individual authors. We are also heavily indebted to our copy editor, Francis Wilson, for his cogent substantive and stylistic improvements. Finally, we would like to express our appreciation to Mrs. Anelle Harris and Mrs. Lois Reisinger for their careful typing of the manuscript, and to Mrs. Dolores McCulloch and Mrs. Maryse McGibney for the preparation of the index.

D. J. H.
C. G. M.
A. L. B.

Contents

PART I

INTRODUCTION

Chapter I

A Pragmatic Approach
to International Stability

CHARLES G. McCLINTOCK, DALE J. HEKHUIS,

ARTHUR L. BURNS, ROBERT C. TUCKER

International relations over the last decade have been conducted in the uneasy atmosphere of a delicate thermonuclear balance of terror between major powers and social revolutions in the underdeveloped areas of the world. Realism can only compel the observation that there is a strong likelihood that these two environmental states will continue to persist over the foreseeable future. The principal purpose of this book is to describe and evaluate the characteristics of these states, to delineate their possible effects on the stability of international relations, and to discuss courses of action which might have a stabilizing effect on the international environment.

The present chapter undertakes to describe initially some of the major threats to international stability anticipated from 1970 to 1975. It then sets forth a pragmatic definition of stability and attempts to outline a possible strategy toward international order. Finally it discusses some specific measures for coping with particular threats to international order.

3

SOME ANTICIPATED THREATS TO INTERNATIONAL STABILITY

The international environment during the next decade will be subject to a number of destabilizing forces. These anticipated threats to international stability, as brought out in subsequent chapters, include the following:

Rapidly Growing Populations

The pressures of population growth may contribute directly or indirectly to internal political instability. It is anticipated that the total number of dependent children (those under 15) in the non-Communist underdeveloped areas of the world by 1975 will be comparable to the total population of the developed countries of the Free World. This continuing increase in the number of dependent children in the underdeveloped areas greatly limits the opportunity for economic growth and economic contributions to stability. This seems particularly likely to be the case in countries where economic advancement is achieved only to be canceled out by the increased consumer demands of a rapidly expanding population.

Furthermore, it has been noted that revolution can occur as a result of the psychological fears experienced when people perceive that recent gains obtained at a cost of great labor and sacrifice may be lost.[1] Since the peoples of many underdeveloped areas are for the first time experiencing rising economic expectations, and since there is a strong likelihood that rapid increases in population will contribute periodically to the frustration of these expectancies, there are increased possibilities for severe internal political upheavals.

The strains on international stability that derive from population growth also have direct implications for the political, economic and military relationships between nations. One need only recall the rationale underlying Japanese, German, and Italian expansionist policies during World War II to illustrate the potential force of population pressures. In many instances, as Warren Thomson has noted,[2] the pressures of population derive not from an absolute growth in population or from absolute poverty but from the "felt" lacks, the "felt"

---

[1] J. C. Davies, "Toward a Theory of Revolution," *American Sociological Review*, Vol. 27, No. 1, February 1962, pp. 5–19.
[2] W. S. Thomson, *Plenty of People*, Ronald Press, New York, 1948.

pressures on resources, and the "felt" discriminations in access to the resources of the world.

Emergence of New Nation States

Considerable strain will be exerted on the maintenance of the international system as a consequence of the dramatic increase in the number of new nation-states and the ineffectual sovereignties of many of these states. These new nations are faced with the almost insurmountable problem of welding heterogeneous and rapidly expanding populations into a body politic and developing a sufficient level of economic well-being to increase the likelihood of social and political stability through time.

An attempt to isolate and analyze the various ways in which these new nation-states produce tensions, that is, threaten the stability of the international system, is made in Chapter 3. As noted in this chapter, one of the major sources of instability is the demise of the classical nation-state system and, consequently, the loss of more traditional methods of decision-making within the international system.

The breakdown of the traditional international system and the lack of an ordered set of relationships to replace it intensify the tensions and ambiguities which derive from relationships among underdeveloped countries, between these countries and the developed nations, and between the developed nations themselves relative to the exercise of influence within underdeveloped nations.

New tensions among underdeveloped areas will arise from many causes, including inequalities in economic growth and attempts to achieve new boundaries and divisions. Tensions between the developed nations and the underdeveloped countries will be rendered especially sensitive by feelings of dependency and inferiority on the part of underdeveloped areas. And the utilization of newly emerging nations as pawns in the Cold War will generate additional instabilities.

Development of New Weapons

One of the most serious threats to the stability of an international order based on mutual deterrence is the qualitative arms race. As A. Burns notes in Chapter 9, a qualitative arms race is initiated and sustained by rapid technological innovation. Innovation may produce marked increases in tension and instability because "breakthroughs" in weapon technology may occur rapidly, without warning, thus causing rapid shifts or changes in the distribution of power. For instance, the development (by a single nation or coalition of nations) of an effective missile defense, a foolproof antisubmarine device, or a cheap and relatively invulnerable attack vehicle could markedly shift the balance of power—a process which leads inevitably to an increase in tension and possibly to a marked destabilization of the international system.

The coincidence of new weapons with both enormous lethality and supersonic speed imposes difficult decision-making requirements on both military and political leaders. Decisions must be made with great rapidity, and simultaneously with maximum validity. Accidental firings, impulsive and irrational actions, represent dire threats to the survival of oneself and one's adversary. Simultaneously, unwillingness to act in the face of overt strategic attack, or at least an appearance of reticence to act, violates the principal assumption on which a military strategy of deterrence is based, that is, credibility of response.

The problem is further intensified, as both Burns and Schelling point out in Chapters 9 and 10, by the fact that given the technological characteristics of current and future weapons, there is a considerable military advantage in striking first. Consequently a nation may feel compelled on the basis of minimal information to attack first in "self-defense." Thus the requirements for rapid decisions and the advantages of a first-strike operate to keep both sides poised for immediate action. And as Schelling notes, in the light of current weapons technology, the things that each side does to make its own strategic force more secure—to make it more alert, less vulnerable to surprise, better able to strike quickly if that is the way the decision goes—are likely to be the kinds of actions that can be interpreted as preparations for attack. They are likely to be actions that increase the danger of "false alarm" on both sides and that could lead to a succession of decisions aggravating each side's perception of the need to pre-empt.

In other words, the preparatory actions in which nations engage because of the constraints of decision-making time, and the advantages of a defensive first strike, may, by a process of mutual feedback and reciprocal actions, increase the level of tension and the likelihood that any given threat, real or imaginary, can touch off a nuclear war. The recognition of this problem is reflected in the recent installation of a "hot line" communication link between Washington and the Kremlin.

Nuclear Weapons Diffusion

If explicit arms control agreements beyond the current ban on nuclear testing are not achieved by 1975, it can be anticipated that the United States, the U.S.S.R., Britain, France, perhaps some European alliance or community (including either or both France and Britain), and Communist China will possess what Burns in a subsequent chapter calls "independent nuclear deterrent" capability, that is, sufficient H-bombs or other high-yield weapons to deter directly an attack from a major power. In addition, the Benelux nations, one or two Scandanavian countries, Italy, Japan, Israel, some of the British Dominions and Latin American countries, and possibly some Middle Eastern and Southeastern nations, may have nuclear weapons that provide them with "triggering" or "minimum atomic" deterrence. "Triggering deterrence" is the capacity of a small nation to place a large nation in a position of vulnerability relative to another major power, whereas a "minimum atomic deterrent" is the capacity of one nation to deter a large or small power from attacking because it has the capability to produce nuclear damage at a level that exceeds the rewards a potential aggressor would obtain through conquest.

Increased instability is likely to occur if smaller and/or more politically unstable or less responsible nations obtain the capability for strategic or tactical use of nuclear weapons. The potential danger will be particularly acute if these smaller nations are in a position to "trigger" the larger atomic powers into overt military conflict—a situation that is most likely to obtain, as noted previously, if the technology of armaments makes a first-strike nuclear attack militarily advantageous. In addition, the widespread possession of tactical nuclear weapons would increase the likelihood of their use in limited wars and would increase the likelihood of escalation from limited nuclear wars to all-out nuclear wars. The danger of the latter is particularly acute in face of the political, economic, and social instabilities attending the development of the underdeveloped nations of the world.

Tension Level

The patterns of response by national leaders and other groups within a society also affect the stability or resilience of the international system. To the extent that decision-makers are subject to irrational behaviors, the system becomes less resilient in the face of both minor and major modifications. The likelihood of irrational behavior is increased under conditions of tension, that is, when decision-makers interpret real or imagined changes in the international system to represent major threats to their relative positions of influence. To a large extent the threat-tension process is cumulative. Threat or fear of loss of influence gives rise to tension, tension produces misinterpretations or exaggerations of environmental events, which in turn generate greater fear and additional tension. The end result of this reciprocal feedback process is to increase rapidly the potential irrationality of the behavior of the decision-makers in the system.

Although tension and international instability tend to be interrelated, tension has several distinguishing characteristics. First, although a system may seem to be stable when judged by some analytic criterion such as the actual distribution of power, the potential for a misinterpretation of the state-of-affairs is markedly increased if the actors are under high tension. Secondly, the level of tension may fluctuate much more rapidly and unpredictably than a rational appraisal of the distribution or potential redistribution of influence would warrant.

The potential irrationality and unpredictability of behavior resulting from rapid changes in tension level have been noted by Riggs, who uses the term "spasticity" to describe the process:

> Spasticity implies not so much a steady tension level between intense and relaxed as it does unpredictable shifts between relatively high and low tension, moments of extreme tension succeeding extreme relaxation. When units in a power structure are spastic, it becomes difficult to predict change in power position. Hence, spastic tension levels are marked by violent and apparently irrational outbursts of violence, often succeeded by apathy and unconcern.[3]

"Perspective-Dissolving" Surprise

"Perspective-dissolving" surprise—the evaporation of weapon planners' expectations in the face of an unexpected revolutionary scientific or technological development—can also lead to instability. Surprise of this variety would arise from such developments as an effective anti-missile defense or a large-scale weather control system. This would represent surprise at the technological level only, since presumably no new basic principle of science would be involved; the as-yet-unknown innovations they employed would comprise new combinations of existing knowledge. Scientific surprise could involve a discovery comparable in significance and novelty to the upset of the principle of parity and having, moreover, some immediate application to military technology. The achievement of this kind of discovery, together with its technological application, could make obsolete most current military strategies and policies. The mere possibility that such discoveries *might* be made forces one to consider many contingencies in planning and to realize that one's perspectives regarding the future are simply imagina-

---

[3] Fred W. Riggs, "International Relations as a Prismatic System," *World Politics*, Vol. XIV, October 1961, p. 156.

tive projections of what is to come, wholly extrapolated from the past and present, and inevitably lacking many determinative elements. It is the presence of such future uncertainties that not only places stress on the decision-maker in the international environment but also makes it difficult for the political analyst to make predictions concerning the future.[4]

One may ask whether technological and scientific perspective-dissolving surprises are necessarily destabilizing. So far as an *a priori* answer to this question is possible, it seems to be, "Not necessarily." As leading powers become accustomed to the prospect of surprise innovations in weapon-systems, they may make less rigid plans, for instance, committing themselves to a variety of weapon systems, and they may also come to tacit understandings about procedures for domestically and internationally coping with the destabilizing effects of such innovations. On the other hand, they may be seized with a kind of tension-induced paralysis and make irrational responses when faced by an unanticipated innovation by their opponents. Also, at the purely technological level, some innovations, for example, invulnerable deterrent systems, may tend to increase stability whereas others, such, as, improved surveillance and targeting, may be destabilizing. Sometimes an innovation, for example, "perfect defense" against missiles, may be destabilizing if made unilaterally but stabilizing if made multilaterally.

PRAGMATIC DEFINITION OF STABILITY

In the preceding section a number of threats that may operate to contribute to international instability over the next decade were outlined. In the present section an effort will be made to define and illustrate more explicitly the fundamental concept of *international stability*.

---

[4] The problem of unforeseeable surprise, that is, "real uncertainty," proves to be a very difficult one for those who attempt to construct formal mathematical models of the international system in order to make predictions concerning future occurrences. Many epoch-making events (scientific and technological discoveries are a notable example, but there are other complex happenings, such as the emergence of new nation-states) are unforeseeable, and the mere possibility of these events sets a question mark against any prospective analysis. The area of real uncertainty is reducible by "educated guessing" and speculation. However, one cannot make precise estimates of the mathematical probability of an event which is unnamed and unforeseen. But since it seems inevitable that something unforeseeable will occur, certain analysts regard the relative prevalence or likelihood of unforeseeable events as indices of instability. See Robert E. Tucker, *Stability and the Nth Country Problem*, Study Memorandum No. 5, Institute for Defense Analyses, Washington, Nov. 8, 1961.

By "international stability" one does not imply absence of change. Nations in themselves and the relations between them are bound to change. Indeed changes are inevitable in the political, economic, military, and social relations between the groupings in the international environment, that is, systemic changes. Men may be gathered into new kinds of major groupings, as unlike nations as nations are unlike nomadic tribes or fiefs of the feudal system; or, while the international system remains a system in which the major groupings are nations, the interrelations between these nations may change radically in kind. These and many other types of change are destabilizing events, but if the national or international systems affected by them are stable, if they have resilience, they will adapt to the changes without major upset. Thus, stability in the present sense refers to the propensity of a system to preserve its constituent members against destruction or elimination, not merely by resisting or precluding change, but by adjusting to it through rearrangement.

A variety of possible rearrangements exists. The potential for alliance adjustments between groupings provides one form of rearrangement that can increase the stability or adaptability of the international system. Limiting the extent and duration of war provides a second means for increasing the adaptability of the system by setting the boundaries or permissible level of destruction of constituent members. Ensuring that there are a large number of behavioral alternatives that are unused within the system increases its stability.[5] In the present international system such alternatives would include, for example, the amalgamations of single-nation defense units into bloc agglomerations, not merely to meet a direct threat from an aggressor but to produce a stable deterrent system within a given bloc. A second example would be the establishment of an economic community between nations, not merely to compete with an adversary but to facilitate a stable domestic economic and political environment.

Stability as a Goal

It should be noted that there is no agreement that international stability is an absolute good. Although war is cited typically as an example of the highest and most undesirable form of instability, the American Revolutionary War is held almost universally to have been good and glorious. By way of contrast, the peaceful Federation of the

---

[5] See R. M. Cyert and James G. March, "Organizational Factors in the Theory of Oligopoly," *The Quarterly Journal of Economics*, Vol. LXX, February 1956.

Australian colonies into the Commonwealth of Australia in 1901 was a stable evolution of an empire, and yet this is not held, even by the Australians, to be as "glorious" as the beginning of the United States.

The "white" British Empire of the nineteenth century was not in itself a stable subsystem, and many Britons of upper class, like Macauley, neither expected nor wished that it should be stable. Many people at the apogee of the balance-of-power system hoped that it would be replaced by a better one. Thus, historically, universal stability was often not desired as an enduring characteristic of the international system.

Today there is gross dissatisfaction among many people on both sides of the Iron Curtain with the presently stabilized "loose bipolar nuclear system." However, any desire to stimulate radical modifications in the system is tempered by two important considerations: First, there is a genuine fear of the spread of weapons, that is, the development of a nuclear system of many powers. Second, there is a concern that changes within the international system in a nuclear era may be accompanied by, or result in, war—that is, whether or not the system itself is objectively stable, any systemic change would generate high levels of tension that might produce symptoms of gross and general instability. However, systemic changes may occur without war. For instance, by integration in Europe and elsewhere, the bipolar system may develop without upset into a stable and relatively long-lived system of four or five great nuclear blocs, which may be no more apt to produce thermonuclear war than is the present system. Nor need it entail more subjugation of peoples.

Indices of Stability

The two variables, *the outbreak of highly destructive wars and the subjugation of a people who were previously free,* may serve as pragmatic indices of instability. That is, one can evaluate the stability of any international system in terms of the likelihood that it will result in either or both these extreme instances of loss of national integrity. ("Likelihood" does not here mean "probability" in any mathematical sense, but rather "evident propensity" to produce either or both these extreme instances of loss of national integrity.[6]) Even these two prag-

---

[6] Long before the calculus of probability or tests of statistical significance were invented, people spoke of the likelihood or probability of events. One could maintain that wars were more likely between neighboring than between distant countries.

matic indices may prove ambiguous. The second, subjugation of a free people, places within the same category conquest by an external foe and subversion by internal revolution. Moreover, it does not include several kinds of challenges to national order or sovereignty that might also be considered destabilizing: the conquest of a despotic power by some other, free or despotic; the overthrow of a despotic government

---

One could judge that the birth of twins was more likely than the birth of triplets but less likely than single births. When in the latter case it was discovered that exact cardinal numbers (the probability that a human conception would produce twins, or triplets) could replace the imprecise and relative expressions, e.g., "more likely" and "less probable," some social scentists were encouraged to hope that vague and relative judgments about the likelihood of wars and of other political, economic, and social outcomes might be similarly replaceable by statistical predictions, i.e., probability statements. (See Lewis F. Richardson, *Statistics of Deadly Quarrels*, London 1960.) This hope now seems premature, having been grounded upon several faulty assumptions. Models concerned with the outcomes of action in the social sciences do not characteristically provide predictions stated in terms of a probability distribution. Statistical generalizations about such events as outbreaks of war are often arbitrary, since many different processes are classified together as wars, and since the moment of outbreak of war can often be fixed only arbitrarily. Most importantly, a common-sense judgment about the relative probability of war is not based upon judgments concerning the frequency of the event. When we maintain that some crisis has increased the likelihood of war, we usually mean that some nations, which before had had no reason to consider going to war, now have some such reason; or that the government of some nation or nations that previously had a reason, now has more reason.

At this point, defenders of the relevance of mathematical probability-judgments can point to the fact that any consistent estimate of the likelihood of an event based upon persons' reasons for following one policy or another, can be expressed in accord with certain logical requirements equivalent to the axioms of the Calculus of Probability (See A. L. Burns, "The International Consequences of Expecting Surprise," *World Politics*, Vol. X, July 1958, pp. 517–520.) This kind of probability-expression, "subjective probability," they would argue, employs cardinal numbers and is in no significant feature different from what is usually called "objective probability."

However, the designation, "subjective probability," seems apposite. Though the grounds of such judgments can be thoroughly objective, e.g., a national leader either does or does not give a certain definite weight, in deliberating about a particular act of policy, to some consideration that for him tells in its favor, those grounds have to be given an evaluation by the likelihood estimator. And though evidence may well be available to the likelihood estimator about the character of the national leader, and about the plausibility of the consideration, this form of evidence is not of the kind that can be quantified. For example, if one judges that nuclear war anywhere in the world in 1964 is rather less than likely ("a bit less than 50%"), one is not implying that somehow there exist fifty-odd chances labeled "No war in 1964," and forty-odd labeled "War in 1964." Clearly such a judgment can be neither rigorously refuted nor validated, though it can be supported or undermined by argument and by the adducing of evidence.

by revolutionaries, whether libertarian or dictatorial; and the fission of a state by secession, or the fusion of two or more states by customs-union, or federation.

Such an arbitrary narrowness in the second of our pragmatic indices of stability may also suggest the effects of ideological bias. There is the danger that, like "progressive" in Soviet vocabulary, the term "stabilizing" will work merely as a euphemism for "favorable to Western interests." The pseudopragmatic sleight of hand suggests that what is favorable to Western interests is favorable to the international system as a whole.

Our two pragmatic indices produce another ambiguity that could be avoided if one could construct a rigorously designed theoretical model of stability. For instance, a free people may be subjugated while (or, in order that) a highly destructive war is avoided. In a formal model, both conquest and wartime destruction could be considered as degrees of damage to agents comprised in the system, and therefore could be discounted against each other. Furthermore, a formal model could provide meaningful evaluations of the likelihood of occurrence of such events. But when indices are defined pragmatically, "probabilities" or "likelihoods" become far too impalpable for practical use,[7] so that one cannot always read the indicator under even a single index, much less under two indices. Consideration of the 1962 Cuban crisis illustrates the point.

Khrushchev installed strategic missiles in Cuba, though they could only be vulnerable and provocative first-strike forces, presumably as a means of controlling United States political behavior and of offsetting American nuclear predominance as evidenced by the counterforce strategy announced by Secretary of Defense MacNamara in June 1962. In contrast to the alternative of building up invulnerable retaliatory forces within the Soviet Union, the deployment in Cuba of vulnerable strategic missiles could in no way reduce the likelihood of a United States counterforce strike against the Soviet Union, but could only increase the likelihood of American attack, probably conventional but possibly nuclear, against the provocative installations in Cuba. If such an attack were initiated, it would enhance the possibility of a conflict's escalating to unlimited nuclear war. Therefore, from a "likelihood of war" index,

---

[7] As has been noted in the preceding footnote, it is difficult to conceive of a theoretical model that would yield valid predictions relating to future international stability because of a formidable number of theoretical problems including the identification and quantification of probability concepts, real uncertainty, and human irrationality. In lieu of such a formal model, this book takes a "pragmatic" approach to the problem of stability.

one can clearly arrive at the conclusion that Khrushchev's action would be and was destabilizing.

No such clear reading would have been available for Kennedy's action in imposing a quarantine on certain strategic shipping to Cuba, at least at the time he initiated it. Its longer-run consequence—the withdrawal of Soviet missiles—seems to have been "stabilizing" in every way except so far as it has called the attention of those NATO allies, not already aware of the fact, to the possibility of their being devastated in a Russian-American nuclear war that had escalated from somewhere beyond Europe. But at the beginning, this stabilized outcome was only one of many possibilities, some of them pointing to a war that might escalate. The quarantine and the declared policy of searching Russian ships could have provoked Soviet resistance and some kind of direct American-Russian hostilities. Other alternatives such as an immediate preventive attack upon the Cuban installations, followed by an invasion and occupation, would have been a "destabilization" under any index except that of United States' national interest. But to have neither attacked nor to have imposed a quarantine upon Cuba, and simply to have allowed the continuing installation of the missiles, would have altered both in degree and in nature, the balance of strategic forces between the United States and the Soviet Union in a way that could only have made unlimited nuclear war more likely.

In short, none of the responses open to President Kennedy after having received confirmation of the Soviet missile installations, including the response he made, could have been determined as "the most stabilizing" by any reading which either of our two pragmatic indices could provide. Even though a statesman has a clear vision of the international order he wants established, and even though he can reliably forecast the short-term consequences of various courses open to him in each particular situation, he is still unlikely to possess the means for constructing a strategic guide, even a pragmatic one, that will indicate particular courses to be adopted. Thus, when in the following chapters various strategies of international order, and policies for coping with threats to stability are proposed, they reflect not a strategy of particular actions, but of broad policies within several areas, political, economic, and military. Similarly, the analyses of sources of instability, which form the greater part of this book are included to indicate the effects of selected political, economic, and military factors upon the stability of the international system.

Allowing for the ambiguities discussed above, international stability will be defined as a condition that exists when an actor or a system of actors, that is, a nation, a community, or some other political unit, in its international aspect, behaves peaceably when confronted with external and/or internal changes that are apt to upset it; insofar as it survives these changes; and insofar as, throughout all these processes, its people or peoples unwillingly become no more subject to others than they were before.

TOWARD A STRATEGY FOR INTERNATIONAL STABILITY[8]

Given the pragmatic definition of stability outlined in the previous section, one can ask what strategy might be followed to decrease the likelihood of general war or the subjugation of peoples previously free? In attempting to devise such a strategy a basic dilemma of the nuclear age becomes evident. Namely, national security has ceased to be attainable by the traditional means of national military strength and a diplomacy of defensive alliances while national security through international order remains unrealized and seemingly quite out of reach. A new strategy to the whole concept of international stability or order may represent one possible way out of this dilemma. If international order remains unrealized and out of reach, may this not derive from thinking that is habitually predicated upon an all-or-nothing concept of international stability? If so, might it not be advisable to scale down the meaning of the idea, to work out a more limited and modest concept of order or stability stated in terms of "more or less," and realizable in one degree or another within the foreseeable future?

All-or-Nothing Versus the Limited Approach

The all-or-nothing approach toward establishing new norms of international behavior is exemplified by equating order with the formation of an integrated, international political community. In this case stability is achieved through the transition from a pluralistic world of sovereign nation-states to a universal political community or world-state.

Both the United States and the Soviet long-term approaches to the problem of world order or stability are of the all-or-nothing variety. Both assume the desirability of international order and both assert international order as a policy goal. Each equates international stability with the establishment of a world community of nations and each infers from this that international order implies the universalization of its

---

[8] This section draws on an unpublished paper by Robert C. Tucker entitled "Toward a Strategy of World Order."

own form of society, that is, either an "open society" or a "Communist society." Obviously, then, to achieve international order, each side strives for the universalization of its own form of society and/or for the replacement of the alien society.

The question arises, however, of whether this very competition may not be a self-defeating means to the end of international order. For such an effort by each side to achieve its own form of universalization may increase the chances of catastrophic violence and destruction instead of creating order in the world.

In order to preclude this possibility, a more limited approach to international order deserves serious consideration. A limited approach would be one that assumes the possibility of making the international system more orderly or stable on a piece-meal basis, without universalizing any one form of society. This approach would depart from the partisan advocacy of individual societies that has characterized both Soviet and American thinking. For example, speeches by the Soviet leadership attribute the high violence potential in the international system to malevolent, ruthless, and irresponsible tendencies of "international imperialism," and maintain that if war should occur, it will be our fault and not theirs. American thinking tends to run along similar lines with roles reversed. This suggests, then, that the international violence potential is partially related to the international political process as determined by the roles that the two great powers are playing in it.

Secondly, the limited approach would concentrate on the specific action patterns of nations. In fact, it would assume a critically important correlation between the international violence potential and the action patterns of individual states, so that the world could conceivably become inherently more stable through a variety of tension-reducing actions by one or more nations even in the absence of general disarmament. If valid, this assumption has certain attractions, for action patterns, unlike broad ideologies, are more subject to change through human volition.

Some suggestions with this observation in mind have been made recently by Charles Osgood.[9] As a possible means for alleviating conflict between Russia and the United States, Osgood suggests that a policy of graduated unilateral disengagement be considered. This policy advocates that the United States take increasingly significant unilateral steps, e.g., reductions in defense expenditure and withdrawal of forces from limited areas, designed to reduce international tensions. These

---

[9] Charles Osgood, "Suggestions for Winning the Real War with Communism," *Journal of Conflict Resolution*, December 1959, p. 324.

specific actions, being perhaps disadvantageous in the military sense, but not cripplingly so in a nuclear age, should be publicly announced and observed, and should include invitations for Russian reciprocation. The steps taken would be graduated in terms of the magnitude of the action initiated and according to the reactions of the enemy.

Further, in analyzing alternative approaches for implementing a deterrent strategy, T. Milburn (see Chapter 8) has suggested that actions that convey a continuous threat of punishment (negative deterrence) as a means for influencing behavioral change, that is, changing the action patterns of other individual states, leave much to be desired, particularly since they tend to increase anxiety and hostility. He notes that for psychological reasons an imaginative employment of both reward (positive deterrence) as well as threat of punishment (negative deterrence) would be a more effective means for one nation to produce behavioral change in other nations.

Competitive Co-existence and International Stability

As pointed out above, the United States and the Soviet Union are committed to the goal of an integrated world political community and each views the achievement of this goal as a universalization of its particular form of society. Moreover, in recent years, both powers have voiced the desirability of conducting their international rivalry in the non-military sphere. In the case of the United States, this has involved no departure from an established policy position. In the case of the Soviet Union, however, it has involved a break with the classical Marxist-Leninist concept that was maintained by Stalin of the inevitability of war with the capitalist world and appears still to be loyally subscribed to by the Chinese Communists.

In this struggle for international predominance by non-military means, competitive co-existence, one side seeks to foster the spread of the Soviet-type system and the other the spread of the open society wherever possible. In practice, of course, both recognize certain more limited aims as worthy of serious pursuit. Thus, the Soviet Union supports the forces of anti-Western nationalism in various non-Communist countries, regarding these as likely forerunners of future Soviet-type regimes, and the United States supports the forces of anti-Communism in many non-democratic nations. Viewed in the broadest terms, therefore, the competitive struggle is one in which the Soviet Union strives to promote the spread of anti-Western and pro-Communist regimes, and the United States strives to promote the spread of anti-Communist and pro-Western regimes. Each side views the desired type of regime as a way-station on the road toward development of the ideal type of world society.

The theory and practice of competitive co-existence has emerged in the context of an international situation that is characterized by (1) a rather delicate and uneasy balance of power between the two great power blocs and (2) a very great internal instability in many of the smaller countries—the so-called uncommitted countries—that do not belong to either of these blocs. Both of these characteristics of the international environment, which are assumed for the moment, and which are dealt with extensively in subsequent chapters, determine the nature of the struggle for competitive co-existence. Similarly, the struggle is affected by the fact that political change in any given area of the world tends to affect not simply the particular country in which it occurs but also other countries within its geopolitical area, for the international system is in reality a congeries of international subsystems (that is, the Middle Eastern, the Southeast Asian, the Latin American, and the European subsystems, etc.). Thus the Iraqi revolution in 1958 had consequences that radiated throughout the Soviet bloc, and the rise of the Castro regime in Cuba affects the entire Latin American political picture.

The essential point of a critique of the concept of competitive co-existence from the standpoint of international order may be formulated briefly. Precisely because there is an uneasy balance of world power between the two great power blocs (a balance inevitably threatened by changes in regime in one direction or another), the game of competitive co-existence tends to remain peaceful only so long as neither side is conspicuously or irretrievably losing. In other words, the game shows a very dangerous tendency to cease to be peaceful (1) whenever a change of regime that is seriously adverse to one side or the other occurs or threatens to occur within any given country, and (2) whenever circumstances permit the application of force to prevent or reverse this adverse change.

With respect to the first of these points, it must be stressed that what makes a change-of-regime situation seriously adverse to one side or another is oftentimes the threat of a "chain effect." Thus, the change of regime in Hungary in October 1956, when Nagy came to power, involved not only the probable departure of Hungary from the Soviet bloc but a possible or probable chain effect threatening to upset the whole East European status quo. Again, the Iraqi revolution in 1958 momentarily threatened, or seemed to threaten, the whole structure of political power in the Middle East. It was probably the fear of such a chain effect that impelled the United States to move into Lebanon with military force for purposes of stabilization of the Middle Eastern situation in the aftermath of the Iraqi development. The Hungarian intervention involved the bloody and brutal suppression of a popular revolution, whereas the Lebanese intervention was mild and bloodless. Yet both illustrate the reasoning process just outlined regarding the dynamics of the potential collapse of competitive co-existence into armed violence. A great many situations that have arisen in the international politics of recent years could profitably be analyzed from this standpoint.

Finally there is an unfortunate tendency in the thinking on both sides to compartmentalize, to separate the military aspects of the world situation from the non-military struggle. Indeed the foregoing analysis suggests that the whole concept of a non-military struggle is an unreal abstraction. As R. Osgood points out in Chapter 5, there is no realistic way of isolating the military from the non-military factors. In this connection he argues that neither should we expect the wisest choice of military deterrents to eliminate warfare from international relations nor should we expect to reverse the historic relationship between arms and politics, in which a stable political environment is a condition for, and not the result of, a stable military environment. Therefore, if the game of competitive co-existence tends intermittently toward international armed violence this would appear to be attributable, at least in part, to the non-military action patterns of the great powers in their relations with the smaller countries.

This analysis suggests at least a fruitful direction for further thought on the requirements of a possible strategy of international stability. One must acknowledge that there is no apparent way in which the international violence potential can be reduced to zero or anything closely approximating it within the foreseeable future. It must also be recognized that there is no way to freeze the internal political status quo in a large number of internally unstable countries. There is room, however, for a strategy of international order that would seek to decrease rather than increase the violence potential resulting from the competition for uncommitted nations. For insofar as the two great powers are themselves responsible for increasing the international violence potential, they have it within their power to work for greater order by changing the accepted code for international behavior, the rules of the game of competitive co-existence.

The basic and essential change called for, from the standpoint of international stability, is the renunciation of types of action calculated to promote the development of pro-Communist or pro-Western regimes and thus to align the uncommitted nations on one side or the other in the worldwide struggle for influence. To the extent that the continuing internal sociopolitical changes in these countries depend less on the predominance of pro-Western or pro-Communist local elements in the regimes concerned, these changes will be less threatening to the international balance of power, will impinge less sharply upon the vital interests of the great powers on both sides, and so will be less likely to generate conflicts involving the great powers.

There remains the problem of spelling out the requisite modification of the international "rules of the game" in terms of norms for more orderly and less threat-provoking behavior on the part of the great powers. To what extent, for example, might it be possible to solve this problem by placing greater emphasis upon the role of international organizations as media of great-power action in relation to the countries concerned, especially in the field of economic assistance? Alternatively, to what extent might it be possible to devise cooperative instead of competitive action by the great powers? By way of example, one might conceive of joint United States-Soviet international aid projects. Another possibility that may be fruitful to explore is the devising of certain mutually accepted restraints upon the pattern of permissible great-power competition for influence. In the latter connection one immediately thinks of regulating assistance in the field of arms.

The analyses presented in the subsequent chapters of this book do not elaborate an integrated program of action patterns that would provide an overall strategy for modifying the "rules of the international game," or for establishing mutually agreed upon restraints. However, many of the analyses do enumerate action patterns, within the context of the specific problem areas discussed, that imply modifications in the current rules of international behavior, or the establishment of new restraints upon action patterns. A brief outline of some of these measures for coping with threats to stability is presented in the next section.

MEASURES FOR COPING WITH THREATS TO STABILITY

Given a limited approach to international order, that is, one which assumes the possibility of increasing or maintaining the stability of the international system by meeting specific threats, it is necessary to identify the threats and to devise more or less specific measures for coping with them. The nature and severity of the wide diversity of threats to stability has already been alluded to in the first section of this chapter. Given these specific threats there exist two possible strategies for coping with them: (1) to eliminate or alleviate, insofar as possible, the threat at its source; or (2) to contain or deter the threat if it cannot be effectively dealt with at its point of origin.

As noted previously, one of the more severe threats to the stability of the international system is the rapid increase in the number of new states with their pressing problems of economic aid and political development. In this instance, it seems likely that positive programs of economic and technical assistance (threat alleviation) as well as concurrent programs of military assistance to deter encroachment from other nations (threat containment) will be required to cope with these problems and to provide a foundation for internal stability. As W. W. Rostow has put it, what is required is ". . . not merely a proper military program of deterrence, but programs of village development, communications and indoctrination."[10] In essence, a wide diversity of threats, for example, those which attend the emergence of new states, calls for a wide diversity of responses and a sense of discrimination and balance with respect to the employment of threat-alleviating and threat-repressing measures. One cannot seriously argue, for example, that the destabilizing propensities of new states can be effectively dealt with by a more finely-honed strategic deterrent system (threat-repression) any more than a malevolent enemy can be resolutely countered by a technical assistance team (threat alleviation). Finally, it needs to be recognized that there are a number of problems that need to be studied, as outlined below, before one can talk intelligently of comprehensive, rational stabilization strategies, and that there is little likelihood that from these studies a set of rigorously defined statements of necessary and sufficient conditions for international stability will emerge.

Economic and Technical Assistance

The principal justification for economic and technical assistance to the developing countries from the standpoint of United States national interests is that some measure of consistent economic growth appears to be a necessary, although not a sufficient, condition for the development of stable societies. It is during periods of rising socio-economic expectations that frustrations generated from perceived economic or political failures often produce marked political and social upheavals. The latter may obviously contribute to serious instabilities within the international system as a whole.

The extent to which economic and technical assistance may succeed

---

[10] W. W. Rostow, address, U. S. Army Special Warfare School, Fort Bragg, North Carolina, June 28, 1961.

in stimulating steady economic growth, and thus contribute to the internal stability of underdeveloped nations is difficult to assess. Even more ambiguous is the relationship between economic development and political evolution. Finally, the degree to which technical and economic aid can be employed as a generalized instrument of influence is speculative.

It would appear, then, that both United States and Soviet policy-makers do not have sufficient information to determine the impact of their respective foreign aid programs. As Lucian Pye notes in Chapter 3, the United States badly requires an integrated body of studies that can provide the information needed for coherent policies toward the newly developing countries. It remains doubtful that even the most carefully devised policies could eliminate all of the uncertainties in aid programs. However, the advisability of formulating and carrying out effective aid programs is of critical importance. As noted in Chapter 2, nearly 2 billion people, or about two thirds of the world's population, live in underdeveloped areas; and approximately 1.25 billion live in non-Communist areas. Further, the gap in per capita income between the underdeveloped and developed countries is increasing over time.

Thus, it is essential for the West to attempt to formulate programs of economic and technical aid that will promote economic growth, political stability, and the adoption and maintenance of democratic institutions. To achieve these goals, the West, (1) must have sufficient information to permit it to establish policies congruent with the economic, cultural, political, and military needs of individual nations; (2) must translate its policies and programs into action in such a manner as not to cause the recipients to view the donor's motives as ones of political and economic exploitation; (3) must provide military assistance in order to increase stability, but only under the condition that this assistance not be used as a means to impede the economic progress of a nation; and (4) must provide, through information and most of all *by example,* a basis for demonstrating the potential strengths of democratic forms of organization in order to combat the prevailing myth that democratic institutions are by definition weak and ineffectual whereas totalitarian institutions are strong and decisive.

Mutual Deterrence

The realities of great power relationships suggest that strategic nuclear and non-nuclear deterrence will continue to be a vital program for threat containment for the West over the foreseeable future. Whether this program will result in a stable deterrent balance between the major protagonists in the international system is the central question that Chapters 5, 6, 7, and 8 of this book address.

The problem of achieving a stable deterrent balance is complicated at the outset because of the inherent instability contained within a system maintained by threat and counterthreat. This is particularly the case when there are technological and military advantages in "striking first," which give rise to what R. Osgood calls "active deterrence," that is, the willingness to strike first when a judgment is made that one's adversary is about to launch an attack.

In his discussion of methods for stabilizing the military environment Osgood also observes that one of the gravest threats to stability is the overdependence of the West upon expensive weapons of all-out war, and a deficiency of preparedness to deter other forms of military conflict. He emphasizes that the West should develop the capability to deter a wide range of conflicts with a military capability that is credible but not provocative and that from this position of overall military strength should attempt to arrive at tacit and informal agreements with the Soviet as well as "to consolidate the many mutual restraints on military power."

T. Milburn in Chapter 8 argues, as does Osgood, that the United States is placing too great an emphasis on the doctrine of retaliation. Milburn notes that the United States has made little effort to determine what levels and what kinds of deterrents, under given environmental conditions, would produce behaviors on the part of an adversary that would be consistent with Western goals. Drawing from the psychological literature, he observes that reward or a combination of reward and threat is a more effective means of influencing behavior than threat alone. Maintaining that there remains a need for the United States to retain a moderate nuclear threat capability, he suggests that the United States strategy should be modified to give greater emphasis to "positive deterrence," that is, deterring Soviet aggression by rewarding actions that are consistent with, or at least not detrimental to, United States goals.

The particular problem of European nuclear deterrence is taken up in Chapter 7. The authors observe that the declining credibility of the use of United States nuclear forces on behalf of Europe, the increasing reluctance of Europe to accept the United States as the predominant, if not sole, decision-maker regarding the use of strategic nuclear weapons, and the unlikelihood that individual European nations can independently develop more than symbolic nuclear forces, that is, relatively few weapons with technologically unsophisticated means of delivery, markedly decrease both the credibility and the effectiveness of the European deterrent.

One method for resolving the above problems that appears to be politically and economically feasible would be the creation of a supranational European organization, similar to and related to the European Economic Community (EEC), to assure responsibility for the procurement and command and control of strategic nuclear weapons. Such a program is viewed as a means of increasing the credibility of European deterrence, reducing current frictions between the United States and Europe and reducing the number of individual European nations that currently or in the future may possess nuclear forces.

In the analysis in Chapter 7 the importance of Britain's becoming a member of the EEC as a prerequisite to a European Community deterrent is noted. Although De Gaulle's refusal in the winter of 1962 to permit British entry into the EEC places an additional obstacle in the path of a European deterrent, the possibility of an easing of French objections to Britain's entry into the EEC with the eventual retirement of De Gaulle, and the precedents established by the 1963 negotiations to establish multinational crews on nuclear-armed naval vessels, would suggest that the eventual establishment of a supranational European deterrent remains a possible program for increasing stability.

Arms Control and Disarmament

The deterrence programs discussed above are based upon the assumption that mutual deterrence will remain a major part of Western and Soviet strategy during the next decade, and that certain modifications of current programs would increase their effectiveness given the goals of the West, one goal being international stability. In their papers on disarmament and arms control (Chapters 9 and 10) both Burns and Schelling are concerned with serious destabilizing forces to which mutual deterrence is subject, including accidental war, escalation, nuclear weapons diffusion, fatigue due to protracted crisis, and technological innovation.

In response to these potentially destabilizing events, Schelling argues the need for mechanisms that would facilitate a "relaxation" of tensions should nuclear war appear imminent. Such mechanisms would necessarily be founded on mutual distrust and the necessity of proving one's intent not to initiate an attack. One mechanism that Schelling suggests is a Special Surveillance Force whose function would be to observe enemy behavior, at the enemy's invitation, and to report findings back to its own country instantly through reliable channels. The negotiations and agreements required to establish such a capability might also provide acceptable ground rules for cooperation in other areas, for example, general disarmament.

In considering practicable measures for disarmament, Burns also affirms the necessity of assuming mutual distrust between East and West. He proposes that an international agent, for example, the United Nations, be given the capability, first for surveillance, and subsequently, for armed policing of its members. The latter, a nuclear-armed, independent Third Force, might serve as a balance wheel at the highest level to deter large-scale aggression.

One major difficulty in evaluating specific proposals for disarmament is the lack of precedent experience. Extremely difficult conceptual and pragmatic questions arise, for example, Can international stability be maintained without military force? How can severe conflicts of national interests and values be mediated and resolved in a disarmed world? How can the stresses and strains which will occur, for instance, within individual underdeveloped nations, be taken up without recourse to military force? Current political and social philosophies do not seem to provide answers for such questions, which have major implications for the future stability of the international system. However, as Burns concludes in Chapter 9, "the prospect of these intractable problems is at least preferable to that of an uncontrolled arms race."

International Instrumentalities

Both Chapters 11 and 12 take a pragmatic and restricted view of the United Nations as a mechanism for preserving the peace and for achieving international integration. As a peace-preserving force, the United Nations record of activities indicates the feasibility of its serving as a non-political, non-interventionist intranational operation as it did in the Suez and Jordan actions. However, generalized resort to force in the achievement of political objectives appears to lie beyond the capability of the United Nations, since the prevailing international power structure would work against an impartial, universal application. It would appear that the United Nations is in great measure simply the formalized part of a largely informal and worldwide political "conversation." That is, the United Nations reflects the current power relationships that exist within the international system. Under these circumstances, both Burns and Haas agree that the United Nations can realistically pursue only "limited" peace-preserving objectives.

In his analysis of regional and international integration, Haas argues that the forces that have led to the establishment of a supranational community in Europe are not found within the United Nations or other regions. The economic development and technical aid activities of the United Nations to establish stable political and economic national units are seen as promoting nationalism and thus operating against the establishment of regional integration, as well as international integration. Should regional integration occur outside of Europe, it would likely impede international integration since the very forces giving rise to this form of organization would likely be antithetical to integration at the international level.

Thus, if regional integration occurs in various areas of the world, for example, Africa, South America, and Eastern Europe, the major actors in the international system would shift from nations to regions. This may contribute to regional peace but not necessarily to universal peace.

PART II

INTERNATIONAL
STABILITY AND
THE UNDERDEVELOPED AREAS

Chapter 2

The Nature of the
Underdeveloped Areas

DALE J. HEKHUIS and JOHN F. YOUNGBLOOD

For purposes of this chapter, the nations of the world are classified as underdeveloped, developed, or Communist bloc. The Communist bloc nations are excluded from the developed-underdeveloped dichotomy to facilitate discussion of United States policy formation and foreign aid programs.

In defining developed and underdeveloped nations, Rostow's five-category classification of the stages of economic growth[1] is a useful and convenient starting point. For our purposes, the first three economic stages delineate underdeveloped nations:

1. Traditional—primarily an agrarian economy in which the level of productivity is curtailed by the lack of capital and technology. Political power is regional and often exercised by landowners.

2. Transitional—an economy in which there is an increase in the rate of investment to a level which substantially exceeds the rate of population growth. Science and technology are beginning to be developed or

---

[1] W. W. Rostow, *The Stages of Economic Growth*, Cambridge University Press, Cambridge, 1960.

imported; capital is being invested. The traditional agrarian economy is slowly being converted to an industrial base, and the traditional social system is beginning to break down.

3. Take-off—an economy in which the rate of investment rises from under 5 per cent to over 10 per cent of national income; in which there are one or more manufacturing sectors that have a high rate of growth; and the development of a social system that highly values and thereby stimulates economic growth.

The remaining two of Rostow's categories describe the economic status of developed countries:

4. Maturity—an economy in which modern technology has been applied to most of the nation's resources and in which there are a large number of manufacturing sectors. The great majority of the working force has shifted out of agriculture and rural areas. Questions regarding the utilization of the fruits of industrialization are beginning to emerge.

5. High Mass-Consumption—an economy in which the focus has shifted from the provision of food, shelter, and clothing to the production of consumers' durable goods and services and from an overriding concern with technology to questions of social welfare.

With this distinction being made between developed and underdeveloped nations, the three major groupings are:

1. Underdeveloped—all of non-Communist Asia (excluding Japan), Africa (excluding the Union of South Africa), Latin America, the Middle East, and the European nations of Spain, Portugal, Greece, and Yugoslavia.

2. Developed—Europe (including Finland), the United States, Canada, the Union of South Africa, Japan, and Oceania (Australia and New Zealand only).

3. Communist bloc—the Soviet Union, China, East European satellites: Czechoslovakia, Hungary, Poland, Albania, East Germany, Bulgaria, and Romania, North Korea, and North Vietnam.

Wide variation is found among underdeveloped countries with respect to almost any characteristic that may be examined. It is necessary then, in discussing basic factors, which when applied to the aggregate of these countries do separate them from developed nations, to qualify statements by such terms as "in general" or "for many (or most, or some) of the areas" and other imprecise expressions.

One of the most important factors generally characterizing underdeveloped areas, and one that tends most to contravene efforts for per capita economic expansion, is rapid population growth. A brief description of this growth provides a background for examining three additional factors: economic status, technical manpower, and educational resources.

POPULATION GROWTH

The projected growth of the world's population through 1976 is illustrated in Table 1. Approximately 50 per cent of the entire world's population growth from 1961 to 1976 is expected to occur in the underdeveloped areas as previously defined. These areas are characterized by birthrates in the range of 30 to 50 per 1000 inhabitants in contrast to the range of 15 to 25 per 1000 for developed countries. The effect of the high birthrates on the population growth has been more pronounced in those underdeveloped areas where modern medicine has been applied to substantially reduce mortality rates and extend life expectancy.

In terms of sheer numbers, the population growth rates of the underdeveloped areas are impressive. In India, for example, with an annual growth rate of about 2 per cent, the net addition per year presently approximates 8 million people. Of particular interest to the United States is the growth in Latin America as displayed in Table 2. With a growth rate exceeding 2 per cent annually, the population is expected to increase from the 210 million in 1961 to about 311 million in 1976.

Such rates of growth are, in general, serious handicaps to securing economic growth and to achieving adequate investment in the social and human overhead that must accompany economic growth. The underdeveloped areas face the tremendous problem of achieving rates of economic development that outstrip the population rates.

In addition to sheer numbers, this problem is intensified by the fact that a rapidly growing population alters the age composition of a nation and hence the fraction of the total population that is in the labor force. To illustrate the relationship between birthrate and labor force, the percentage of working-age population (aged 15–59) is calculated in Table 3 for model stable populations for three levels of life expectancy (at birth) and four levels of crude birthrate based on populations with four age-specific fertility rates. The age-specific fertility rates selected in Table 3 encompass those actually found in developed and underdeveloped areas. From such an analysis, Spengler concludes:

. . . if fertility declined from levels such as are found in much of Asia, Africa, and Latin America to those found in Europe, the fraction of the population of working age would be something like one-sixth higher under stable-population conditions. This amounts to an increase of one-sixth or more in potential productivity per capita. This theoretical finding is borne out, of course, in the real world; for example, 66.28 percent of the Swedish population but only 56.69 percent of the Brazilian population is aged 15–64 years.[2]

Underdeveloped countries would derive two main benefits in terms of age composition if high fertility rates were reduced: (1) potential per capita productivity would rise 15 per cent or more by an increase in the proportion of persons in the labor force age group, and (2) this increase would reduce the need to employ children in the labor force and thus enable them to receive educational training that in the long run would lead to further increases in productivity.

TABLE 1. *Population of the World, 1961–1976*

Region	1961		1976		Pop. Growth 1961–1976 (Millions)	Per cent of Total Growth 1961–1976
	Population (Millions)	Per cent of Total	Population (Millions)	Per cent of Total		
Developed areas						
United States	184.6		220.0			
Western Europe	261.0		284.6			
Canada	18.3		22.3			
Japan	94.8		116.0			
Oceania	16.1		20.5			
South Africa	15.2		21.9			
	590.0	19.7	685.3	18.3	95.3	12.5
Underdeveloped areas						
Asia	779.8		983.8			
Middle East	106.1		145.7			
Africa	205.8		238.3			
America	210.1		299.6			
Europe*	66.8		77.7			
	1368.6	45.7	1745.1	46.5	376.5	49.5
Communist bloc						
Soviet Union	215.0		274.0			
China	694.0		900.0			
Eastern Europe	99.6		114.4			
North Korea	9.5		11.4			
North Vietnam	16.7		23.2			
	1034.8	34.6	1324.0	35.2	289.2	38.0
World Total:	2993.4		3754.4		761.0	100.0

Sources: P. N. Rosenstein-Rodan, "International Aid for Underdeveloped Countries," Center for International Studies, Massachusetts Institute of Technology, Cambridge, January 1961; and "The Future Growth of World Population, "United Nations Population Study, No. 28, United Nations, New York, 1958.
* Spain, Portugal, Greece, Yugoslavia.

---

[2] J. J. Spengler, "Population and World Economic Development," *Science*, May 20, 1960.

TABLE 2. *Estimated Population Growth
for Underdeveloped Countries, 1961–1976*

Region	Rate of Annual Increase (Per cent)	Population (Thousands)	
		1961	1976
Argentina	1.6	21,487	27,399
Bolivia	2.4	3,523	5,027
Brazil	2.8	67,549	102,710
Chile	2.0	7,688	10,297
Colombia	2.8	14,519	21,861
Ecuador	3.0	4,397	6,818
El Salvador	3.1	2,683	4,262
Guatemala	3.0	3,883	6,109
Mexico	3.0	35,246	54,916
Paraguay	1.7	1,785	2,298
Peru	2.7	10,902	16,338
Uruguay	1.4	2,831	3,523
Venezuela	3.0	6,906	10,812
All Other Central America		26,746	38,536
Total Population:		210,145	310,906
Total Growth, 1961–1976: 100,761,000			

Source: P. N. Rosenstein-Rodan, "International Aid for Underdeveloped Countries," Center for International Studies, Massachusetts Institute of Technology, Cambridge, January 1961.

TABLE 3. *Crude Birthrate and Percentage of Population
Aged 15–59 in Model Stable Population*

Life Expectancy at Birth (Years)

40		60.4		70.2	
Birthrate per 1000	Per cent, Aged 15–59	Birthrate per 1000	Per cent, Aged 15–59	Birthrate per 1000	Per cent, Aged 15–59
46.0	52.5	43.8	49.6	42.9	48.4
31.7	58.8	30.6	55.8	30.1	54.7
23.1	61.6	22.5	58.7	22.3	57.7
13.6	62.6	13.3	59.4	13.3	58.6

Source: J. J. Spengler, "Population and World Economic Development," *Science*, May 20, 1960.

ECONOMIC STATUS

Table 4 shows the absolute 1961 real Gross National Product and the GNP per capita for the underdeveloped, developed, and Communist bloc areas. These data, when considered in conjunction with the world population estimates presented above, reveal that the underdeveloped countries account for approximately 46 per cent of the world's population but dispose of only 17 per cent of the world's gross national product.

The factors contributing to this imbalance in world product generation and distribution are numerous and have been studied extensively.[3] A few will be mentioned briefly here.

Agricultural products and raw materials characterize the production of underdeveloped nations. The ratio of the economically active male population engaged in agriculture to that engaged in manufacturing lies between 0.1 and 1.0 in developed countries but between 2 and 20 (or more) for the underdeveloped areas.[4] In the aggregate, approximately two thirds of the people in underdeveloped areas earn their living in agriculture. The preponderance of agrarian economic pursuit in these areas is in itself characterized by low output per worker, low output per acre, and a small amount of land per worker. Contributing to these in many areas are systems of land tenure and tradition-bound, feudal systems of land tenancy. The low output per worker may be at a near subsistence level and give rise to "disguised unemployment" in which withdrawal of agricultural workers could be made without reducing agricultural output. Forced redistribution of land holdings has been a feature of some approaches by underdeveloped nations to the problem of initiating economic growth.

The underdeveloped areas are capital poor, and the rate of capital accumulation in some areas is barely sufficient to maintain a constant per capita income for the expanding populations. At a capital-output ratio of 4 to 1, investment of 8 per cent of national income is required to supply a population growing at 2 per cent per year with constant capital per head. The net domestic savings of most underdeveloped regions fail to reach this percentage of national income. The capital-output ratio appropriate to specific nations may be substantially lower than 4 to 1, however.

---

[3] G. M. Meier and R. E. Baldwin, *Economic Development*, Part 3, John Wiley, New York, 1957.
[4] *Statistical Yearbook, 1955*, United Nations, New York, 1955, Table 6.

TABLE 4. *World Gross National Product, 1961*

Region	GNP Real Terms* (US $ Billion)	Per cent of World Total	Real GNP per Capita (US Dollars)
Developed Countries			
United States	515.0	29.4	2790
Western Europe	384.9	22.0	1472
Canada	37.5	2.1	2048
Japan	58.1	3.3	598
Oceania	24.4	1.4	1513
South Africa	9.1	0.5	598
	1029.0	58.7	
Underdeveloped Countries			
Asia	119.8	6.8	154
Middle East	29.3	1.7	257
Africa	33.7	1.9	164
Latin America	89.3	5.1	422
Europe	33.5	1.9	501
	305.6	17.5	
Communist Bloc			
Soviet Union	212.0	12.1	986
China	115.7	6.6	167
Eastern Europe	82.1	4.7	825
North Korea	2.0	0.1	211
North Vietnam	3.3	0.2	199
	415.1	23.7	
World Total:	1749.7		

Source: P. N. Rosenstein-Rodan, "International Aid for Underdeveloped Countries," Center for International Studies, Massachusetts Institute of Technology, Cambridge, January 1961.

* "Real" GNP indicates the purchasing power of the GNP compared to U.S. Prices

Foreign economic aid programs (considered in Chapter 4) may supply part of the necessary capital inflow—the external push—to alleviate the capital poverty, to increase savings, and to accelerate economic growth toward a self-sustaining state. While this inflow is necessary for such acceleration, it is not sufficient; for the capital poverty of these areas is in part a consequence of cultural and social factors that have hampered economic change and dampened incentives for it.[5] Religions and caste or family systems in some areas, and the land tenure systems mentioned above, are examples. The interplay of these numerous factors has stultified entrepreneurial activity and has in part resulted in low labor efficiency, low occupational mobility, and elites ignorant in economic organization and operation. The requirements for economic change in these areas, hence, include more than economic factors per se. Basically, there must be an indigenous desire for economic advance and a willingness to accept the social changes demanded by it.

TECHNICAL MANPOWER RESOURCES

A condition that characterizes most, if not all, of the underdeveloped nations is a lack of qualified technical personnel (scientists, specialists, engineers, and technologists in the physical, mathematical, biological, medical, and agricultural sciences) to implement the plans for economic development. The deficiencies may not, of course, exist in all technical realms. For example, according to one estimate the shortage of engineers in Mexico is not so acute as to seriously impede planned industrial expansion.[6] Nor are the deficiencies necessarily of number only. The past need of Communist China to bolster her 250,000 scientists and engineers with additional thousands of technologists imported from the Soviet Union stemmed in part from inadequacies in China's technical training programs. It is likely, for instance, that many of those designated as engineers in China would be classed as technicians in the United States.

The histories of the underdeveloped areas reveal the forces that have operated to inhibit the nucleation and growth of technical manpower resources. For example, farming methods in some areas have been so constrained by tradition or religion as to restrict appropriate utilization of natural resources. In some areas, disease, poverty, and tropical climate have drained human resources and vitality, and little energy

---

[5] For a discussion of the multiple causation and interrelation of social, economic, and political factors involved see *Economic, Social and Political Changes in the Underdeveloped Countries and Its Implications for U.S. Policy* (A study prepared at the request of the Committee on Foreign Relations, U.S. Senate), Center for International Studies, Massachusetts Institute of Technology, Cambridge, March 30, 1960.

[6] H. C. Mattraw, "Capabilities for Scientific Research and Engineering in Selected Latin American Countries," *Tempo*, General Electric Company, Santa Barbara, California, September 1960.

has remained for pursuits other than securing simple necessities. Feudal systems left little motivation or time for innovation. Some religions, although they sanctioned investigation of limited aspects of the physical world, spurned the pursuit of material goods. Some of these forces persist and oppose the application and diffusion of technical knowledge from the developed nations.

The preceding factors which have inhibited technical growth are more or less indigenous in origin. Other factors are to be found in the histories of colonial rule in some, but not all, underdeveloped areas. Perhaps the principal oversight by the colonialists was the grossly inadequate investment in schools for the native populations and the strong prohibitions against native social mobility.

The consequences of deficiencies in technical manpower within a nation are manifold. Some apply quite generally to all underdeveloped areas even though each nation has its own peculiar requirements regarding the total number and type of technical personnel. One such consequence is a lack of knowledge concerning local resources and various characteristics of the agricultural environment. Such information is a prerequisite to extensive developmental planning.

Another consequence of deficiencies in technical manpower is a nation's inability to adapt modern technologies to local requirements. Modern agricultural technology, for example, can seldom be transferred wholesale from one area to another. On-site applied research may be required to adapt modern agricultural technology to local peculiarities of soil, moisture, insect infestation, and a myriad of other factors. Industrialization efforts are also hampered by the same manpower limitations in establishing and operating manufacturing facilities. In many instances, engineers, supervisors, and technicians must be imported to solve the construction and installation problems and to train indigenous supervisors and laborers.

A further consequence is a nation's inability to develop diversified products that best exploit the physical and agricultural resources of the various underdeveloped areas. A lack of this innovative activity forces continued dependence of some nations on the sale of one or two commodities to more industrialized nations. In turn, the economies of those countries that depend upon a few export commodities are particularly vulnerable to the fluctuations of international markets.

EDUCATIONAL RESOURCES

Probably the most critical deficiency in underdeveloped areas is in school systems capable of providing only a minimal, or better, education to an appreciable fraction of the population. Even now, most of the areas are characterized by inadequate investment in schools, poor educational programs, and shortages of adequately trained teachers. All of these restrict the supply of qualified native technical personnel.

From the standpoint of economic growth, the lack of technical manpower perhaps overshadows deficiencies in other professions. However, industrialization and significant agricultural advance cannot be achieved in a vacuum of well-trained administrators, civil servants, teachers, and political leaders. Nor can communication with and improvement of the labor force be achieved in the face of a high illiteracy rate. The illiteracy rates presented in Table 5 provide a dramatic example of inadequate educational programs. In underdeveloped areas the illiteracy rates range from 40 to 90 per cent, while for the developed countries they are about 10 per cent or lower.

For instance, Latin American nations are faced with severe problems of illiteracy, especially in the rural areas. There the rural illiteracy ranges from 37 to 83 per cent, while for the urban population the range is 8 to 40 per cent. A few nations have made strong efforts to reduce illiteracy. Mexico, for example, reduced its national rate by 31 per cent between 1940 and 1950. This reduction was made despite a population increase of 30 per cent (19.8 to 25.8 million) in the same period. For most of the Latin American nations, however, the illiteracy improvements were more moderate, ranging from 5 to 10 per cent reduction during the same ten-year period.

The shortage of well-trained teachers throughout underdeveloped areas is perhaps the most serious block to educational advancement. The number of elementary school teachers per 1000 inhabitants may be used as an indicator to compare developed and underdeveloped nations in this regard. In 1950, this ratio for developed nations was found to be in the range of about 4 to 5.5 teachers per 1000 inhabitants; for underdeveloped areas it ranged from a few tenths to about 2.5 and rarely exceeded 3. Latin America may again serve as an example. Even though 90,000 teachers were added between 1956 and 1959 (an increase of 16 per cent), 400,000 additional teachers would have been required to ensure only an elementary education for the entire school-age population. Further, 48 per cent of primary school teachers in all but four Latin American countries have not received special training and the proportion is even higher in secondary education. An expected Latin American increase in population of the age group 7 to 14 years from about 40 million in 1960 to about 65 million in 1980 is a measure of how the educational problems will intensify in Latin America.

TABLE 5. *World Illiteracy, 1954–1955*

Region	Number of Illiterates per 1000 Population
North America	
United States	20–30
Canada	20–30
South America	
Brazil	500–550
Argentina	100–150
Bolivia	750–800
Colombia	450–500
Peru	550–600
Africa	
Nigeria	800–850
Liberia	900–950
Morocco	850–900
Libya	850–900
Sudan	900–950
Union of South Africa	550–600
Middle East	
Egypt	750–800
Israel	50–100
Iraq	850–900
Iran	850–900
Saudi Arabia	950–990
Asia	
Afghanistan	950–990
India	800–850
Burma	500–550
Ceylon	400–450
Japan	20–30
China (continental)	500–550
Europe	
United Kingdom	10–20
France	40–50
Denmark	10–20
U.S.S.R.	70–100

Source: UNESCO, "World Communications, Press, Radio, Film, Television,' 3rd Edition, 1956.

A review of educational programs in Latin America[7] reveals many problems more or less characteristic of the underdeveloped areas: high illiteracy rates; high drop-out rates at all levels; endemic diseases which reduce vitality and school attendance; inadequacies of school buildings and equipment, textbooks and supplies, and libraries and laboratories; unqualified teachers; insufficient teachers; curriculums that are not geared to the needs of industrial and agricultural development; totally inadequate financial resources; and cultural barriers impeding the universalization of education.

The critical educational problems of Latin America have been used to illustrate the problems that face most underdeveloped areas. Their task of advancing the material and human facilities and the curriculums of schools to a point anywhere near modern levels and creating resources of trained specialists, including technical manpower, is a prodigious one.

It is not in educational and technical manpower resources alone that these areas find common problems. The Prime Minister of Nepal, speaking of the similarities of problems facing the new states of Africa and Asia, has noted:

Because of the differences of background, the problems might differ in degree and emphasis, but in general outline there is fundamental unity not only in the nature and the variety of the problems but in the availability or resources to cope with them too. In general terms, the problem is that of a country trying to live up to the complexities and responsibilities of the twentieth century, which is equipped with the tools of the seventeenth or eighteenth century.

Lack of technical know-how and technical skill in the people in general, results in low productivity, low national income, and a consequent low standard of living. Unless the new nations find means of acquiring technical know-how and train people fast enough to man the jobs to implement the development plans, all our efforts may remain pious intentions only.[8]

---

[7] Evelyn L. Harner, "Changing Patterns of Education in Latin America," *Tempo*, General Electric Company, Santa Barbara, California, August 1960.
[8] International Conference on the Role of Science in the Advancement of New States, Rehovoth, Israel, August 1960.

Chapter 3

The Underdeveloped Areas

as a Source of International

Tension Through 1975

LUCIAN W. PYE

INTRODUCTION

The dominant theme of the 1950's, second only to the Cold War, was the dramatic increase in the American awareness of, and sensitivity about, the problems of the underdeveloped areas. The popular press has given the American people a general sense, which is still vague and diffuse, that these areas are of crucial importance to our national security. The American people have been informed that ominous dangers are somehow associated with the problems of the newly emerging countries. During the last decade, a national consensus was established over the need for foreign aid and for technical and economic assistance.

Presently, however, the American response still is largely one of mood, for it has not been based upon a clear and precise knowledge of the specific nature of the potential dangers of the underdeveloped areas or how they might, in fact, become a threat to American security. In spite of this, the diffuse sense of the ominous in American thinking about such areas represents a significant shift in basic opinion. Im-

41

mediately after World War II the American public was still largely
wedded to its classical anti-colonial views, and American policy reflected little awareness of the profound problems that can plague a
traditional society seeking to become a part of the modern world. In
the past, the American response to the problems of colonial and primitive areas was largely an irrational, sentimental one, which at best saw
national development as a spontaneous, creative act. Indeed, in our
thinking about the colonial world, we saw the main problem as simply
one of removing foreign political domination. We assumed that the
indigenous people, after a brief period of adjustment, would soon be
able to create their own society and realize their own objectives.

The initial American approach to the underdeveloped areas was
hence an easy and optimistic one that rested upon a moralistic and
somewhat magical view of the universe. We were, at the time, largely
insensitive to the difficulties and frustrations that a traditional society
is certain to experience when seeking to adapt to the impact of both
modern technology and liberal Western values. During the decade immediately after World War II there was, indeed, an odd congruence
in American thinking and Marxian views of the colonial problem,
wherein both ourselves and the Communists tended to see the central
problem as that of the strong unjustly exploiting the weak. We were
prepared to go quite far in accepting the Communist prediction that
once the shackles of colonial control were removed, the freed peoples
should be able to realize readily their destinies. We fully distrusted suggestions about the need for preparation and for tutelage in self-govern-
ment.

The 1950's have taught us that colonialism can readily disappear, but
the problems of traditional societies run far deeper and will persist far
longer. During the early 1950's, American thinking on the underdeveloped areas shifted to the realization that the end of colonialism
might usher in a period during which the new countries would be
particularly vulnerable to Communist penetration. Thus, as we saw the
problem of colonialism receding, we quickly fitted the question of the
underdeveloped areas into our thinking about the Cold War. Our
struggle with the Soviet Union dominated our foreign policy commitment during the 1950's, particularly after the outbreak of the
Korean War, and we came to treat the problems of the underdeveloped
areas as a function of our basic conflict with Communism. The Cold
War thus provided the shock necessary for a drastic revision of our
thinking about the underdeveloped areas.

Our new perspective left us with a distorted and only partial appreciation of the problems of the transitional regions. In our anxiety over

the Soviet threat, we became peculiarly sensitive to the need for support among all the peoples of the world. Through our search for allies and, more important, for a means to isolate Communist China during the Korean conflict, we came into direct conflict with the sentiments of neutralism in many of the newer emerging countries. American thinking about the underdeveloped areas thus gradually became that of seeing them as potential friends and admirers or as hostile critics and easy dupes of Communism. We became readily convinced that we were the victims of a cruel dilemma: our relations with underdeveloped areas could threaten our vital alliance relationship with the European colonial powers, while our NATO associations would certainly make it impossible for us to realize our deserved popularity in the underdeveloped regions. The Suez crisis both highlighted this problem in our thinking and proved, as it receded in time, that we had exaggerated the dilemma.

By the early 1960's, American thinking had progressed to a new position beyond that of just viewing the problems of underdeveloped areas as functional to the Cold War. Increasingly we had to acknowledge the problems of the underdeveloped areas to be part of a profound historical process which would constitute a fundamental challenge to international stability even if the threat of Communism were to disappear. We could also take a more balanced view toward Asian neutralism, and see more advantages to our national interest in honest commitments to neutral policies. We have also begun to realize that the need for foreign aid might be of long duration. Indeed American thinking has reached a point of discerning two conflicts relating to the underdeveloped areas: first, the East-West conflict between Communism and the Free World, and second, a North-South problem involving the relations between the industrially advanced northern half of the globe and the poverty stricken southern half.

These developments in American thinking all represent an ever-increasing understanding of the complex nature of social change in transitional societies. As we became actively involved with all aspects of the building of new nations, we became considerably more proficient in numerous technical aspects of foreign aid. Unfortunately, however, we are still without a body of theories and doctrines that might provide intellectual guidance and coherence in our policies toward the newly emerging countries. We can neither explain to them nor to ourselves why these societies are economically and politically behind the West. More seriously, our lack of doctrine means that we cannot provide leadership in evolving strategies for political and economic development.

It is a disturbing fact that the very essence of Marxism is to convey a sense about the processes of historical development and to suggest appropriate revolutionary strategies toward the goal of modernized national power. It is not only that the Communists claim to have the answers to rapid industrial development; they do in fact have doctrines that are concerned precisely with the questions of how feudal societies give way to the emergence of modern industrial societies. That we can point to fallacies in their doctrines is not enough; we must be able to provide the material for a democratic non-Communist course of national development if we are to continue to aspire to the leadership of the Free World. This need for a body of theories and doctrines will clearly be a matter of the highest urgency during the coming decades. It should be the goal for American thinking on the problems of the underdeveloped areas, and it will serve as the prime theme throughout the remainder of this analysis as we turn to a search for more specific sources of tension.

Since the problems of the underdeveloped areas tend to affect so many aspects of international relations, it is not easy to isolate clearly separable tensions that might threaten the peace. For purposes of discussion, however, they have arbitrarily been divided into four categories: (1) the strains the underdeveloped areas place on the continued maintenance of the interstate system as a coherent system; (2) the tensions emerging from the relationships between advanced and underdeveloped societies; (3) the tensions rising from the relationships of the underdeveloped countries with each other; (4) the tensions between the major powers arising from the existence of underdeveloped countries.

The first category includes problems which affect those in the other three categories and it also includes problems that are the sum consequences of the others. Therefore, some of the problems in the first category are discussed as an introduction to the other categories, and the remainder are discussed in the concluding section.

THE UNDERDEVELOPED AREAS AND THE CONTINUITY OF THE NATION-STATE SYSTEM

In the immediate post World War II period, it was generally assumed that the new countries, on achieving independence, would take their place within the nation-state system without violently or appreciably altering the basic characteristics of that system. The individual countries were expected by Western policy-makers to adapt themselves to the standards of behavior of the classical nation-state system. In the West, relatively little concern was expressed over the need of the new countries in joining the international community to adapt themselves to a system that had evolved out of the European cultural complex, the norms of which were deeply embedded in a particular culture that might be classified as being a "world" or "cosmopolitan" one, but which strongly reflected its European origins. Thus, at a time when the system was being mortally threatened by revolutionary Communism, it also had to withstand the shock of absorbing within its operations new units that did not possess all the attributes basic to the members of the classical nation-state system.

The task of isolating and analyzing the various ways in which the underdeveloped areas constitute sources of tension can be greatly facilitated by first briefly outlining the essential features of the traditional nation-state system and then noting the types of adjustments that will have to be made to accommodate the typical underdeveloped countries. In presenting such an analytical model of the nation-state system we cannot expect to capture all aspects of reality; we shall be emphasizing only the most relevant aspects for our analysis.

Specifically the Western state system depended for its self-maintenance upon the continued existence of certain peculiar conditions, the most important of which were:

(a) All the member states shared a relatively homogeneous cultural base, particularly in the scope and function of government. It was presumed that new participants might be inducted into the system if they accepted the minimum set of norms for governmental behavior. Thus the story of much of the nineteenth century was the effort of the European powers to induce the leading non-European candidates for statehood (Turkey, Japan, and China) to accept the standards of international usage that rested upon the European cultural concepts of the nature of law.

(b) All member states shared a relatively common level of technology. One state might be "larger" and more "powerful" than another, but the question of whether one was "superior" and the other "inferior" was not particularly appropriate or frequently raised.

(c) All member states represented governments based upon distinct institutions that to a degree functioned autonomously from the other spheres of that society. That is, the governments were expected to be able to maintain themselves according to the norms of the international system and not to be so vulnerable to domestic events as to be unable to preserve the standards of the international system.

Above all else, however, the classical nation-state system was based upon certain assumptions about the nature of a "state" and about the characteristics of "sovereignty." Specifically, it was assumed that the ultimate test of the sovereignty of a nation-state was the ability of the government to commit the society, over which it claimed to rule, to courses of action and to ensure that the society would adhere to the standards of the international system and to any commitments made within it. The concept of sovereignty upon which the nation-state system was built was thus directly related to the concept of effective action, and in turn the test of effective action was assumed to be the ability to make commitments of indefinitely long time durations.

The classical nation-state system as it emerged out of the European complex also developed certain mechanisms for preserving its own stability and identity. In effect, the nation-state system sought to ensure that all non-states and all societies that could not meet the qualifications of sovereignty were so controlled and regulated as not to disrupt the effective operation of the nation-states. Viewed from the perspective of the system as a whole, it is possible to identify colonialism as the chief mechanism by which the nation-state system sought to protect itself from the intrusion of influences that, for the preservation of the system, had to be considered as disruptive, random, and irresponsible. Colonialism functioned to regulate and control societies that had not achieved the capacity to be full states and to operate according to the standards of state behavior.

A second function of colonialism in the classical nation-state system was to provide a mechanism for facilitating the diffusion of culture and technology while preventing the more explosive consequences of social change from disrupting the system. Under the auspices of colonial authorities, "primitive" people could experience the inevitably painful process of modernizing all phases of their life without dislocating the entire world order.

In summary then, the essence of the classical nation-state system was the close connection between predictability and stability. Forces within the system worked to make the behavior of all actors as predictable as possible and to prevent the introduction into the system of unpredictable elements.

Since World War II the nation-state system has experienced drastic changes that have challenged its fundamental premises. The emergence of newly independent countries with low states of technology, primitive economic systems, unstable governments, and restless populations has reduced the accuracy of predictability. Thus at a time when a revolution in weapons technology has made total annihilation a possibility, the emergence of new states has made the nation-state system inherently less stable.

In noting the trends since 1950, we may select those which appear likely to become increasing sources of tension in the next decade and a half. In particular, three sources of potential tension stand out: the increase in the total number of sovereign states, the lack of effective sovereignty in many of the states, and the need for functional equivalents to certain aspects of colonialism.

Tensions Caused by the Increased Number of Actors

Much of the predictability inherent in the classical nation-state system was derived from the limited number of states; each was in a position to scan the total field of actors before engaging in any significant action. This did much to reduce the likelihood that any given state(s) would encounter unexpected developments. During the 1950's the increase in number of nation-states in itself made questionable the possibility of maintaining many of the traditional forms of the nation-state system. This problem was most conspicuous in terms of membership within the United Nations, but it exists aside from the United Nations and is likely to become increasingly disturbing over the next decade. In 1955 there were only five African UN members; in 1961, the African total was twenty-nine, more than the entire Latin American bloc or the Asian states within the Afro-Asian bloc. By 1970 it is likely that Africa will be composed of at least 38 or more states. By the end of 1965, there will be over 110 nations recognized as sovereign states and as members of the United Nations.

This spectacular growth in the number of states is certain to cause serious problems of communication and to tax the capacity of the system to maintain itself. Consequently pressures will probably develop within the system to control and minimize the disruptive consequences of erratic behavior on the part of new and fragile states. Such tendencies will conflict with the demands of the new states to be considered similar to the more established states.

The increase in numbers will probably foster the belief that the new states should (and probably they will) join in various associations in order to heighten their international influence. However, for reasons we shall be noting in discussing the relationships among the underdeveloped countries, there is little likelihood of effective blocs or even regional alignments developing within the United Nations except for marginal issues. Nevertheless, it is likely that the European powers will feel for some time that such potential groupings of the underdeveloped countries are a threat. Already sensitive over their relative decline in power, they will probably tend to exaggerate the dangers of the advanced societies being overwhelmed by the sheer numbers of new states.

The test for the United States will be the devising of new mechanisms for controlling the disruptive consequences of the increased number of states while reassuring the European powers that the danger is not one of a simple clash between the few advanced societies and the numerous underdeveloped ones.

Ineffectual Sovereignties

A second distinction that the emergence of the underdeveloped areas has produced is the need for accepting groupings of persons within the nation-state system which do not have all the classical attributes of sovereignty. The legal fiction of sovereignty has had to be granted to all of the newly emerging states even though many of these are unable to meet the crucial tests of sovereignty of the classical system. Most of the governments of the underdeveloped areas cannot commit their people to courses of action in the same fashion as a classical state, for they are often in tenuous positions of power. Rapid changes in such societies not only alter the positions of the existing elites, but also cause rapid shifts in policy.

The problem of ineffectual sovereignties brings into question the appropriateness of the classical device of the treaty as a basic element in the nation-state system in relations with the new countries, since treaties rest upon the assumption that governments are able to make commitments of indefinite duration. In the early 1950's, the United States sought to employ in its relations with underdeveloped countries the classical principle of the treaty, and possibly the greatest compliment that the United States has ever paid to the newly emergent countries was the decision to ask them to join with it in the solemn act of international covenants. The ability, however, of the new countries to meet the obligations of treaties is so limited as to make their treaty commitments of dubious value. Indeed, by asking new governments to bind themselves in international covenants, we have underlined the very ineffectualness of such governments and emphasized the questionable powers that they have in dealing even with their own peoples. Also the gross distinction in relative power between the United States and the new countries is so great that the element of mutuality that was basic to the concept of the treaty in the classical system has been lost.

Thus, it seems that the treaty, which was the most honored act in the classical nation-state system, has lost its relevance for relations with unstable and drastically changing societies. It will be necessary during the 1960's for the United States to rely on other methods and devices in seeking to stabilize and normalize our relations with the less developed countries.

The Need for Stabilizing Mechanisms in a Post-Colonial World

A prime source of tension in the international system through 1975 will be the conflict between the need of the underdeveloped countries to modernize their societies, and hence experience dislocating and even explosive social changes, and the need for the international system to maximize stability, and hence to control disruptive influences. As we have noted in describing the elements of the classical nation-state system, these two conflicting developments were traditionally controlled by colonialism. In the post-colonial era, new methods must be found for facilitating the spread of modern culture and for protecting the international system as a whole from the disruptions of such change.

By the end of the 1950's, the methods of economic aid and technical assistance had been fairly well institutionalized as appropriate means for speeding societies through the disruptive stages of modernization. It should be noted, however, that by 1960—in spite of a greatly increased worldwide awareness of the problems of economic and social development in the transitional societies—the total transmission of resources from the advanced industrial countries to the underdeveloped regions was on the decline. In fact, this trend is a reflection of the persisting decline of private international investments over the last half century. In part, the decline stems from the fact that there were numerous hidden forms of social overhead investments under colonialism which the industrial countries will no longer be making in the less developed areas. For example, the early education and training of colonial administrators was undertaken by the metropoles, while in the post-colonial era there have not been matching investments.

The crucial questions for the future are whether foreign aid will be sufficient to facilitate the process of modernization and protect the stability of the world order and whether the West will be able to provide effective aid without unduly disturbing the sense of sovereign independence of the new societies. There is a genuine danger, not frequently recognized, that there may be an explosive reaction against American foreign aid similar to the reaction against colonialism. If the United States is to lead in the establishment of a new world system based on sovereign states, it must be certain that our prime method for supporting and easing the process of transition is not compromised.

At this stage in our analysis we must turn directly to the problem of future relations between advanced industrial powers and the under-developed countries.

TENSIONS BETWEEN THE ADVANCED POWERS AND THE UNDERDEVELOPED COUNTRIES

Throughout the 1950's the problems of the underdeveloped areas were largely viewed within the context of the direct, bilateral relation-ship between major advanced powers and newly emerging states. At the beginning of the decade, Americans tended to assume that the prime problem was the struggle between colonial powers seeking to maintain their position and subjugated peoples seeking their independ-ence. The clash over colonialism seemed to define the basic problem of the underdeveloped areas. As the decade progressed, the issue of colonial-ism receded into the background, but the problem of the underde-veloped areas was still seen largely in a bilateral context. The problem was now felt to be one between the "have" and the "have not" coun-tries, between the rich and the poor, the powerful and the vulnerable.

At the beginning of the decade, United States policy-makers were concerned with avoiding any entanglement in the colonial problem. In a diffuse, general fashion, we supported our anti-colonial sentiments; but for practical purposes we often found it necessary, because of our European alliances, to support the position of the colonial powers. Whenever we sought to bypass the ex-colonial relationship and deal directly with the newly emerging countries, we were charged with trying to supplant the former colonial influences. In order to avoid this charge, we sought wherever possible to continue to deal with the newly emerging countries through the former metropole. In this way, we endeavored to reduce the tensions between former mother coun-tries and the newly independent states.

By the end of the decade, it had become apparent that the problem of the underdeveloped areas could no longer be seen as primarily one of weakened and vulnerable societies needing protection from the great powers. An equally serious problem was that of preventing the small powers from irresponsibly exacting demands from the larger powers by threats of disrupting the stability of the world order. In the early 1960's, many examples could be found in which the logic of anti-colonialism had been easily twisted into a pretext for championing threats against the international order. With the decline in the realities of colonialism, anti-colonialism was being turned into anti-internationalism.

Consequently, American policy-makers have had to search again for internationally acceptable methods by which small powers can be controlled and prevented from exploiting their nuisance value. Events in Cuba and the Congo have graphically demonstrated the extent to which relatively impotent countries can cause immeasurable threats to the stability of the entire world system.

In the future, it seems likely that the relationship between the great powers and the underdeveloped countries will remain extremely delicate and psychologically complex. The old issue of the injustices of colonialism is likely to decline, for the governments of the newly independent countries cannot indefinitely attribute their difficulties to the evils of a former colonial master and hope to gain the confidence of their own citizens. However, such governments may feel the need to find new scapegoats abroad to rationalize their failings. Thus, the decline of direct anti-colonial sentiments may not lead to an easing of the relations between the individual great powers and particular underdeveloped countries. Governments confronted with a fear of failure may become desperately anxious to return their countries to an emotional state of anti-Westernism.

A different form of tension between advanced and underdeveloped countries may also emerge, even if the latter are relatively successful in their efforts at economic and political development. The very process of development tends to highlight, at certain stages, the extent to which an underdeveloped country must be economically, culturally, and technologically dependent upon the great powers. The transmission of skills and arts, of capital goods and services, creates webs of dependent relationships. The leaders of a new country can come to feel that they are losing control in their own house as they are forced to act in increasingly responsible ways. This sense of dependency may stimulate a sense of inferiority. Consequently, governments which seem to be moving ahead and improving the standard of their own societies may build up within themselves frustrations leading to periods of defiance against the "great" powers.

Thus, the basic problem of the relationship between the developed and the underdeveloped nations will continue in the next decade in spite of the decline in colonialism. This is because the basic disrupting element in the relationship is a gross difference in technology; hence the idea of inferior ability is never easily pushed out of the thinking of the underdeveloped nations. The leaders of such countries tend to feel that even when they are treated as equals there is an element of condescension in the behavior of the advanced country.

If we were to chart this pattern of responses, we would first note that historically, during the earlier phases of colonial control when the Western technology was first impinging upon a traditional society, there was a relatively low level of tension. It was only as the colonial peoples became more and more aware of the modern world and became more skilled in performing certain minimum technical and economic activities that tensions built up. These tensions centered around the issue of national independence, and when independence was realized another plateau was reached and the conflict between the two types of societies tended to decline. However, in varying degrees this plateau tends to be short-lived and soon the tensions increase again. People learn that they cannot fully escape from having to see the advanced countries as being their superiors. It is extremely significant that this second phase of frustrations has a more diffuse character, for the people cannot direct their hostilities against any particular colonial power. Instead, they feel a need to strike out against the demands of the modern world. The reaction can be unexpectedly explosive, and it may focus upon any power that seems to be the symbol of the modern world.

Hence, it must be assumed that over the next ten to fifteen years the United States will become a principal target of the hostility engendered by the frustrations attending the process of modernization. We will find it hard to understand why we should be the objective of such hostility. We must not, however, be provoked to emotional counter-reactions. Our response should be to concentrate on the problem of improving the methods by which the process of cultural diffusion can be accelerated while tensions are minimized. The crucial question is whether or not we can, through more indirect methods than the outmoded methods of colonialism, achieve a more effective transmission of skills and knowledge to transitional peoples. We should not assume that the task will be easy simply because we can picture ourselves as assisting others to achieve their desired objectives of modernizing. The process of national development is extremely complex and difficult. We should not underestimate the danger that our indirect methods may accelerate the demand for the rewards of a modern world, but not provide the discipline of action necessary for achieving such a world.

TENSIONS AMONG THE UNDERDEVELOPED COUNTRIES

One of the most striking characteristics of the foreign policy orientations of most of the newly emerging countries is their lack of awareness of their immediate neighbors and their intense concentration upon the West. The pattern of colonialism was one of creating blinders on the peoples of Africa and Asia as far as viewing their neighboring countries. In particular, the focus of attention of the Westernizing elite in these countries was all in the direction of the mother country and the modern world.

Only with independence have the peoples of Africa and Asia had to learn about the rest of the underdeveloped areas. Lack of actual experiences caused the new governments to base many of their mutual relations upon ideological considerations. In the early 1950's, the leaders of the underdeveloped countries tended to assume in a vague and diffuse way that they shared a common set of interests with all of the other former colonial countries. Indeed, both in the Western world and in the underdeveloped countries, it was assumed that in time a block of countries representing the newly independent states would emerge. The Cold War, in providing a clear logic for a neutralist position, encouraged this sense of a common orientation. Concrete efforts at creating such a force included the Bandung Conference in 1955 and the establishment of the Afro-Asian bloc within the United Nations.

By the end of the 1950's, it became increasingly apparent that the newly emerging countries did not necessarily share such a common set of interests. The Bandung Conference did not usher in a new era, but rather, climaxed a dying one; it was followed only by the Communist-dominated Cairo Conference in 1957. Within the United Nations, the Afro-Asian bloc has only acted as a unit when the issue has been an unambiguous matter of colonialism. On other questions the gap, particularly between the African and the Asian countries, has been increasing during the latter 1950's and early 1960's.

Indeed, as the Asian and African states have come to know each other better it has become increasingly apparent that new grounds for tension and conflict have been introduced into the international system. For example, every state in Southeast Asia has had some conflict with a neighboring state. It is certain that in the next few years there will be increasing tensions within the African continent as new states try to achieve boundaries and divisions that will seem to them to define their physical identity more adequately than the arbitrary boundaries they inherited from the colonial powers.

Already there has been considerable latent conflict among the leading African personalities as they seek to expand their influences on a regional basis. Sentiments of pan-Africanism exist, but there are no effective vehicles for making such aspirations into political realities. Thus, although the idea of pan-Africanism or of Afro-Asian solidarity may continue to exist as a general ideal during the next decade, it is likely to become more a source of frustration than inspiration. Governments seeking to shift attention from their own difficulties may tend to exploit it, and it may become the tool of subversion against extremely fragile states.

Aside from an increase in this form of conflict, the next decade is likely to see a relatively novel source of tension emerging to affect relationships among the underdeveloped societies. When we compare the economic growth rates of the countries currently underdeveloped, it is clear that by 1975 some of these will be well on their way to self-sustained economic growth while others still will have stagnating economies. In short, the future is certain to reveal increasing differences among the underdeveloped countries, and more and more countries will feel that they have less in common with the other underdeveloped societies. Some countries will, indeed, feel that they have risen above the crude and uncomplimentary category of being a mere "Afro-Asian" state.

This pattern of development should reduce lateral tensions among the underdeveloped societies. However, it will still have disquieting effects on those societies that are lagging behind and, as pointed out previously, the more rapidly advancing nations may transfer their tensions to the developed powers. During the past decade, it has been possible for all of the underdeveloped countries to feel a certain bond of solidarity among themselves as they faced the advanced world, and individual governments found comfort in knowing that their difficulties and failures in modernizing and strengthening their country did not justify harsh judgments from their people because they were common to many other countries. The possibility of sharing misery and of sharing a sense of failure has maintained the expectations of some of the new governments. In the next decade, however, examples of successful development will threaten the security of elite groups in nations which have been less successful.

There have been some indications of how such anxieties may affect the stability of underdeveloped areas. For example, some leading Burmese Army officers became dramatically aware of the desperate state of their own country after visits to Thailand, a country they assumed to be less developed than their own, but which they found to be rapidly modernizing. They felt a need for action, which culminated in the Burmese "caretaker" government. In a different pattern of response, the opposition elements in Indonesia appear to have become only discouraged and despondent on observing the rapid improvement of conditions in Malaya. In the next decade, it is likely that those governments that have been faltering will be agitated by deeper feelings of frustration. Plagued with self-doubts and with their citizens questioning their abilities, such elites may find it even more difficult to manage their affairs. Thus, the very example of some governments solving their problems may become the source of new tensions.

TENSIONS BETWEEN THE UNITED STATES AND THE SOVIET UNION

The danger to the international system of the weaknesses and instabilities of the new countries becomes immediately apparent when our analysis turns to United States-Soviet Union relations. There is no underdeveloped country with the potential for threatening our security if it independently develops its power base. The danger is that the weaknesses of such countries will create a power vacuum that will in turn affect our position relative to the Soviet Union.

During the 1950's, our conflict with the Soviet Union expanded to include competition in economic aid to the underdeveloped areas. We have come to a fundamentally ambivalent attitude toward this competition: we see it as a part of a total world struggle with the U.S.S.R. and feel that it constitutes a major challenge to our position in the world, but we also sense that such competition in economic matters may reflect a decline in tensions in the world and that possibly we and the Russians share a common interest in preventing the underdeveloped areas from becoming a powder keg which might set off a third world war.

Such an ambivalence on the part of a major power toward competition in the underdeveloped areas is not unique, for in the classical nation-state system one of the functions of colonial rivalries was to reduce conflict and tension at the centers of power and move it out of Europe and into the marginal areas of the world. Thus Britain and France could contend with each other in Africa and in Southeast Asia with the expectation that the clashes would not bring the two countries into total conflict.

Unfortunately, it appears that certain factors in the current situation will prevent this form of competition among the powers from performing the same function as colonial rivalries did for nineteenth century Europe. First, it is probable that despite the shift in emphasis from aircraft to missile armament during the next decade, the question of overseas bases will continue to be a matter of highest importance to the United States. The competition between ourselves and the U.S.S.R. in the underdeveloped areas is thus likely to continue to be influenced by the advantages we are assumed to derive from our advanced base structure. Even though technological advances will reduce the value of such bases by the end of the decade, there will remain a strong geographical dimension to our conflict with the Russians. We will continue to feel the need to preserve the existing lines of division between the free world and the Soviet bloc.

Secondly, our present conflict with the Soviet Union is too deeply ideological to permit the competition over the underdeveloped areas to perform the function of reducing tensions at the source as was the case in the nineteenth century. We will continue to see any decline in our popularity and in our areas of influence as a threat to what we feel we represent in the world. Similarly, the Soviets will see any decline in the Soviet position as a threat to their total security.

These military and ideological considerations ensure that the intensity of the competition will remain high, but they also suggest that the vital interest of neither side is involved in the underdeveloped areas. Only by miscalculation and irrational policies could these areas become the cause of total war. In the next decade, the military significance of such areas will continue to decline more rapidly than their political and ideological significance. The gap between our vital concerns (including the avoidance of nuclear war) and our concern for the underdeveloped areas is one which the Soviets are likely to exploit with a greater degree of recklessness than in almost any other aspect of the total struggle. Thus, there has been a calculated basis behind the Soviet use of "atomic blackmail" and threats of missile diplomacy during crises in the underdeveloped countries. This was the pattern during the Suez crisis, the Lebanon landings, and during the Congo crises. The assumption that we know our vital interests are not directly involved apparently encourages the Soviets to use bluffs and threats in order to maximize uncertainty and hence to deter us from effective actions. It would appear that in the case of the secret installation of Soviet missiles in Cuba, the Soviets miscalculated what the United States would perceive as in its vital interests. In this instance, the United States acted resolutely and effectively to force the Soviets to withdraw their missiles.

These efforts at maximizing tensions and disorder point to the significant difference between what the underdeveloped areas mean to the United States and to the U.S.S.R. Our concern in these areas involves more than just bilateral competition with the Soviets. We are committed to the maintenance and the remodeling of an international system. They are concerned with disrupting and radically changing the system.

At a basic political and psychological level we do, however, find ourselves involved in a bilateral form of competition with the Soviets in the underdeveloped areas. This is at the level of our ultimate faith in our abilities to devise a system of government whereby all the people may enjoy the full fruits of modern knowledge. If by 1975 the Soviets could prove that they have a superior method for helping the underdeveloped areas modernize, it could so shake us in our fundamental self-confidence that we might no longer be able to offer effective leadership in striving to build a stable and just international system.

Thus, although the military and economic significance of the underdeveloped areas in the next decade of Soviet-American competition may be overestimated, it is impossible to exaggerate the psychological and political significance of our competitive roles in seeking to create new societies for transitional peoples. In the future, as the ideological appeals of Communism continue to decline for peoples in the advanced industrial societies, it is likely to become increasingly apparent that the ultimate issue that is at stake is whether America will be able to lead effectively in developing new societies and a new international order.

PROSPECTS FOR AMERICAN POLICY

These considerations suggest that in looking to the future, the crucial task for the West will be to develop the techniques necessary for modernizing the new countries while at the same time maintaining the stability of the international order.

Soviet strategy, in a perverse fashion, does focus on precisely these two objectives. The Russians have been able to devise the means for conveying the necessary sense of discipline and order that individuals must have if they are to become active participants in a modern society. By imposing their own strait jacket of discipline on such people, they have been able to achieve certain minimum conditions for modernizing a traditional society. At the same time, they have also been able to offer to these people a feeling that they are going to become a part of a new, modern, international order. Thus, on the one hand, they are disciplined, and on the other, they are, in form at least, elevated to becoming partners in the Socialist camp.

As was suggested earlier in this analysis, there is a fundamental need for Western or American doctrines or theories about the process of modernization to provide not only guidance and encouragement to the leaders of the new countries, but also an intellectual framework for coordinating the management of our own policy instruments. We must, during the 1960's, be able to convey to the transitional people a sense that we know what their problems are and that we can help them deal with these problems realistically.

Once the intellectual basis for a democratic approach to development has been established, the next step will be to create a stronger emotional climate appropriate to the enterprise of national development. American policy must be oriented to strengthening the necessary frame of mind for building democratic societies. For example, with probable Chinese Communist developments in mind, it will be particularly important in the next decade for the United States to fight the perverse notion that somehow "democracy" is equated with inefficiency, incompetence, and administrative slovenliness, while "totalitarianism" is equated with efficiency, intelligence, and steadfastness of purpose. For too long we have permitted the leaders of the underdeveloped areas to rationalize all manner of human failings as manifestations of their "democratic approach." It will be necessary to spread an understanding that democracy demands the rigid adherence to professional standards of competence and effectiveness in the performance of all technical activities.

Another general matter which will be crucial in determining the prospects of American policy in the underdeveloped areas is the need for a clearer understanding of the basis of our relations with developing countries. During the last decades, the United States has assumed the lead in creating a wide range of policy instruments for influencing developments in transitional societies. Such new instruments as economic aid, technical assistance, information programs, cultural exchange and the like, all have in common the feature of being designed to go beyond the range of formal, official international relationships and influence domestic developments. Thus, there is always a potential source of tension in our relations with such countries because of the possibilities of interpreting our assistance as a violation of the cardinal principle of the classical nation-state system: the principle of non-interference in the domestic affairs of other countries.

The situation calls for the development of new standards that will make it possible for us to support effectively the diffusion of modern culture and technology while leaving the recipient governments re-assured on the matter of their sovereignty. United States strategy should be one of utilizing the United Nations machinery for technical assistance for testing out and for forcing any issues in this area of international conduct while preserving our bilateral instruments for the bulk of our effective efforts at developing the countries. In short, it is appropriate for the United Nations to take the lead in establishing the principle that external agencies can appropriately, and without compromising a country's sovereignty, influence decisively a society's movement toward the modern world.

Another aim of United States policy efforts should be to obtain general acceptance of the proposition that the world as a whole must not tolerate the spreading of the Cold War to the underdeveloped areas. Specifically, we must decisively "call" any Soviet threats of blackmail during crises in the underdeveloped areas, and we must be equally firm if any underdeveloped countries seek to act irresponsibly in playing upon our basic struggle with the Communists. In this situation, the advantage lies entirely with us if we adopt the posture of champions of the international order.

A final general principle that American policy should support is that there can no longer be any easy changes in the "real estate" lines that divide us from the Soviet bloc. The understanding must be established that although political and social chaos may engulf particular under-developed countries from time to time, it will be intolerable for any power to seek to exploit such developments in order to alter the general power balance.

The Specific Aspects of American Policy

The trends that we have outlined in this chapter suggest that the underdeveloped areas will continue to be a major source of international tensions into the 1970's. With respect to the specific aspects of American political and military policy, the need will be more for improved performance and for greatly expanded programs along current lines than for drastic innovations. There is the need to accept the fact that the problems of the underdeveloped areas will be of long duration. This means that we must be able to lengthen our horizons in planning. We must also give ourselves the ability to make long-run commitments for developmental aid.

Furthermore, as gaps in the rates at which the various new countries are developing begin to appear, our policy instruments will have to become increasingly sensitive to the unique and distinctive character of the individual countries. In the past, it was possible to treat the underdeveloped countries as all falling within the same category and hence it was possible to employ approximately the same techniques in all countries. We must now be prepared to recognize that at different stages of development quite different methods and combinations of policies are needed.

With respect to military policy, two particular problems are likely to become increasingly important.

First, as we move from the Air Age to the Missile Age, there will be some decline in the military significance of our overseas bases in the underdeveloped areas—although not in their political significance as communication and transportation centers capable of ensuring that the United States can act as a worldwide power. However, this same trend also suggests that there will be a decline in the risks of total war arising out of peripheral crises, and hence there is likely to be an increase in the possibilities for limited wars in the underdeveloped areas. The gap between our deterrence strategy and our ability to control marginal disturbances will increase unless we develop more effective limited war forces.

Secondly, our efforts at military assistance to underdeveloped areas is likely to continue to affect the relative position of the military among the elites of the new countries. There is every likelihood that armies will continue to play significant, if not dominant, roles in countries faced with serious difficulties in development. It will become increasingly necessary to ensure that American military aid contributes to and does not inhibit the prospects for economic and social development. It will also be especially important to utilize our opportunities in training military officers in the underdeveloped countries to give them a better appreciation of the processes of national development so that they can perform their extramilitary roles more effectively. The military can play an essential part in modernizing such societies, but they also can become a force retarding progress.

Finally, it may be said that it seems likely that there will be an increased dramatization of the problems of the underdeveloped areas. The American public is likely to be exposed increasingly to discussions of the significance of the areas, American idealism may become increasingly responsive to the apparent challenge, and certainly American ingenuity should be adequate to the task. The crucial question is whether we will be able to act fast enough to get a sufficient start on the developmental process. For if we do not take full advantage of the time available to us until about 1975, we shall be faced with tremendously more difficult problems. This is because by that time the world's population will be growing so rapidly that it will be almost impossible to improve per capita standards of living if all the preparatory work has not been done. The note of urgency stems less from Soviet capabilities or from any particular trend; it comes from the inescapable fact that if successful actions are not taken promptly to assist the processes of modernization, it may become too late for anything to be done at existing levels of technology. America must help to keep alive the hope that a stable world order can yet be created which will be composed of independent communities, bound together by the fruits of man's most advanced knowledge and skills.

Chapter 4

Programs for Alleviating Instability

PAUL N. ROSENSTEIN-RODAN and DALE J. HEKHUIS

In Chapter 3 it was pointed out that the ultimate issue at stake in Soviet-American competition in the underdeveloped areas is whether the United States can effectively lead in developing new societies and a new international order. It was also suggested that the very process of modernization of the underdeveloped countries might serve to enhance or create some instabilities as well as to alleviate others. The present chapter, although mindful of the former, is concerned with the provision of economic and technical assistance as a means of satisfying a minimum condition for the achievement of political stability, namely, a minimum rate of economic development. In the sense that Soviet-American competition in the economic realm may divert tensions to a less explosive area, these assistance programs may also be considered to alleviate international instabilities.

SOME CONTRASTS BETWEEN UNITED STATES AND SOVIET APPROACHES IN FOREIGN AID[1]

Foreign economic and technical aid in the modern sense is essentially an American innovation in foreign affairs. What has been notably lacking in our exploitation of this innovation, as indicated in Chapter 3, is an intellectual basis for understanding the requirements of the development and modernization of transitional societies. We have rather loosely regarded economic aid as a proposition that works to our long-range advantage by creating and supporting a process of social change in which a steadily increasing gross national product is expected, in time, to provide the essential basis for a stable political process. A major goal of our economic aid has thus been to help under-developed economies reach a stage of self-sustaining growth. We expect that our long-range political objectives will be served by supplying the outside push to stagnant economies so that in a short time they can reach a stage in which they continue to grow without outside help. In the process we also see advantages accruing to us that stem from the resultant psychological atmosphere: aid programs help create a sense of constructive purpose for the outlet of strong nationalistic feelings, and the commitment of the underdeveloped areas to serious programs of economic development should reduce irrational tendencies, weaken the appeals of Communism, and strengthen the growth of democratic institutions.

The goals of Soviet foreign aid programs appear to be more immediate and more directly political in nature than those of the U.S. As Robert C. Tucker notes, ". . . economic assistance is regarded as having a political purpose of prime importance: to help along the on-going process of self-detachment of non-Communist countries in the 'anti-imperialist bloc' from economic dependence upon the West and Western political influence."[2] This is not to say that the Soviets can afford to be overtly political in their aid programs. In fact, the neutralist policies and nationalist fervor of many of the underdeveloped areas presents a policy dilemma to the Soviet leaders also. Although they

[1] For a more detailed discussion on this subject see L. W. Pye, "Soviet and American Styles in Foreign Aid," *Orbis*, Vol. IV, Summer 1960, p. 159. Foreign Policy Research Institute, Univ. of Pennsylvania. We are indebted to Prof. Pye and the editors of *Orbis* for permission to draw freely from this article and to reprint the paradigm in this section.

[2] Robert C. Tucker, "Russia, the West and World Order," *World Politics*, Vol. 12, October 1959, p. 15.

expend aid to gain direct political influence, if they attempt directly to exert that influence they risk loss of the aid-program entree to the area.

The contrasts between United States and Soviet goals and views of how foreign aid can work are summarized in the following paradigm:[1]

American	Soviet
1. Great social change can come from marginal investments. Possibility of small input resulting in large output because of "multiplier effect."	1. Social change is extremely costly; big investments of effort yield slight changes.
2. Change is progress and it is popular.	2. Change is progress but people resist it.
3. People will "naturally" work for self-improvement.	3. People will "naturally" slip back into lazy ways.
4. The long run is all important, but short run considerations tend to absorb all one's time and energies.	4. The long run is predetermined, but people tend to waste time and energies in idle speculations about the distant future. Need is for people to channel their energies into the short run.
5. One's enemies and competitors have the advantage of being able to reflect on the long run.	5. One's enemies and competitors have the advantage of being able to direct effectively all their attentions to immediate problems.
6. All aspects of society are interrelated; secondary and tertiary effects important because of our mechanistic vision of society.	6. Secondary and tertiary effects unimportant; necessity for a frontal assault in achieving all objectives because indirect manipulations ineffectual.
7. Indirect effects of policy predictable and hence direct controls not necessary.	7. Limited possibility for predicting immediate effects of policies and hence need for constant control.
8. Different bodies of knowledge have their own "laws" and hence possible to have "apolitical" policies.	8. All specialized knowledge the servant of political considerations and hence no action can be "apolitical."

Especially noteworthy of these observations are the Soviet views that all the various special fields of knowledge must bow to the logic of politics (there are no such things as apolitical acts in international affairs) and that social change is extremely costly (the processes of social change are comparable to war; the old order must be stormed and overpowered). It follows that in the Soviet view economic aid is a means of establishing relations that will eventually lead to direct political influence.

These contrasting approaches to foreign aid hence reflect the ideological differences of the goals of the chief competitors seeking to mold the ultimate nature of the developing new international order. That the development of transitional societies and American leadership in this transformation will be basic determinants in the molding of the new order has already been discussed in Chapter 3. These considerations offer a perspective for gauging the real costs to the Free World of foreign economic and technical aid, costs which include not only the allocation of resources to that purpose but also the business dislocations resulting from the growth of new, subsidized competitors. To some, the importance of maintaining the West's political and economic dynamic is so great as to warrant granting a new status for "development diplomacy." [3]

ECONOMIC ASSISTANCE REQUIREMENTS OF UNDERDEVELOPED COUNTRIES

Criteria for Evaluation of Requirements

A basic objective of Western international aid programs for underdeveloped countries is to accelerate their economic development to a point where a satisfactory rate of growth can be maintained on a self-sustaining basis. That is, foreign capital is provided to increase the rate of domestic capital formation to a level (for example, 12 per cent yielding a 2 per cent increase in per capita income per annum) which can subsequently be maintained without further aid.

This inflow of foreign capital provides additional resources and technology which, in turn, generate additional income. Of this additional income a larger proportion can be saved (marginal rate of savings) than was saved on the average (average rate of savings) at the previous income level. For example, while the average rate of savings for Asia is approximately 7 per cent, the marginal rate could be stepped up, through international aid, to 20 to 25 per cent. Thus a marginal rate of savings which is substantially higher than the average rate of savings

---

[3] Eugene R. Black, *The Diplomacy of Economic Development*, Harvard University Press, Cambridge, 1960.

is the main lever of a development program and should be the principal condition of aid to underdeveloped countries.

Absorptive Capacity. The extent to which increased investments with a high marginal rate of savings can be realized depends on a country's capacity to absorb capital which, in turn, varies directly with the stage of economic development. For example, the capital absorptive capacity of a country with a low level of economic development, where a higher proportion of technical assistance must precede a large capital inflow, is narrowly restricted. With a rising level of development, however, the marginal rate of savings can increase.

The capacity to absorb capital in many underdeveloped countries can, within a few years, be increased by 20 to 30 per cent above present levels. Furthermore, the expectation by an underdeveloped nation that capital will be available over a decade or more up to the limits of its absorptive capacity and its capacity to repay will, in many cases, act as an incentive to greater effort. Thus assurance of continuity of aid may be as important a consideration as the amount of aid.

For most of the underdeveloped countries, however, there are fairly narrow limits to the rate or the extent to which absorptive capacity can be expanded. These limits are a function of a country's administrative capabilities, the skills and size of its non-agricultural labor force, the development of markets, and the extent to which social overhead facilities—power, transport, communications—have been developed.

Estimates of the capital absorptive capacities of individual nations can be made by recourse to three indices, two of which are quantitative, one qualitative. First, actual investment rates for the recent past can be used to set limits to future rates. Second, the actual gap between the average and marginal rates of saving can be ascertained. In the event that a country has been able to maintain or widen this gap during the recent past, a similar performance over the next five-year period may be projected as a lower limit. On the other hand, a changing composition of output, for example, more industry with high marginal rates of savings, could justify a projection of a marginal savings rate significantly higher than past achievements. Finally, qualitative judgments on the ability (relative to other underdeveloped countries) of a country to organize its economic development (administrative apparatus) could be made.

Capacity to Repay. The foreign capital inflow to an underdeveloped nation should be within the limits of its technical absorptive capacity, on the one hand, and within the limits of its capacity to repay on the other. While the first should influence the amount of aid, the second limit should largely determine the method of financing it. For example, where the capacity to repay in low-income underdeveloped countries is below their absorptive capacity, a proportion of aid will have to be given in grants, or "soft loans" repayable in local currency which will be re-lent for subsequent investment.

The capacity to repay should not be assessed by a static projection of the present situation but should take into account the increase in income and the increase in the rate of savings that will result from the adoption of a development program. Nor is it sensible to assume that the foreign debt of each country should be amortized within twenty or thirty years, since it is by no means rational for each country to reduce its foreign indebtedness to zero. The rational question to ask is: "How much foreign indebtedness can a country maintain in the long run?" In exactly the same way in which any national debt (or corporate debt) need not be reduced if it is within sound limits, the foreign debt of debtor-countries need not be amortized to zero in a sound world economy.[4]

Definition of Economic Aid. Foreign capital inflow and foreign economic aid are not synonymous terms. Aid, properly speaking, refers only to that portion of capital inflow that normal market incentives do not provide. It consists of (1) long-term loans repayable in foreign currency, (2) grants and "soft loans" and (3) sale of surplus products for local currency payments.

Long-maturing loans (twenty years or more) are preferable to shorter-term loans. The former reduce the annual burden of amortization to a fraction (one quarter to one half) of the burden imposed by short- and medium-term loans. Furthermore within the definition that economic aid constitutes that part of capital inflow that normal market incentives do not provide, neither short nor medium-term loans can be considered as aid. These loans are largely selling devices for achieving increased exports of the investor's equipment goods.

There is one partial exception to the inclusion of private foreign investment as capital inflow (see Table 6). Oil and mineral investment into "foreign enclaves" in "dual economies," for example, Bahrain and Kuwait, is not considered to be capital inflow where it constitutes the total foreign private investment in an underdeveloped economy. In other countries where foreign private investment flows largely but not entirely into extractive industries, one half of that investment is included

---

[4] For further elaboration see M. F. Millikan and W. W. Rostow, *A Proposal: Key to an Effective Foreign Policy,* Harper and Brothers, New York, 1957.

as capital inflow since, although such industries provide important taxes and other revenues, their diffusion and complementary effects are markedly smaller than those of other industries.

"Soft" loans, including loans "repayable in local currency," are of many varieties. Soft loans are in effect contingent part-grants. That is, a loan is made with the expectation that repayment will depend on the future ability to pay. These loans include very long term (ninety-nine years) loans repayable in foreign currency at a low rate of interest, loans with a long grace period (ten to twenty years) for payment of principal and/or interest, and loans repayable in local currency, which is then reloaned to the borrower for further domestic investment. According to the future success of development, which is unforeseeable and uncertain for each country at the beginning of its development, a part of the local currency loans may be repaid at a later date, while a part will, in fact, have to be written off.

The sale of surplus products for local currency payments (under Public Law 480 in the United States) is also a form of economic aid. In this connection surplus food as well as producer durables can be said to constitute capital. For example, if sufficient indigenous food-stuffs cannot be supplied by an underdeveloped country to support those additionally employed on construction or other investment-type projects, then either more "circulating" investment capital would have to be allocated for imports or the amount of the additional investment would have to be reduced. It cannot be said in reality, however, that the whole of imported surplus products will be used for additional investment, although a good economic development policy will insure that a major portion is used for raising investment, while a lesser portion is used to bolster domestic consumption. In practice, therefore, a withdrawal of surplus product sales would lead to a reduction in both consumption and investment. In the present analysis two thirds of surplus product sales is considered as investment or aid. On this basis Public Law 480 sales constitute approximately 33 per cent of United States aid to underdeveloped countries.

A portion of defense support is also included as economic aid since a portion of it may well contribute to the development of the recipient countries. The estimates of United States economic aid presented in Table 6 include 25 per cent of defense support.

The Burden of International Aid

General principles of how the burden of international aid should be apportioned among developed countries have not been generally agreed upon. However, this analysis suggests that all developed countries (those with income per capita above 600 dollars) should contribute a specified proportion of their Gross National Product to aid, perhaps one-half per cent per annum. Alternatively their contributions could be computed by applying the United States income tax progression to the number of families of each developed country, counting a family as having four times the country's income per capita.

If only countries with GNP per capita in excess of $600 are to be contributors to economic aid, Japan and South Africa would be excluded. Japan should certainly provide short and medium-term loans and technical assistance, but she is not yet a capital export country.

Applying the progressive income tax principle to the real GNP of the developed countries, the United States share of foreign aid would be about 65 per cent of total aid with the remaining 35 per cent to be shared among Europe, Canada, and Oceania. We shall accordingly assume that the United States would supply 65 per cent of the total economic aid provided by the Free World.

The Aid Requirements of the Underdeveloped Areas

In 1960, United States aid and capital outflow to underdeveloped countries approximated 1.8 billion dollars, as shown in Table 6. Private foreign investment from the U.S. totaled 0.7 billion dollars, giving a total capital outflow of 2.5 billion dollars. Technical assistance amounted to 0.2 billion dollars and the Emergency Fund about 0.2 billion dollars. Other sources, principally the International Bank, the United Kingdom and France, provided 1.25 billion dollars.

Summary estimates of capital inflow per annum required by the underdeveloped countries during the 1961–1976 period are presented in Table 7.

Table 7 [5] shows a steadily declining aid requirement with aid decreasing from 4.3 billion dollars per annum during the 1961–1966 period to 1.9 billion dollars during the 1971–1976 period. Simultaneously private investment increases from 1.4 billion dollars per annum in the 1961–

---

[5] The summary estimates are the result of an examination of each underdeveloped country's gross national product, gross and net investment, and average and marginal savings rates in the recent past and the projection of these figures for the 1961–1976 period. The foreign capital inflow is to fill the gap between possible investment (according to each country's absorptive capacity as reflected in her projected rate of growth and her domestic savings) and actual predicted investment. Investments needed for the assumed rate of growth are calculated on the basis of a capital-output ratio of 2.8:1.

TABLE 6. *Capital Outflow to Underdeveloped Countries by Composition and Source, 1960 (Billion Dollars)*

United States	
Development Loan Fund	0.7
Export-Import Bank (gross 0.4, net 0.3)	0.3
PL 480 (two-thirds of total sales of 0.9)	0.6
25% of "Defense Support" (75% is considered "Military Aid")	0.2
Total Economic Aid	1.8
Private Foreign Investment (gross $1.0, net $0.9, minus ½ of oil investment)	0.7
Total Capital Outflow	2.5
Other Free World Sources	
International Bank (gross 0.42, net 0.35, on commitment basis)	0.35
United Kingdom Public (0.2) and Private Investment (gross 0.6, net 0.52 minus ½ of oil investment)	0.35
French Public (0.5) and Private Investment (gross 0.7, net 0.65, minus ½ of oil investment)	0.45
Other Countries	0.10
Total	1.25

Note: The U.S.S.R. supplied economic aid of about $0.5 billion.
Source: P. N. Rosenstein-Rodan, "International Aid for Underdeveloped Countries," Center for International Studies, Massachusetts Institute of Technology, Cambridge, January 1961.

TABLE 7. *Foreign Capital Inflow per Annum Required for Underdeveloped Countries, 1961–1976 (Million Dollars)*

Region	1961–1966			1966–1971			1971–1976		
	Capital Inflow	"Aid"	Private Invest.	Capital Inflow	"Aid"	Private Invest.	Capital Inflow	"Aid"	Private Invest.
Africa	430	275	155	605	395	210	740	415	325
Latin America	1550	840	710	1495	585	910	1010	180	830
Asia	2695	2395	300	2380	1965	415	1250	910	340
Asia (alt. India)*	(2520)	(2240)	(280)	(2910)	(2430)	(480)	(2270)	(1710)	(560)
Middle East	640	475	165	750	525	225	400	180	220
Europe	385	305	80	455	305	150	360	185	175
Total I	5700	4290	1410	5685	3775	1910	3760	1870	1890
Total II (alt. India)	(5525)	(4135)	(1390)	(6215)	(4240)	(1975)	(4780)	(2670)	(2110)

* Asia (alt. India) and Total II (alt. India) reflect an alternative assumption that the capital output ratio for the Indian Third Five Year Plan may be too low and that the capital inflow required is higher than that assumed in the plan.

1966 period to 1.9 billion dollars per annum during the 1971–1976 period. It is also of interest to note that Africa is practically the only region for which aid requirements increase over the 1961–1976 period. Asian aid requirements fall off sharply in the 1971–1976 period. Latin America's aid requirement declines substantially between the periods 1961–1966 and 1966–1971 and dwindles to 0.18 billion dollars per annum in the 1971–1976 period. This is a reflection of the fact that by 1971 many Latin American countries—including Argentina, Brazil, Chile, Colombia, Mexico, Uruguay, and Venezuela—according to this analysis, will, no longer require aid.

Of the total aid requirement shown in Table 7 the International Bank is assumed to supply 0.5 billion dollars per annum; the United States share would amount to 2.46 billion dollars per annum in the 1961–1966 period; 2.13 billion dollars in the 1966–1971 period; and 1.41 billion dollars in the 1971–1976 period.

In order to match the low-income countries' (mainly in Asia) limited capacity to repay, these loans should be distributed as follows: 65 per cent of "soft" and 35 per cent of "hard" loans in the 1961–1966 period; 50 per cent soft and 50 per cent hard in the 1961–1971 period; and 40 per cent soft and 60 per cent hard in the 1971–1976 period.

TABLE 8. *Allocation of Aid Responsibility and "Other" Aid Required per Annum 1961–1976 (Billion Dollars)*

	1961–1966	1966–1971	1971–1976
Allocation of Economic Aid			
Development Loan Fund	1.50	1.20	0.80
	(1.2 soft)	(0.8 soft)	(0.3 soft)
	(0.3 hard)	(0.4 hard)	(0.5 hard)
Export-Import Bank	0.26	0.33	0.21
⅔ of PL 480	0.70	0.60	0.40
Total	2.46	2.13	1.41
Other Aid Required			
Technical Assistance	0.25	0.25	0.20
⅓ of PL 480 (for "Consumption" purposes)	1.34	0.30	0.20
Social Development "Budget Support" etc., (not examined in this chapter)	0.30	0.30	0.20
Special Contingencies Fund	0.20	0.20	0.10
Total	1.10	1.10	1.70

The allocation of "economic" and "other" aid in typical years might be as shown in Table 8.

Thus, total United States government expenditures for underdeveloped countries under this plan would amount to about 3.6 billion dollars per annum in the 1961–1966 period, 3.2 billion dollars per annum in the 1966–1971 period, and 2.1 billion dollars per annum in the 1971–1976 period.

Prospects for Economic Development

In appraising the long-run prospects for economic development of the underdeveloped areas, it must be recognized at the outset that economic assistance can only make available a basic requisite, capital, for economic development. The actual effectiveness of the aid itself would depend upon the extent to which it succeeds in eliciting increased national development efforts, which is not necessarily coincidental with a maximum increase in income. For example, the investment required to produce an additional unit of income varies with the stage of development. In instances where the bulk of available capital must be devoted to the establishment of social overhead facilities only small increases in income will be generated. However, once these overhead facilities have been constructed, higher income-yielding investments can be undertaken. Thus, from the point of view of progressing toward self-sustained growth, a direct increase in income is less significant than an increase in investment opportunities.

Assuming, therefore, that the basic objective of an aid program is to provide an opportunity to achieve sustained (continuous) growth and not to equalize incomes in different countries, what degree of development for the underdeveloped countries can be foreseen, provided these countries grasp the opportunity proffered them?

In summary, it is projected from the previous considerations that the gross national product of the underdeveloped areas as a whole would increase by about 4 per cent per annum during the 1961–1976 period while population growth would approximate 2 per cent per year.[6]

---

[6] To the extent that the projection of the population growth rate is underestimated, the economic growth rate is overestimated. It may well be the case that the average rate of population growth will exceed 2 percent per annum. No allowance has been made, for example, for spurts in population growth which might be induced by the process of economic advance itself. Furthermore, no explicit allowance has been made for the costs of fertility control programs which may have to proceed concurrently with the economic assistance program in order to achieve the estimated rate of economic growth. These costs are highly unpredictable, since they are a function of future developments in birth control technologies.

These data are for anticipated aggregate performance, however, and consequently do not reflect the different rates of progress of the individual underdeveloped nations. In order to gain an appreciation of the widely disparate progress which would be achieved let us attempt to list those countries which could achieve either sustained or self-sustained growth during the 1961–1976 period.

Sustained Growth. Basic conditions for the achievement of sustained growth include: a level of investment approximating 10 per cent or more of the national income, the rapid expansion of one or more sectors of industry, the ability to imitate and absorb other countries' methods of production (technological progress), and the development of an entrepreneurial class.[7] An important characteristic of this stage of development is that the need for foreign capital is greater than during any other period.

None of the countries in Africa has reached or is very likely to reach this stage during the next decade. Latin America, with about one sixth of the total population of the underdeveloped countries, has one third of their income and approximately 37 per cent of their investment. This region consists, however, of three unequal groups. First, there are five countries with a high, sustained rate of growth: Argentina, Brazil, Chile, Colombia, and Mexico. (Within a few years, Uruguay and probably Jamaica can be added to this group, and within a decade Ecuador and Cuba can possibly be added.) Second, there are countries with a lower and less sustained but nevertheless satisfactory rate of growth like Peru, Ecuador, and Venezuela. Third, there is a large group of stationary countries in Central America which, partly because of very high rates of population growth, cannot "get off dead center." Costa Rica has a special position among these countries, having a relatively high level of income but no growth in output. The example of Mexico, on the other hand, shows that a high rate of population increase is not an insuperable obstacle to economic growth.

In Asia, both India and Communist China have achieved sustained growth. While Pakistan's tempo of development appears to be somewhat lower, it has promise of being sustained. Burma should be able to achieve a high, sustained rate in the near future. "Economic factors"

---

[7] Economic factors are a necessary but not sufficient condition for sustained growth. For a discussion of the multiple causation and interrelation of the social, political, and economic factors involved see *Economic, Social and Political Changes in the Underdeveloped Countries and Its Implications for U.S. Policy* (A study prepared at the request of the Committee on Foreign Relations, U. S. Senate), The Center for International Studies, Massachusetts Institute of Technology, Cambridge, March 1960.

such as the rate of savings appear to be favorable in Burma and the capacity to organize development may follow soon. Malaya's satisfactory rate of growth does not yet show symptoms of being sustained. Obstacles to achieving sustained growth in Ceylon include a rapidly increasing population and a relatively low capacity to organize development. Indonesia is an example of a limited capacity to effectively absorb economic assistance.

In the Middle East, Turkey, Egypt, and Iraq are possible candidates for sustained growth in five or ten years. The task appears to be most difficult in Egypt because of a high density of population. Yet there are symptoms of development vigor which may show some results in five years.

In Southern Europe, both Yugoslavia and Greece seem to have reached the stage of sustained growth, and Spain and Portugal may follow within five to ten years. None of the countries in Africa have reached or are likely to reach sustained growth during the next decade.
Self-Sustained Growth. Self-sustaining growth marks a stage in which economic assistance is no longer required for economic growth. In Latin America several countries will probably reach this stage within five or ten years. Colombia, Argentina, and Mexico will gradually approach it during the 1966–1976 period with more than half of total capital inflow provided by private investment. Chile's progress is less clearly foreseeable. In Asia, India should reach this stage in the early 1970's if her third and fourth five-year plans can be implemented. While realization may lag behind the austere and ambitious targets, she may reach the self-sustaining growth stage with a few years delay, say in 1976. Pakistan may reach this stage three to five years later; the Philippines probably only after 1975. None of the countries of the Middle East appears likely to reach this stage by 1976, with the possible exception of oil-rich Iraq. In Southern Europe, Yugoslavia should achieve self-sustained growth by 1966 and Greece during the latter part of the 1960's.

TECHNICAL ASSISTANCE PROGRAMS

Some General Requirements and Specific Functions

The importance of planning and executing technical assistance programs in a context of economic, political, and social considerations is recognized in the United States Mutual Security Program. Technical assistance is defined therein[8] as:

---

[8] U. S. Mutual Security Act, 1960, Section 302.

Programs for the international interchange of technical knowledge and skill, designed to contribute primarily to the balanced and integrated development of the economic resources and productive capabilities of economically underdeveloped areas. Such activities (are) limited to economic, engineering, medical, educational, labor, agricultural, forestry, fishery, mineral, and fiscal surveys, demonstrations, training, and similar projects that serve the purpose of promoting the development of economic resources, productive capabilities and trade of economically underdeveloped areas, and training in public administration.

Another general requirement is for shaping development programs to the highly individual needs and resources of the individual recipient nations. For example, while some degree of industrialization is probably essential to the growth of all underdeveloped areas, the rate and degree of industrialization and the types of industries will not be common among areas. In fact, industrialization does not represent the only path to economic growth and consequently should not necessarily be conceived as the *raison d'être* of assistance programs.

This implies the need for comprehensive development planning for individual nations so that priorities are established for the various development tasks. The basic problem is to secure the most effective use of all resources—human as well as material. Assistance programs that fail to take account of this requirement may act more as diversions from, rather than contributions to, the main stream of economic development. It may be seriously questioned, for example, whether the need for reactor research activity has been correctly assessed under the Atoms for Peace program for countries such as Vietnam and Thailand. Such countries are in the transitional stage of economic growth and their developmental needs are numerous. Investments of their scarce technical manpower and financial resources in reactor research appear premature for either future atomic-power applications or medical and agricultural experimentation.

Factors of tradition and culture in underdeveloped areas often impede social change and deter acceptance of it. The ability to adapt to the changes engendered by science and technology is an important prerequisite for modernization and varies widely among the underdeveloped areas. "It is this ability to absorb and apply modern technology (to agriculture and raw materials as well as industry) which distinguishes a modern growing economy from a traditional economy. In one sense, the most basic economic change required is therefore psychological." [9] Acceptance of these changes can hardly be decreed. To

---

[9] *Economic, Social and Political Changes in the Underdeveloped Countries and Its Implications for U.S. Policy, op. cit.*, p. 23.

reach full effectiveness, assistance programs must allow for these impediments and be designed to facilitate acceptance of modernization.

Planning technical assistance programs for the individual nations is hence complicated by their peculiarities, which demand differences in the approaches, the content, and the phasing of the various elements of the programs. However, there are certain basic functions of technical assistance which appear to apply to all cases.

Economic Planning and Establishment of Development Priorities. Essential to these activities is knowledge of the physical resources and agricultural environment (for example, water, mineral, soil, and power resources) and the trade potential of products which could exploit the natural resources. Technical assistance is generally required by underdeveloped areas in order to secure such pre-investment survey data.

Training Indigenous Technical Manpower. As previously noted, inadequate resources of indigenous technical manpower are in general a critical impediment to modernization in the underdeveloped countries. The immediate and practical needs of any particular country do not encompass all specialities of technology. One function of technical assistance is to provide special training programs for rapid development of specialists to meet these more immediate needs. However, the deficiencies in technical manpower reflect a more basic deficiency in educational resources. Hence, another function of technical assistance is to aid in establishing educational facilities and training teachers to eventually secure a body of technical specialists and workers skilled in vocational arts.

Although the immediate and short-term manpower needs of the underdeveloped areas predominantly fall into the realm of technology, the training of at least a limited number of scientists and their employment in basic research is a necessary adjunct to national technological development. One reason for this is that basic research aids in the training of teachers highly competent in their technical subjects. Another is to prevent delay in the future flow of innovation which will increasingly stem from basic science.

Adaptive Engineering. There is a growing realization that traditional modes of foreign aid and technical assistance that have often attempted to utilize alien technologies from developed countries are frequently inappropriate for newly developing countries and that an approach which involved a measure of adaptive engineering—adapting technology to the particular needs and environments of the less developed areas— could sometimes be more effective. Thus, the jeep is an example of adapting known technology to a particular need—transport of military personnel—and environment—rugged terrain.

Actually little adaptive engineering, other than of the superficial variety, has been accomplished with respect to the specific needs and environments of the developing countries. In a very real sense this is not surprising when it is recognized that (1) the potential market has frequently been too small and too specialized to serve as an inducement for adaptive engineering programs leading to commercial products or processes and (2) the U.S. foreign aid program, until recently, has not regarded research and development on new or improved technologies for developing countries as falling within its purview.

Moreover a note of caution should be injected with respect to apparent needs for new or adapted technology. Upon a careful review, it may be discovered that an already existing technology is quite sufficient for a particular requirement. The difficulty here is the considerable amount of time and effort required to establish an international inventory of existing technologies. Furthermore in many cases the transfer of technology from a developed country to a less-developed country is straightforward and there is no particular requirement for adaptation. This is especially true with respect to large scale facilities in such areas as power generation, petroleum refining, and rail transport.

It should also be pointed out that although it may be desirable to develop new products or equipment which are cheaper for the developing countries, less costly to operate, simple to operate, easy to maintain, and highly reliable, it is seldom that all of these criteria can be satisfied simultaneously. Under these circumstances a problem of systems engineering is involved from the standpoint of determining optimal design and performance characteristics.

Establishing Applied Research Facilities. Because of scarce economic and technical manpower resources, most of the underdeveloped nations are without applied research facilities. In many instances their manpower is not qualified to organize such facilities, to plan programs, or even to maintain equipment. The need for external aid may go beyond the mere establishment and organization of the facilities; experienced and inventive foreign personnel may be needed to serve, at least part-time, as research staff members and as consultants.

Underdeveloped nations may require several, or even networks, of these applied research facilities[10] organized and equipped to engage in a wide range of problems, from those of immediate consequence for infant industries and agriculture to problems of longer-range consequences for maintaining a flow of invention.

---

[10] For some suggestions along these lines see *Recommendations for Strengthening Science and Technology in Selected Areas of Africa South of the Sahara*, National Academy of Sciences, Washington, D.C., July 1959.

Transferring Knowledge and Skills for Specific Development Projects.
The developed nations have long been accumulating a fund of practical
experience often referred to as "know-how." This experience can be
effectively gained through job apprenticeship. The transfer of know-
how is an important function in development projects where newly
trained and inexperienced indigenous personnel are bolstered by foreign
technologists skilled in the complexities of the task. The transfer need
not always be made in connection with an assistance project; it can
be accelerated through planned apprenticeships of trainees from underdeveloped nations in the more or less ordinary technical activities in
the industrialized nations.

Recommendations for Improving Technical Assistance

The importance of improved application of science and technology
in the service of the United States policies toward underdeveloped
areas is generally recognized. In particular, more conscious direction
must be given to technological activities in the United States that can
assist in the achievement of American international goals. New emphasis should be given to implementing technical assistance, for example, programs for international exchange of knowledge and skills.
This is true especially in the training of indigenous technical manpower,
the transfer of knowledge and skills for specific development programs,
and the establishment of indigenous applied-research facilities. The
goals of technical assistance are to create pools of technically experienced personnel within the underdeveloped areas, to provide them
with the wealth of know-how from the developed countries for the
more immediate tasks, and to provide them with facilities for adaptive
development.

Beyond generally expanding the present programs for technical cooperation, a major step towards attainment of these goals would result
from a greater use of the technical and managerial resources of United
States industry. In attempting to aid the underdeveloped areas to develop their resources and raise their standards of living, it is paradoxical
that "the greatest reservoir of industrial growth talent the world has
ever witnessed, American free enterprise, has not yet been successfully
enlisted to contribute to the goals." [11]

The following suggestions for more effective implementation of
technical assistance programs are perhaps worthy of consideration.

---

[11] *Significant Issues in Economic Aid to Newly Developed Countries*, Stanford Research Institute, Menlo Park, California, 1960, p. 2.

They are principally aimed at aiding in the solution of some practical and immediate technical problems of the underdeveloped areas.

1. Identify requirements for adaptive engineering in such areas as small-scale industry, water purification, tillage techniques, protein extraction, and small-scale power sources.

2. Increase radically the number of training positions made available by United States industry to engineering, science, and business administration graduates of the underdeveloped nations. A recent report[12] revealed that of 26 Free World nations participating in a job-training exchange program, the United States ranked eighteenth in the number of openings (81) made available. Some nations offered several hundred openings each.

3. Investigate means for motivating and involving the United States scientific and engineering community in the technical assistance.

4. Determine the types of engineering training and curriculum most appropriate for technical assistance personnel and for engineers and technicians in the underdeveloped countries.

5. Explore potential working relationships between laboratories and institutes in the United States and research organizations in the less developed countries for the purpose of carrying out applied research on technical problems and conducting pilot projects.

6. Consider the establishment of a United States technical institute for the underdeveloped areas with the purpose of providing facilities for applied research on technical problems of development. An additional function could be the translation and dissemination of applied research and technological information. The facility could be operated in the United States under the sponsorship of a private foundation or technical society. Some research personnel would be "on leave" from the underdeveloped areas, and some "on leave" from United States industrial firms and universities.

In addition to adaptive development of devices, processes, or techniques of various kinds, which might be treated in the technical institute mentioned above, there is a need for a systems-development approach to some of the basic problems that inhibit economic growth in the underdeveloped areas. An example are the problems of illiteracy and untrained workers. Mobile educational systems employing selected audio-visual aids and other mechanical teaching aids could be designed for use, particularly in the rural areas of underdeveloped countries. Power supplies, resistance of devices to temperature and corrosion, and

---

[12] *Engineer,* Engineers Joint Council, Vol. 1, No. 3, Fall 1960.

modes of mobility might have to be varied to suit different climates. Such systems could not only help to increase literacy but could also aid instruction in sanitation and health problems, birth control, improved agricultural practices, domestic and animal husbandry, and in the training of teachers, industrial workers, and medical aids. Development of such systems would require a high degree of cooperation between governmental, industrial, educational, and psychological specialists.

PART III

INTERNATIONAL STABILITY AND MUTUAL DETERRENCE

Chapter 5

Stabilizing the Military Environment

ROBERT E. OSGOOD

Ever since President Eisenhower broached the "open skies" proposal in 1955, American "disarmament" policy has assigned priority—apart from diplomatic and propagandistic purposes—to stabilizing the military balance of power rather than to abolishing or reducing the arms that sustain the military balance. So Secretary of State Herter on February 18, 1960, described the first goal of America's disarmament policy as creating "a more stable military environment" by reducing the risk of war resulting from a surprise attack launched by miscalculation or from the promiscuous spread of nuclear weapons production.[1] And so on May 25, 1960, President Eisenhower took the occasion of the U-2 incident to reiterate the urgent need for an international agreement providing mutual assurance against surprise attack; and on September 22, 1960, in an address to the United Nations General Assembly, proposed a United Nations surveillance body to help nations to prove

---

This chapter originally appeared in the March 1961 issue of the American Political Science Review.
[1] *New York Times*, February 19, 1960, p. 4.

to each other that they are not preparing to launch a surprise attack.[2]

If stability is the objective, then arms control is clearly the comple-ment rather than the antithesis of defense policy. Yet in the absence of an overall strategy of stability, linking arms control with military strategy, the two may work against each other. Thus in the context of missile technology, stabilizing the military environment requires the American government to make a basic decision, not only about arms control, but about the whole strategy of deterrence. That decision should be based on a sober appraisal of the element of instability in the balance of terror, the diverse and interrelated requirements of de-terrence, and the relationship of military stability to the political en-vironment.

Such an appraisal will indicate, I believe, that the most effective con-tributions to military stability under foreseeable technological and political conditions are measures in the realm of military capabilities, strategy, and pronouncements that the United States and her allies can readily take by themselves, rather than in the realm of elaborate inter-national agreements that require the formal cooperation of the Com-munist bloc.

THE MILITARY BASIS OF STABILITY

Stability of the military environment is measured chiefly by the absence of a tendency toward war among the major military powers and their allies. Since war grows out of conflicts of national interest, military stability cannot be dissociated from the stability of the political environment. However, the contemporary military environment is widely supposed to be distinguished from previous military environ-ments by the extent to which its stability depends upon the autonomous influence of military technology, which is now based upon radically novel weapons. Some hold that this technology promotes stability in spite of serious political conflicts; others hold that it incites instability in spite of a common interest in avoiding war. Both may be right, de-pending upon the strategy and capabilities nations adopt. In any case, the novel characteristics of contemporary military technology seem to have placed an unprecedented burden upon the stability of the military environment as a condition of relative international order.

Stability is an old ideal in international relations, expressing the goal of moderating and regularizing the competition of power among states

---

[2] Radio and television address to the nation, *ibid.*, May 26, 1960, p. 6; *ibid.*, Sep-tember 23, 1960, p. 14.

so as not to disrupt the political system, which they have a mutual interest in preserving. The most effective instrument of stability in modern times was the balance-of-power system of the middle of the eighteenth and nineteenth centuries, which in theory—and, to a notable extent, in practice—constrained the great powers by confronting them, on the one hand, with the prospect of countervailing alignments and alliances and by offering them, on the other hand, opportunities for limited adjustments of power without the hazards of unrestricted competition. But the conditions that enabled this system to stabilize international relations as well as it did—principally, a fairly equal distribution of power among several states, a rudimentary moral consensus among rulers and ruling classes, and a war potential of relatively limited destructive capacity—no longer exist. Instead, we live in a more or less bipolar political system dominated by two states with intensely antithetical interests and aims. Either of these states could drastically alter the configurations of power in a single military encounter. Neither has access to the non-military balancing mechanisms of the old political system, such as shifts of alliances and territorial compensations, even if it wished to use them.

With the disappearance of the non-military balancing mechanisms of the balance-of-power system the stability of the general confrontation of state power and interests has come to depend more upon the stability of the military balance. At the same time, with the revolutionary increase in the destructive capacity of war potential in the last half century, the resort to armed conflict, which was a primary instrument for maintaining the balance of power before the "century of total war," could destroy not only the balance of power among states but perhaps some of the states themselves. Consequently, in the Cold War the status quo powers have aspired to build stability on the foundation of deterrence, on the assumption that the very capacity of the United States and the Soviet Union to destroy each other gives both an overriding interest in observing strict restraints upon the overt use of armed force.

This is an essential assumption upon which to base contemporary foreign and military policies; yet it would be dangerous to underestimate the difficulties of translating a hypothetical common interest in stable deterrence into actually stable relationships. Even assuming that revolutionary powers share this interest with status quo powers, in order to act upon it both must observe an unprecedented degree of deliberate restraint upon the conduct of their military and political policies, considering the risks and consequences of the competition getting out of control. This means that the United States and the Soviet Union can buy stability only at a price of adopting carefully planned reciprocal restrictions upon the most "efficient" instruments of military power. In planning these restrictions, both powers must take account of the inherent element of instability in a military balance that depends so heavily upon threats and counterthreats of reprisals which are intended to constrain the adversary by sheer terror.

THE SOURCES OF INSTABILITY

In order to stabilize the military environment we must understand its basic sources of instability. All military balances have been subject to instability resulting from the natural failure of statesmen to estimate intentions and capabilities correctly and to act upon a strict and prudent calculus of risks and gains, subordinating concrete, immediate interests to the general interest in preserving a hypothetical and always nebulous state of equilibrium. The contemporary military balance is also subject to this kind of human failure. Consider the opportunities for miscalculation, even if there is mutual will to follow the rules of the system.

The maintenance of the balance of terror puts an unprecedented premium upon prudent and accurate calculations of the will or intention of adversaries to impose upon each other a disadvantageous ratio of costs to benefits, even though neither would be likely to gain an advantage if both employed their full capabilities to impose such costs. The heavy dependence of military power upon the credibility of reprisals and counter-reprisals rather than upon opposing capabilities to attain or withhold military objectives, creates a far more complex and uncertain relationship between military capabilities and the will to use them than existed under the balance-of-power system in its heyday (which was itself far from being the automatic regulator of power that its proponents sometimes claimed). Whereas deterrence under the balance-of-power system depended ultimately upon estimates of relative military capabilities—which were relatively simple to measure and were assumed to have a fairly straightforward relationship to the will to employ them—deterrence under the balance-of-terror system depends, primarily, upon a complicated process of mutual mind reading based upon some such highly subjective and conjectural calculus as the relationship between the value of an objective at stake and the estimated effectiveness and costs of an action in the light of the probability of a particular response. The management and control of deterrence as an instrument of policy is, correspondingly, more unpredictable and more subject to miscalculation. At the same time, the consequences of even a small miscalculation could be enormous.

Stability is further jeopardized by the rapidly changing and untried weapons systems upon which deterrence must now be based. The whole complex calculus of deterrence rests upon assumptions about the consequences of employing a military technology that has never been tested in war. Merely by the normal process of technological innovation and obsolescence, one configuration of capabilities that seems to assure stability can be rapidly supplanted by another that seems to upset the balance.

The saving grace of the system of deterrence is that, up to a point, the very uncertainty of the requirements of deterrence, combined with the disastrous consequences of miscalculation, may stabilize a condition of reciprocal restraint, since states will be proportionately cautious not to make a military threat or action that might lead to war. But, carried to its full logic, a strategy based upon the stabilizing effect of this uncertainty leads to a dangerous reliance upon the balance of terror to deter the whole range of possible military threats. It leads to a kind of strategic monism that relies too heavily upon the undeviating self-restraint and low risk-taking propensities of statesmen. It ignores the provocative effect of the fearful uncertainties themselves. It overlooks the tendency of any apparently stable military balance, even one based on great uncertainties and risks, to breed unwarranted confidence in the regularity and predictability of that balance, which in turn diminishes the restraints upon military action. And, connected with this phenomenon, it overlooks the tendency of the stability of deterrence against one kind of threat—for example, the initiation of strategic nuclear strikes—to create instability with respect to another—particularly, limited conventional military action.

In the light of these hazards, one of the greatest threats to stability in the contemporary military environment is the proclivity of democratic nations to economize in acquiring increasingly expensive weapons systems by relying upon deterrence of the most catastrophic contingency —an all-out nuclear attack—to deter a wide range of lesser contingencies, while tailoring their estimates of the uncertain requirements of deterrence to fit the capabilities they are willing to buy.

THE DECLINE OF CONFIDENCE IN STABILITY

In spite of the inherent element of instability in the balance-of-terror system, the great Western powers were inclined, until the onset of the missile age, to assume that the stability of the military environment is an automatic result of technological advance in the means of destruction, that the requirements of stability and maximum striking power are identical. When the United States held a monopoly of nuclear striking power, stability was supposed to be a function of the continued advancement of her capacity for massive retaliation. When the United States lost her atomic monopoly, stability was supposed to be assured by a balance, or parity, instead of a monopoly of terror.

Thus Western leaders eagerly embraced the view expounded by Sir Winston Churchill in his famous address to the House of Commons on March 1, 1955, that as strategic nuclear striking capacities increased, even an inferior capacity could deter the aggressor from "snatching an early advantage" by threatening to inflict "swift, inescapable, and crushing retaliation." "Then it may be," he foresaw, "that we shall, by a process of sublime irony, have reached a stage in this story where safety will be the sturdy child of terror, and survival the twin brother of annihilation." Churchill even anticipated the realization of that ultimate condition of stability, nuclear sufficiency, which would remove any security incentive to continue the nuclear arms race except for technological adjustments to continue sufficiency; for in three or four years, he said, nations might reach a point of "saturation" in their nuclear capabilities, when, although one nuclear power might be stronger than the other, each would be capable of inflicting crippling damage upon the other.[3]

After Churchill gave the balance-of-terror its most eloquent and hopeful expression, however, a marked decline of Western confidence in its automatic stability set in. This decline of confidence was a result of three major changes in the military environment: (1) the spectacular growth of Soviet nuclear striking power; (2) the increasing range, speed, accuracy, and explosive power of nuclear missiles; and (3) the prospect of other powers acquiring strategic nuclear capabilities. It was manifested, principally, in four ways: (1) doubts about the efficacy of America's capacity for massive retaliation to deter aggression upon other states; (2) doubts about the efficacy of this capacity to deter a direct strategic attack upon the United States; (3) fears that the strategic nuclear capabilities of the United States and the Soviet Union might provoke a thermonuclear war by accident, miscalculation, or misapprehension of surprise attack; and (4) fears that the spread of nuclear capabilities to other powers will lead to wars provoked and initiated by third powers.

---

[3] It should be noted that Churchill, unlike those who took his statement as a confirmation of the universal efficacy of massive retaliation as a deterrent, recognized that stability in the strategic sector of the military environment would create instability in the tactical sector unless local conventional forces were enlarged to deal with piecemeal, limited aggressions.

Quite apart from the possible adverse effects of the diffusion of nuclear capabilities, including the difficulty of stabilizing a multipolar
balance of terror, even these doubts and fears about the bipolar balance
created a far more complex view of the requirements of stability and
their relation to strategic nuclear striking power than the view prevailing before the appearance of accurate long-range missiles. By 1960,
these requirements were being discussed and proposed in the West,
explicitly or implicitly, in terms of three concepts of deterrence—active,
passive, negative.[4] These concepts are distinguished by different objectives and methods and are related to stability in different ways. Yet
Western governments were slow to take full account of the conflicts
among these diverse requirements of stability and of the implications
of these conflicts for existing strategies and capabilities of deterrence.
This was conspicuously true of the Eisenhower administration.

ACTIVE DETERRENCE

Active deterrence refers to the deterrence of military aggressions upon
allies and other powers. If it depends upon nuclear reprisals rather than
upon local resistance (whether by limited nuclear or conventional warfare), it requires convincing a potential aggressor that one will counter
aggression with a first strike (first and second strikes referring here to
the initial and secondary use of strategic nuclear blows),[5] which will
inflict unacceptable costs in relation to the aggressor's anticipated benefits.

Exercised against an aggressor with a substantial counterstrike capability, active nuclear deterrence clearly puts a premium upon the
credibility of a first strike, not just upon the capability to inflict great

---

[4] "Active" and "passive" deterrence are words invented in 1958 by John Grant, the
Defense Correspondent of the London *Times*, and subsequently popularized in
Parliamentary defense debates. See *The Times* (London), October 15, 1958, p. 13;
October 16, 1958, p. 13. They are less precise but, perhaps, more descriptive than
other designations of these two types of deterrence, such as Herman Kahn's Types II
and III and Type. I. As explained below, "negative" deterrence is my own invention.

[5] "Strike first" and "strike back" might be less confusing terms, since a "first strike"
can be construed to refer solely to a surprise attack that starts hostilities, whereas
it actually refers to a retaliatory nuclear attack against non-nuclear aggression as
well; and "second strike" may be construed to refer to the second nuclear blow
delivered by the state initiating the nuclear exchange, whereas, in the special sense,
it refers only to the first retaliatory nuclear blow launched by the state receiving
the initial nuclear strike. However, "first strike" and "second strike" are by now
too firmly fixed in their special meanings to justify supplanting them.

damage. But the credibility of a first strike depends upon convincing the aggressor that in a strategic nuclear exchange one's own costs would not be unacceptable in terms of one's anticipated benefits. Therefore, the growth of Soviet striking power has seriously diminished the credibility of America's willingness to deliver a first strike on the Soviet Union and its allies in response to their aggressions upon America's allies, except, perhaps, in the case of aggressions taking the form of local nuclear attacks. It has diminished the credibility of active nuclear deterrence in inverse proportion to the dimensions of the threat that such aggressions directly pose to America's security and prestige. The emergence of substantial Chinese Communist nuclear striking power would diminish the credibility of active nuclear deterrence to the point of zero.

What is required to stabilize the military environment, to maintain deterrence, against the threat of aggressions upon America's allies and other powers? The principal requirement of active nuclear deterrence is a first-strike capability that can disarm enough of the nuclear adversary's striking power to confine its retaliatory damage to an acceptable level. A device that would stop second-strike missiles by "killing" them or disrupting their electronic systems might contribute to the same end; but the contribution is likely to be negligible, since it would seem to be much easier to counter such a device than to make it effective and since one power is unlikely to enjoy a significant unilateral antimissile capability for long. A tremendous civil defense program might also, conceivably, contribute to the credibility of active nuclear deterrence; but this, too, would be relatively easy for the nuclear adversary to counter by increasing his capacity to inflict civilian damage with bigger warheads, "dirtier" bombs, the use of gas, and other means.

Can the United States, then, maintain a nuclear striking power adequate for active deterrence? Let us assume that anything approaching the destruction of thirty of America's major cities would be regarded as an unacceptable price to pay for countering aggression upon her allies. By the late 1960's a first-strike capability against Russia that would give American statesmen confidence in their ability to keep Soviet retaliatory damage below this level will probably require the maintenance of such a vast and effective "counterforce" capability as to be economically and technically infeasible.[6] For as the numbers, accuracy, dispersion,

---

[6] A U.S. "counterforce" strike would be one directed against Russian missiles and planes (and their bases, command centers, and other supporting elements), as distinguished from "countercity" or "countervalue" strikes, which would be directed against fixed civilian targets—primarily, Russian cities and industrial facilities.

mobility, concealment, and protection—in short, the relative invulnerability—of Soviet long-range missiles increase (as they must, if only to neutralize America's first-strike capability), the United States will find it prohibitively difficult to maintain a counterforce capability that she can safely rely upon to destroy enough of Russia's retaliatory power. At the same time, the effort to maintain such a capability would lead to an immensely expensive arms race, if only because each side would fear that its second-strike capability was in serious jeopardy. And, of course, even a perfect counterforce capability would not guarantee deterrence of a great variety of lesser aggressions; for even when the United States enjoyed a virtual monopoly of nuclear striking power, such aggressions occurred.

Only if the United States bases active deterrence on a strategy of limited or graduated nuclear reprisals—that is, a strategy of striking a small number of selected targets as a means of imposing disproportionate costs in a bargaining process leading to a political settlement —will she be able logically to reconcile available counterforce capabilities with a first-strike strategy. But the obvious difficulties of getting the Soviet Union to cooperate in a war of controlled nuclear reprisals and counter-reprisals, let alone the political and psychological liabilities of declaring such a strategy as a deterrent against non-nuclear aggressions, would seem to preclude relying upon limited nuclear retaliation as a substitute for local resistance. On the other hand, when the United States can no longer hope to confine Russia's retaliatory strike to a tolerable level of damage, limited retaliation will be an indispensable substitute for massive retaliation, if some form of active nuclear deterrence remains essential as a last resort. It could be especially useful as a counter to Soviet and, in the distant future, Chinese Communist threats of direct limited nuclear strikes against allied bases. For this option some counterforce capability in addition to a minimum countercity capability would be essential.

It follows that successful active deterrence will depend increasingly, although not necessarily exclusively, on local resistance forces capable of denying the aggressor the attainment of his immediate objective at an acceptable cost to the defender,[7] rather than upon a nuclear striking force designed either to disarm the aggressor in order to confine his retaliatory damage to an acceptable level or to inflict disproportionate

---

[7] I believe that such local resistance forces should rely principally upon conventional weapons, reserving tactical nuclear weapons for selective retaliation in order to deter the enemy from using them and to induce him to limit and terminate an aggression that cannot be contained conventionally.

costs upon him through limited reprisals—even though the creation of such denial forces may somewhat hasten the declining credibility of active nuclear deterrence.

Alternatively or in addition, it has been proposed that the United States give her NATO allies—either individually or, preferably, collectively—control of their own nuclear striking power, in the expectation that their initiation of nuclear reprisals against direct conventional attacks upon them would be more credible than America's use of nuclear reprisals in their behalf. However, considering the physical vulnerability of nuclear-armed allies to devastating Soviet pre-emptive or retaliatory strikes, it is doubtful that their nuclear capabilities—even if integrated under joint control and consisting of numerous mobile, sea-based, and solid-fuel missiles—would give them the confidence to play the deterrence game as effectively as the United States, independently of the United States. And if their nuclear capabilities would serve only as a trigger upon America's striking power or as an instrument of policy outside allied purposes, they might only compel the United States to limit the obligation to become involved in their conflicts and so undermine not only deterrence but political collaboration as well. Therefore, the diffusion of nuclear capabilities among America's allies is no substitute for America's active deterrents, whatever its utility may be for other military and political purposes.[8]

Of course, a nuclear force capable only of supporting a first-strike strategy of very low credibility may nevertheless be an adequate deterrent against aggressions upon allied and other states, since the potential aggressor may place a very low value on the pursuit of his objectives by military means in the light of attractive non-military alternatives. There are indications that the Soviet Union, if not Communist China, places some such low value upon military aggression in the present phase of "peaceful co-existence." It would be dangerous, however, to assume that the Communist powers, under changed circumstances— say, the frustration of their present ambitions in the "zone of peace"

---

[8] There are good arguments for the United States giving her allies an equitable share in the control of a joint nuclear capability under central command as a means of dissuading them from seeking independent nuclear capabilities, of consolidating the alliance politically by relieving them of exclusive dependence upon America's decision to employ nuclear weapons, and of enhancing NATO's collective second-strike capability and protection against "nuclear blackmail." See, especially, Alastair Buchan, *NATO in the 1960's*, Praeger, New York, 1960, Ch. V; and the articles by Buchan, Aron, and Knorr in the *Bulletin of the Atomic Scientists*, XVI, September 1960. However, it is probably politically infeasible for the allies to agree upon a workable method of sharing the decision to use nuclear weapons.

or the vicissitudes of internal or bloc politics—may not decide to exploit opportunities for military aggression, if the "relationship of forces" appears to permit them to do so at a tolerable risk. The Soviet nuclear striking power which today may be intended only to deter the United States from supporting her allies with massive retaliation, could some day convince the Russians that they can assume the risks of limited warfare with impunity in spheres of interest where they enjoy local conventional superiority.

Finally, even if the United States did achieve a first-strike capability that assured stable deterrence against limited attacks on her allies, this would tend to destabilize the military environment by increasing the incentive for the Soviet Union to strike first herself. Against the threat of a Soviet first strike, only effective passive and negative deterrents can promote stability.

PASSIVE DETERRENCE

Passive deterrence refers to the deterrence of a direct offensive assault upon one's own nation. Essentially, it requires convincing a potential aggressor that one can inflict unacceptable damage upon him with a second-strike attack. As added insurance beyond this "minimum" or "finite" deterrence, some counterforce capability would be essential in order to avoid being compelled to strike only at cities or industrial complexes while the enemy could strike at military installations, and in order to help terminate a strategic war short of catastrophe if deterrence should fail.[9] Aside from the moral opprobrium attached to a strategy that aims exclusively to inflict maximum damage, a minimum deterrent striking force has the disadvantage of foreclosing the possibility of responding to a Soviet first strike confined largely to military targets with graduated countermilitary strikes. Such a response could be the only way for the United States to avoid choosing between surrender and placing all its cities in jeopardy by initiating civil strikes, and the only way to enable both sides to terminate the war short of extensive countercity exchanges leading to catastrophic destruction. It seems exceedingly unlikely that the Soviet Union would incur the great risks and costs of initiating a strategic nuclear war on the highly problematical supposition that the United States might not respond to counterforce blows with countercity blows; but it is conceivable that, if Russia did for some reason launch a first-strike counterforce attack,

---

[9] See Herman Kahn on the uses of a counterforce capability to provide strategic options, *On Thermonuclear War*, Princeton University Press, Princeton, N.J., 1960.

while sparing American cities, and then decide that she did not wish to engage in extensive nuclear exchanges, she might seek an advantageous settlement by confronting the United States with certain obliteration if the United States should strike at Russian cities. The proper American response to such a tactic might be to bargain with limited retaliation upon comparable military targets, rather than to launch an automatic all-out attack intended to win the war or inflict maximum damage. In any circumstance, the United States should try to maximize the opportunity of fighting a limited, controlled, politically-guided nuclear war, however difficult this may be in practice. For this purpose the United States would need some counterforce capability that could be used without diminishing her countercity capability. However, this capability would not be designed to "win the war" by protracted nuclear exchanges or to blunt an imminent attack by a preemptive blow. Both of these courses would result in unacceptable damage to the United States and to other Western nations.

Since the *credibility* of a massive second strike in response to an all-out attack could hardly be discounted by the aggressor, passive deterrence puts a premium upon one's *capability* to inflict unacceptable retaliatory damage. We must assume that the objective of a premeditated Soviet offensive first-strike would be at least to disarm the United States so as to confine her retaliatory damage to acceptable levels and at most to eliminate the United States as a major competitor. The Soviet Union might be willing to accept substantial damage if she were quite sure of eliminating the United States, although probably not so substantial as to destroy her great-power status in relation to other nations, especially Communist China. Since no one, including Khrushchev, can prescribe the level of retaliatory damage that would be unacceptable in such a hypothetical situation, it is probably prudent not to set this level short of the destruction of Russia's major cities and industrial facilities. One must hope that by the time Communist China obtains a significant independent nuclear striking force, she will operate under the same inhibitions against striking first at the cost of subjecting her cities and industrial facilities to retaliatory obliteration.

The maintenance of a second-strike force capable of inflicting unacceptable retaliatory damage will depend heavily upon its relative invulnerability; that is, its ability to survive a first strike and to strike back. In the long run, as the numbers, accuracy, and penetrating power of the potential aggressor's missiles increase, the ability to escape detection by concealment and mobility will probably be the most useful attributes of invulnerability.

Might not the United States, with a sufficiently invulnerable strik-ing force, achieve such an effective second-strike capability as to con-vince the Soviet Union that there would be no advantage in her trying to build up a massive first-strike counterforce capability at great ex-pense? As early as 1960, the Soviet Union appeared to have con-vinced at least the United States Navy and Army that second-strike "finite" deterrence was the only feasible objective of America's strategic striking force, while all military and civilian representatives of the government (except, occasionally, Air Force officers) publicly justified their recommendations concerning the composition and size of Amer-ica's strategic striking force exclusively in terms of its ability to survive a surprise attack and deliver unacceptable damage in return.[10]

The Russians seemed equally conscious of the disastrous damage that would be inflicted upon them in a nuclear war, and they too justified their strategic power in terms of a second-strike capability. In fact, Soviet strategic doctrine and defense policies gave far less indication of first-strike intentions than American doctrine and policies.

Khrushchev, in a speech to the Supreme Soviet on January 14, 1960, hailed the adequacy of Russia's missile force on the identical grounds upon which American officials were at the same time assuring Congress that there was no "deterrent gap." He conceded that in the event of a general war Russia "would suffer heavy misfortune, would sustain great losses of life"; but he expressed confidence that, even if some capitalist states were to gain parity with Russia in modern armaments, they would not rationally launch a first strike, because the Soviet Union had a sufficiently secure retaliatory missile force—by virtue of dispersion, camouflage, duplication, and triplication—to "literally wipe the coun-try or countries that attack us off the face of the earth." [11]

In October 1960, General Nicolai A. Talenski, a leading Soviet mili-tary theorist, reinforced Khrushchev's argument in a prominent Rus-sian magazine on foreign affairs.[12] His statement was by no means an

---

[10] Thus on January 13, 1960, Secretary of Defense Gates, when asked to define the "deterrent gap" before a subcommittee of the House Committee on Appropriations, said, "If you can be satisfied that your deterrent power . . . will survive a surprise attack, regardless of what force he can attack you with, then you have no deter-rent gap." And he assured the committee that "even a surprise attack by all the missiles of the Soviets could muster would not suffice to destroy enough of our retaliatory strike forces to enable him to make a rational decision to attack." Sub-committee of the House Committee of Appropriations, *Hearings, Department of Defense Appropriations for 1961*, 86th Congress, Second Session, pp. 4, 26, 136.
[11] *Current Digest of the Soviet Press*, XIV, No. 2, p. 11.
[12] "On the Character of Modern Warfare," *International Affairs*, X, October 1960, pp. 25–26.

isolated example of Soviet military thinking. Talenski contended that in a nuclear war "the world population would be reduced by one-half . . . the most active, capable, and civilized portion of mankind would be wiped out . . . the material and technical basis for life would be destroyed . . . humanity would be thrown back and its way to Communism would become immensely longer." Therefore, no power, Talenski implied, could derive an advantage from a surprise attack. "The 'saturation level' of nuclear weapons, their disposition, and methods of using them are at present such that the attacked country would always be left with sufficient nuclear means to inflict a counterblow of sufficient proportions to cause tremendous losses and destruction." He did not claim that this situation applied only to the Soviet Union.

Therefore, an old question arises anew: Will the nuclear powers reach the state of sufficiency or "saturation" in second-strike capabilities that Churchill envisioned? This is doubtful, considering the tendency of technological innovations to perpetuate an unstable equilibrium between offensive and defensive capabilities (not to mention the effect if Russian and American allies were to develop independent nuclear capabilities). Each side must continue to develop its striking force, especially qualitatively, if only to protect itself against the other side's achievement of a sudden offensive or defensive capability that would vitiate passive deterrence. Nevertheless, it is conceivable that the nuclear powers might, through a tacit understanding, forfeit first-strike strategies because they found it physically impossible or economically disadvantageous to maintain sufficient counterforce capabilities, yet were confident of maintaining adequate second-strike capabilities at tolerable expense. In this event, the strategic arms race might be more in the realm of research and development and less in the production of weapons.[13]

---

[13] Judging from the reciprocal interaction in the arms race so far (for example, the Soviet decision to concentrate on building missiles instead of competing with SAC, or the American decision to base strategic capabilities on the downward revision of estimates of Soviet ICBM production in 1958), the United States and the Soviet Union probably have sufficient knowledge of each other's weapons to limit the arms race reciprocally to the maintenance of second-strike capabilities and to determine whether such a limitation is observed. There are obvious technical obstacles to maintaining a mutual abnegation of first-strike capabilities. For example, most of the weapons suitable for a second strike are also suitable for a first strike; the distinction between a first-strike and purely second-strike capability will be somewhat blurred by maintenance of counterforce insurance in addition to "finite" deterrence forces; and advancements in defensive and offensive nuclear technology (as in anti-missile devices) will continually seem to threaten the invulnerability of second-strike forces. Yet as the concealment, mobility and protection of missile

Concomitantly, the West would, logically, have to build up its tactical (especially non-nuclear) capability, where no arms race has existed. But, whether the arms race as a whole were mitigated or accelerated, the primary objective of promoting a tacit agreement against first-strike strategies would be not to diminish or end the arms race but rather to stabilize its effect upon the military environment. In fact, an arms race limited quantitatively but covering a broad spectrum qualitatively seems likely to provide far greater assurance of stability than a formal agreement to control armaments and reduce arms levels, as long as technological innovations and serious conflicts of interest continue.

A tacit or informal agreement recognizing, in effect, that neither side has an interest in building a large counterforce first-strike capability as long as the other side refrains from doing so could not be secure against violation as long as the fundamental conflict of interests and aims that generates the Cold War persists. Mutual suspicions and imperfect knowledge of intentions are inherent in this underlying political conflict. Nevertheless, an agreement of this kind should be at least as reliable as, and technically and politically much more feasible than, a formal agreement for the limitation and inspection of long-range strategic weapons, intended to stabilize a balance of striking power at a level at which small violations would not upset the balance.[14] Such

---

bases, as well as their number and dispersion, increase, it should become increasingly easy to determine whether one side or the other is building a counterforce capability adequate for a rational first strike. Tacit understandings renouncing first-strike disarming capabilities could be implemented and reinforced by announced conditional unilateral limitations, by private talks among Soviet and American military and civilian personnel, by emphasizing anti-first-strike measures in disarmament discussions, and by unilateral measures designed to de-emphasize a first-strike strategy (chiefly, those negative measures by which states would conspicuously refrain from deployments and actions that threaten the adversary's second-strike capability.) Thomas C. Schelling makes some suggestive observations on the value and tactics of tacit and informal arms agreements in "Reciprocal Measures for Arms Stabilization," Daedalus, Vol. 89, Fall 1960, pp. 892–914.

[14] One technical difficulty in a formal agreement would be agreeing upon the ratio that represented a stable balance—a problem that has traditionally plagued disarmament schemes. The problem of ratio would be compounded by the fact that invulnerability is a product not only of relative numbers of missiles but also of qualities such as protection, dispersion, concealment and mobility. It would also be compounded by the rapid rate of technological development in armaments. The development of an effective anti-missile device, for example, could vitiate the whole agreement.

A trustworthy inspection system capable of verifying the ratio without undermining the invulnerability it was intended to guard (especially by disclosing the location of missiles) would require a complex and exacting procedure. However, if such an inspection system could be devised, it would probably give more assuran agreement would be self-enforcing, since a violation could be re-dressed simply by unilaterally resuming the arms race for a first-strike force. It would certainly be less cumbersome and expensive than a formal agreement. More important, it would be less conducive to the distrust and misunderstanding that would accompany the continual operation of an elaborate inspection system, which would be highly susceptible to technological obsolescence.

Therefore, barring a really decisive unilateral technological advance by one side or the other, which becomes increasingly less likely, it is conceivable that through a tacit agreement the balance-of-terror might become very stable in terms of mutual deterrence against first strikes, at least until other states gain significant nuclear capabilities. Judging from official pronouncements, this kind of stability became a major American objective under the Eisenhower administration. However, it is not clear that the Eisenhower administration also took account of the tendency of the stability of passive deterrence to destabilize active deterrence.

Assurance of America's ability to deter a Soviet first strike must, realistically, be bought at a price of conceding Russia's ability to deter an American first strike. But to the extent that Soviet and Chinese Communist leaders are assured that the United States will not initiate nuclear strikes, they may be encouraged to undertake aggressions short of a direct massive blow upon the United States; and these limited aggressions might spiral into general warfare. Indeed, the outbreak and "escalation" of limited warfare is the most serious threat to the stability of the military environment. Against this threat, the stability of active deterrence can be sustained only by building up local resistance capa-bilities, not by expanding first-strike reprisal capabilities.

In effect, the American government, during the Eisenhower admin-istration, undermined the credibility of its announced first-strike strategy of massive-and-selective nuclear retaliation against major conventional attacks when it proposed and defended its strategic striking capabilities entirely in terms of the objective of passive deterrence. At the same time, it encouraged instability in the lower sector of the military environ-ment when it denigrated the need for local-resistance forces to deal with anything but minor conflicts, while neglecting to build the kind of forces that could effectively resist major limited aggressions without resorting to nuclear warfare.

---

ance of stability if there were not a formal agreement on missile numbers and ratios, since this would leave the powers free to make adjustments in response to technological changes without violating an agreement and calling into question the whole basis of reciprocal restraint.

NEGATIVE DETERRENCE

As if tacitly conceding the obsolescence of active nuclear deterrence, the public debate on the alleged "missile gap" or "deterrent gap" was concerned entirely with the question of whether the United States had an adequate second-strike capability for passive deterrence. Yet, certainly, a massive Soviet attack upon the United States "out of the blue" was the least of our deterrent worries. Nothing that we know of Soviet foreign policy or military thought, or of the trend of the Cold War, supports the implicit assumption behind much of this debate that the Kremlin takes such a desperate view of its opportunities for advancement through "peaceful co-existence" as to assume the risks of launching a knock-out blow against the United States on a problematical calculation that Soviet costs might be confined to a certain number of "mega-bodies" or obliterated (even if evacuated) cities.

However, there is another possibility of a massive Soviet first strike: the possibility of a defensive strike launched in anticipation of an imminent American attack. Considering America's and NATO's announced strategy of meeting conventional attacks with nuclear retaliation, while both American and Soviet leaders denied the possibility of limiting nuclear warfare, one should not dismiss the danger that Russia might strike at the United States because she expected the United States to strike her first, especially during some intense international crisis or a limited war.

However improbable a defensive first strike incited by misapprehension of a surprise attack may be, it is at least more plausible than a Soviet "Pearl Harbor" attack, a prospect which continued to dominate American official strategic thinking throughout the 1950's. In any case, the announced fear of such a defensive strike carried the government, by implication, beyond the objective of passive deterrence to that of "negative deterrence" or "mutual assurance," which aims to discourage a first strike by assuring the adversary that one does not intend to strike him first;[15] whereas active deterrence depends upon convincing him that one might strike first, and passive deterrence depends upon con-

---

[15] Properly speaking, negative deterrence is not deterrence at all, if to deter is to discourage a hostile action by frightening the actor. However, since there is no English word for preventing an action by negating or alleviating fear, there may be some advantage to calling such preventive assurance "negative deterrence" in order to suggest that fear and the negation of fear can serve the same purpose.

vincing him that one can deliver unacceptable retaliatory damage if he strikes first.

Thus in his statement on February 18, 1960, Secretary of State Herter, in suggesting measures for exchanging information with the Soviet Union through aerial and ground inspection, said,

If these safeguards are effective, there will be less chance of one side being moved to surprise attack by a mistaken belief that the military moves of the other side portend such attack. This danger may be particularly acute in a major international crisis, when tensions are high and both sides are moving to heightened readiness.[16]

President Eisenhower, in presenting his proposal for a United Nations surveillance body to the General Assembly on September 22, 1960, explained its purpose in similar words:

The advent of missiles, with ever-shorter reaction times, makes measures to curtail the danger of war by miscalculation increasingly necessary. States must be able quickly to assure each other that they are not preparing aggressive moves—particularly in international crises, when each side takes steps to improve its own defenses which might be misinterpreted by the other. Such misinterpretation, in the absence of machinery to verify that neither was preparing to attack the other, could lead to a war which no one had intended or wanted.

"The United States," he said, "wants the Soviet Union and all the nations of the world to know enough about United States defense preparations to be assured that United States forces exist only for deterrence and defense—not for surprise attack." [17]

As President Eisenhower's remarks indicated, the concern about negative deterrence arose chiefly because of the rapidly increasing speed, range, accuracy, and power of nuclear missiles. For missiles with these qualities might deliver a devastating surprise attack with very little warning. The potential victim of such an attack, in order to preserve his second-strike capability or, perhaps, to limit his damage by blunting the aggressor's striking power, must reduce his reaction time to a warning of attack to the minimum; and, at best, the United States and the Soviet Union could receive scarcely thirty minutes' warning from the time of launching. The reduction of reaction time, in turn, increases the possibility that the imagined victim may feel compelled to launch a defensive first strike himself because he mistakenly believes that the adversary is about to launch or has already launched a first strike on him; for even if the advantage of a defensive nuclear

---

[16] *New York Times*, May 26, 1960, p. 6.
[17] *Ibid.*, September 23, 1960, p. 14.

attack were in doubt, the prospective victim might prefer to take the risks of delivering the first strike rather than the risks of receiving it. Thus, although neither power wished to launch an offensive strike, either side might initiate a defensive strike on the misapprehension that the other had launched or would imminently launch the first strike, if only because *he* feared receiving a first strike. This misapprehension might arise from a miscalculation of intentions or a misinterpretation of warning information.

The appearance of a doctrine of pre-emptive attack in Soviet military writings in 1955 lent credence to Western fears of a Soviet defensive strike.[18] Although some military specialists suggested that the Soviet pre-emptive doctrine was the guise for an offensive knockout blow, in the light of the Soviet preference and opportunities for less drastic forms of offensive action it seems more plausible to suppose that it was aimed at deterring or blunting an American offensive first strike. For that matter, although a pre-emptive doctrine received only partial and unofficial support in American military and civilian circles, the government's frequently proclaimed fear of a Pearl Harbor-type aggression suggested that the United States might also feel compelled, during some intense crisis, to launch a defensive first strike because of a misapprehension of Russian intentions.

Officially and unofficially, a number of measures—some unilateral and some requiring international agreement—have been suggested to stabilize negative deterrence.[19] The most obvious unilateral measure is to abstain from the provocative mobilization, deployment, and maneuver of nuclear weapons.[20] To the extent that one's second-strike

---

[18] The Soviet doctrine of pre-emptive attack is discussed in Raymond L. Garthoff, *Soviet Strategy in the Nuclear Age*, New York, 1958; and, at greater length, in Herbert S. Dinerstein, *War and the Soviet Union*, New York, 1959; and Garthoff, *The Soviet Image of Future War*, Public Affairs Press, Washington, D.C., 1960.
[19] See Thomas C. Schelling's seminal discussion of different kinds of safeguards against surprise attack, "Surprise Attack and Disarmament," in Klaus Knorr, ed., *NATO and American Security*, Princeton University Press, Princeton, N.J., 1959.
[20] The flight of manned bombers is a case in point. The Air Force argued for the continued utility of manned bombers in the missile age partly on the grounds that, because they can be called back, they can be launched on less than certain warning information and also on the grounds that, in an airborne alert, they serve a psychological purpose as a visible sign on Communist radar screens of American preparedness. However, as Chief of Staff General Thomas D. White conceded, these qualities might also be provocative, in that they could suggest that the United States was launching a first strike. Testimony on February 3, 1960, before the Preparedness Investigating Subcommittee, Senate Committee on Armed Services, *Missiles, Space, and Other Major Defense Matters*, 86th Congress, 2d session, pp. 137–38.

capability depends upon a quick and irrevocable reaction to early warning of a surprise attack, this kind of provocation will be difficult to avoid. This suggests that a second-strike capability so invulnerable that it need not react precipitantly is a virtual prerequisite of negative deterrence. Such a capability would, on the one hand, logically compel a state contemplating a defensive first strike to interpret the adversary's probable intentions and actions very conservatively in the light of the certainty of receiving unacceptable damage in retaliation against a first strike. It would, on the other hand, relieve a state of the necessity of keeping such a quick trigger finger on its retaliatory force as to preclude a thorough and cautious appraisal of the existence or source, scope, and intention of an enemy attack before delivering a counterstrike. And, if an enemy strike did occur, such an invulnerable second-strike capability could at least hold open the possibility of ending hostilities short of a catastrophic sequence of unrestrained nuclear exchanges, which might otherwise be automatic regardless of the political circumstances. Furthermore, it would avoid the implication, which might be conveyed by a vulnerable striking force, that one's striking power was intended only for delivering a first strike because it would not survive a surprise attack. Concealment and mobility will be not only the most effective attributes of invulnerability as the numbers and accuracy of missiles increase; they may also be less provocative attributes than increasing the numbers and dispersion of missiles, since they do not so directly threaten the invulnerability of the adversary's striking force.

If the United States were confident of possessing a sufficiently invulnerable second-strike force to survive a first strike and deliver unacceptable damage in return, she could afford to renounce unconditionally recourse to a pre-emptive blow and to adopt publicly a policy of not launching missiles until hostile missiles had actually struck her territory or bases, along with a policy of graduated or controlled strategic retaliation to suit the nature of the attack. Even if the Russians did not trust the renunciation of pre-emptive strikes, the policy itself would be a considerable safeguard against the precipitation of a thermonuclear war by miscalculation, accident, or (in the age of nuclear diffusion) anonymous or pseudonymous attack.

Pursuing the rationale of unilateral renunciation further, the United States might explicitly renounce a first-strike strategy as an instrument of active as well as passive deterrence, at least to the extent of declaring that she would use nuclear weapons only if they were used against her or her allies. She might then secure the agreement of her NATO allies to this principle and even seek the endorsement of the

United Nations General Assembly. To enhance the credibility of this renunciation, she might make it as obvious as possible—by conspicuously foregoing or disclosing certain weapons and their deployment—that she did not possess and did not intend to acquire the kind of capabilities that would be useful for a first strike. Thus, instead of undertaking an ambitious program of satellite reconnaissance, designed to discover military installations and deployments, the United States might publicly renounce the use of such satellites and invite Soviet inspectors to verify the renunciation.

Carrying the logic of negative deterrence still further, the United States might unilaterally grant the potential aggressor an invulnerable second-strike capability, too. For, logically, negative deterrence is served as well by the adversary's possession, as by one's own possession, of the kind of striking force that permits the conservative appraisal of intentions and actions, obviates the need for a trigger-quick response, and avoids a provocative posture. It follows that any American capability or action that threatens the invulnerability of Russia's striking power—like great counterforce capabilities, aerial reconnaissance, or harassment of Soviet communications, radar, or missile-launching submarines—works against the stability of the military environment. Although it is not easy to draw an obvious distinction between first-strike and second-strike capabilities, the objective of providing mutual assurance against surprise attack requires, as a necessary condition for the effort, that second-strike capabilities should be maintained by increasing one's own invulnerability, not by trying to decrease the enemy's.

The advantage of all these unilateral measures of negative deterrence is that they do not necessarily require the formal collaboration of the adversary in order to achieve their purpose, yet most of them could be the object of an appeal for informal reciprocity on the basis of mutual interest. For example, if orbiting armed missiles seem particularly provocative, then instead of seeking an international agreement to prohibit this, the United States might borrow a leaf from the Soviet tactic with a nuclear test moratorium and announce that we would not orbit armed missiles if the Soviet Union also abstained; and we might even offer to exchange inspection teams at missile-launching sites in order to verify the pledges.[21]

---

[21] The assumption that orbiting armed missiles render an adversary more vulnerable to a first strike—whether delivered intentionally, accidentally, or by miscalculation—than land-based or sea-based missiles probably has more to do with psychology than military logic. However, this does not make them any less provocative.

Even without inspection, both sides might have sufficient information to verify each other's adherence to the mutual abstention; for if the missiles were intended

Or, on the other hand, if orbiting armed missiles were to seem like a stabilizing measure of invulnerability, we might promise not to shoot down Russian missiles if the Russians would refrain from shooting down ours.

In a period in which the complexity and uncertainty of the requirements of deterrence and a rapidly changing military technology combine with a fundamental political conflict to render any military cooperation between potential belligerents rudimentary, fragile, and tentative, the promotion of reciprocal restraints requires the flexibility of informal and tacit agreements (or simply mutual restraints without an agreement), which can be formed, altered, or abandoned without directly involving the prestige or good faith of the parties concerned. Given a suitable military strategy and capability in the West, what is needed to consolidate a base of mutual interest in negative deterrence are not complicated formal schemes of cooperation, verification, and sanctions but, rather, the development of simple, obvious, and reliable informal restraints and the cultivation of purposeful communication between the parties.[22]

In a more stable international political environment, mutual assurance against surprise attack might be served better by formal agreements which specified, elaborated, and regularized the modes of military cooperation, so that the parties to the agreement would have less ambiguous tests of each other's observation or violation of reciprocal restraints—especially during crises, when informal cooperation and communication might break down. Presumably, the Eisenhower administration's proposal for international machinery to enable states to verify each other's abstention from surprise attack reflected a lack of faith in the power of tacit and informal understandings to provide this mutual assurance and also a belief that any formal agreement with the Russians would be a confidence-building step to further agreements. Yet, in the present atmosphere of well-founded international suspicion,

---

for deterrence, they would be announced; and, if they were not announced, the great number of missiles that would have to be orbited in order to be useful for an offensive surprise attack would arouse suspicions of their purpose.

[22] Henry A. Kissinger and Thomas C. Schelling have suggested that, physically, such communication could be promoted by the establishment in the United States and the Soviet Union of observation and communications teams with special equipment capable of instantaneous communication to the Soviet and American governments and between the two. Kissinger, "Arms Control, Inspection and Surprise Attack," *Foreign Affairs*, Vol. 38, July 1960, pp. 566–67; Schelling, "Arms Control: Proposal for a Special Surveillance Force," World Politics, Vol. 13, October 1960, p. 11.

it is doubtful that mutual assurance of peaceful intentions can be more readily achieved by precise and explicit formal tests than by ambiguous and tacit informal tests. Rather, the formal tests, in proportion to their elaborateness, are likely only to increase the opportunities for, and therefore the suspicions of, one signatory or the other dissembling its intentions and manipulating the modes of cooperation for hostile purposes. If only because of their high rate of technological obsolescence, elaborate international inspection and surveillance schemes would be peculiarly susceptible to subversion or simple misunderstanding, so that, in proportion to the cooperation they required, they might actually incite the fear and suspicion they were intended to allay.

This is not to rule out the possibility that limited formal bilateral and multilateral agreements might incorporate reassuring methods of disclosure and verification and yet contain sufficient safeguards against deception and subversion to enhance mutual assurance against surprise attack.[23] Whether formal agreements would actually provide such mutual assurance is impossible to determine in the absence of detailed negotiation and perhaps actual trial of specific agreements. It would be foolish, however, to enter any agreement in the expectation that the very experience of engaging in formal obligations would foster mutual trust. The history of international politics is full of refutations of this naive hope.

In any case, from the standpoint of overall military security both formal and informal agreements encounter a double obstacle: not only might they not achieve their objective of enhancing negative deterrence but, whether they achieved it or not, they might conflict with active and passive deterrence. If active deterrence depends upon the credibility of one's threat of initiating the use of nuclear weapons against conventional aggressions (and one does not rely upon limited nuclear war as an alternative to conventional resistance), the efficacy of this first-strike strategy must certainly depend upon exploiting the advantages of striking with some element of surprise. Therefore, only a strategy of active deterrence that does not depend upon the threat of a nuclear first strike is compatible with a strategy of providing assurance against surprise attack. A nation that wishes to avoid provoking a defensive first strike but does not wish completely to renounce the resort to nuclear war against non-nuclear aggression must logically strive for some balance between two objectives: on the one

---

[23] Kissinger and Schelling, *op. cit.*, outline such agreements, designed to enable the parties to provide each other with positive evidence that they are not preparing a surprise attack.

hand, assuring the adversary that one does *not* intend to strike first in most circumstances and, on the other hand, convincing him that it *might* strike first in some circumstances. A commitment, especially a formal treaty, designed to achieve only the first objective would be distinctly uncongenial to maintaining such a balance.

Furthermore, we must recognize that, quite apart from reducing the credibility of a deliberate, calculated first-use of nuclear weapons, measures of negative deterrence that mitigate the danger of an automatic, unauthorized, and unrestricted nuclear response to conventional aggression will tend to reduce the latent risk of nuclear warfare in any armed conflict and, hence, diminish an important restraint against such aggression. Even the basic safeguards against accidental nuclear blows—the central command, the control system, and the technical safety devices—will make conventional aggression less risky to the aggressor. Of course, this is not a reason to refrain from taking such measures if establishing strict political control over nuclear weapons is more valuable—and I think it is—than enhancing the deterrent effect of the latent risks of nuclear warfare in armed conflict. Rather it is another reason to attain a greater capacity for non-nuclear resistance in order to compensate for a reduced reliance upon nuclear catastrophe.

We must also recognize that some measures of negative deterrence might be incompatible with passive deterrence. For if passive deterrence depends upon an invulnerable second-strike force, and invulnerability depends upon concealing one's striking force and creating uncertainty about its numbers, composition, and deployment, then measures that reveal the nature and location of one's striking force might actually encourage a surprise attack.

The practical difficulty of balancing negative deterrence with active and passive deterrence is particularly significant with respect to multilateral agreements of military cooperation which are designed to increase information about striking forces and to formalize obligations that restrict them. This difficulty would be only partially mitigated by agreements designed to disclose positive evidence of peaceful intentions by occasional inspections rather than to provide negative evidence by continual surveillance. Technically, President Eisenhower's proposal of international surveillance machinery would not obligate a nation to submit to inspection if it did not wish to "prove its own peaceful intention." But although the Soviet Union might readily use this provision to request or prevent inspection, as expediency dictated under different circumstances, the United States would find it awkward to turn the machinery off or on depending upon whether she wished to rely upon active nuclear deterrence, enhance negative deterrence, or protect passive deterrence. The very existence of the machinery might create irresistible pressures upon her to use it. Yet to turn the machinery on during a crisis might jeopardize active or passive deterrence; whereas to turn it off would destroy its future utility and constitute a serious provocation in itself.

Therefore, if the United States undertakes the simple unilateral measures of negative deterrence—particularly, avoiding provocative deployment of weapons, guarding against the unauthorized use of nuclear weapons, maintaining an invulnerable second-strike capability, and de-emphasizing a first-strike strategy—it need not depend upon Russian acceptance of elaborate cooperative schemes of mutual assurance in order to mitigate the danger of a defensive surprise attack. However, the soundest conclusion one is warranted in stating at this stage is not that all formal multilateral agreements of mutual assurance are unprofitable but that any measure of negative deterrence should be integrated with measures of active and passive deterrence within an overall strategy of stability.

THE NEED FOR AN OVERALL STRATEGY OF STABILITY

Let us summarize these observations on the stability of the military environment. The stability of the military environment is not an automatic result of the strategic nuclear arms race. On the contrary, in the present international system the balance of deterrence upon which such stability must rest contains an inherent element of insta-bility, which is aggravated by rapid technological change. To mitigate this element, stability must be achieved in all sectors of the military environment, lest stability in one sector create instability in another. This means that comprehensive stability can be achieved only at the price of foregoing or de-emphasizing some deterrent capabilities and strategies for the sake of a balanced combination of active, passive, and negative deterrents. In the future, the most significant price must be paid by de-emphasizing and perhaps eventually renouncing active deterrence by nuclear reprisals. But the de-emphasis upon nuclear re-prisals can purchase stability only if it is accompanied by a substan-tial increase in local resistance capabilities. If stable active and passive deterrence is achieved, the greatest threat to military stability in the missile age will be the possibility of a defensive strike by accident or misapprehension, a contingency that must be prevented by technical and organizational safeguards and by negative deterrence (or mutual assurance against surprise attack). In deterring defensive surprise attacks, the most significant contributions to stability are measures that the West can undertake unilaterally and by tacit agreement; but to achieve its purpose, any measure of negative deterrence must be integrated with measures of active and passive deterrence within an overall strategy of stability.

Considering the complexity of the problem of stabilizing the military environment when deterrence is, essentially, a relationship between two nuclear powers, one must expect the diffusion of independent nuclear capabilities to other powers—and especially to powers not aligned with the United States—to create instabilities of a new dimension. However, the momentous military and political consequences of the prospect of nuclear diffusion and its relation to military stability is a subject in itself, beyond the scope of this essay.

The preceding discussion should be sufficient to suggest that, merely in terms of bipolar deterrence, the pursuit of a stable military environment as a primary disarmament goal amounts to a major policy decision with significant implications for national and allied military strategy and defense policies. If the American government does not consciously weigh this decision in full recognition of these implications within the context of an overall strategy of stability, it is in grave danger of drifting into the anomalous position of remaining dependent upon a strategy of active deterrence by nuclear reprisals, while in the name of stability it steadily undermines the credibility of this strategy and encourages instability below the threshold of direct nuclear aggression.

The Eisenhower administration largely failed to reconcile the contradictions within its deterrent strategy or the contradictions between its military strategy and its arms control policy. Thus the United States continued to rely primarily upon the threat of nuclear retaliation to deter non-nuclear aggression in the NATO area; for it had declared that NATO is dependent upon a nuclear response to any conventional aggression larger than a border incident or probing action and had denied the possibility of fighting even a conventional limited war in the area.[24] Yet President Eisenhower, while proclaiming America's un-

---

[24] For an analysis of SACEUR General Norstad's position on this point, see Robert E. Osgood "NATO: Problems of Security and Collaboration," *American Political Science Review*, Vol. 54, March 1960, pp. 121–23; for Secretary of Defense McElroy's denial of the possibility of limited warfare in Europe, see his statements to the House Appropriations Subcommittee in April, 1958, *Hearings, Department of Defense Appropriations for 1959*, 85th Congress, 2d session, p. 370 and in January, 1959, *Hearings, Department of Defense Appropriations for 1960*, 86th

willingness and inability to fight a war of local resistance on the ground
and emphasizing his conviction that any war in Europe would become
a thermonuclear war, had also declared that such a war would be
"self-defeating" and would bring about "the destruction of civilization
as we know it." [25]

This declaratory position logically left the United States dependent
upon a first-strike strategy for deterring aggression upon its NATO
allies (although it is difficult to see what advantage there could be in
striking first in a self-defeating war). Yet the Eisenhower administration, despite certain concessions to the Air Force's appeals for full-scale
counterforce capabilities, did not remotely begin to undertake the
massive buildup of the only kind of strategic striking capability that
could conceivably give the United States an advantage in striking
first by the late 1960's; that is, a counterforce capability that could
knock out enough of Soviet striking power to confine her retaliatory
damage to an acceptable level. Nor did it show any interest in the
kind of civil defense program that might contribute to the same purpose. Instead, in the debates of 1959 and 1960 on the "missile gap" or
"deterrent gap," as in the debates on airpower in 1956, it proposed and
defended the size and composition of America's strategic striking
power entirely in terms of passive deterrence and a second-strike capability, while apparently striking a rough compromise between the minimum counter-city capability, advocated by the Navy and Army in terms
of "minimum deterrence," and the counterforce win-the-war capability
proposed by the Air Force.[26]

At the same time, the Eisenhower administration, to the end, was

---

Congress, 1st session, p. 68; see also his statements on May 29 and June 6, 1958,
New York Times, May 30, 1958, p. 3; June 7, p. 9.
[25] Remarks on the Berlin crisis in a press conference, *New York Times*, March 12,
1959, p. 12; remarks at state dinner in Manila, *ibid.*, June 16, 1960, p. 14.
[26] For explicit statements of the guiding concept of deterrence and deterrent capa-
bilities by military and civilian officials, see *Subcommittee on the Air Force, Senate
Committee on Armed Services Hearings, Study of Airpower,* 84th Congress, 2d ses-
sion, pp. 10, 102; *House Committee on Appropriations, Department of Defense
Appropriations for 1960,* pp. 71, 329–30, 477, 591, 594; *Preparedness Investigating
Subcommittee, Senate Committee on Armed Services, Hearings, Missiles, Space and
Other Major Defense Matters,* p. 194; *Subcommittee of House Committee on
Appropriations, Hearings, Department of Defense Appropriations for 1961,* 86th
Congress, 2d session, pp. 4, 26, 36. In these hearings only Air Force spokesmen
occasionally suggested that the purpose of a strategic striking force might also be
to deliver a first strike in response to an attack upon America's allies or in order
to pre-empt an imminent strike upon the United States: *House Committee on
Appropriations, Department of Defense Appropriations for 1960,* p. 929; *Department of Defense Appropriations for 1961,* pp. 232–33.

adamantly opposed to compensating for the declining credibility of active nuclear reprisals by enlarging local resistance forces. Instead, it remained wedded to the thesis (with which neither the Army, the Navy, nor any prominent outside observer agreed) that nuclear firepower would compensate for a reduction of mobilized manpower, and that the forces that would prevent a big war would also prevent a small war, since the chances of even a limited war growing into a thermonuclear conflagration would supposedly deter all overt military aggression.

In this context of military strategy and capabilities the American government pursued in its disarmament policy the prime objective of creating a more stable military environment chiefly by measures of negative deterrence intended to provide mutual assurance against surprise attack. Whether or not these measures would actually promote negative deterrence if the Russians should agree to them, the mere desire to achieve them was bound to help undermine the strategy of active nuclear deterrence upon which the West still largely depended. It was bound to undermine that strategy, not because a formal treaty to provide mutual assurance against surprise attack would actually contribute much toward that end, but simply because the emphasis upon securing such a treaty indicated as clearly as existing military capabilities that the government had turned from stressing its determination to deliver a first strike, as at the time of Dulles's "massive retaliation" pronouncement in 1954, to stressing its common interest with the Russians in *not* delivering a first strike. This shift of emphasis represented nothing less than America's tacit acceptance of the psychology of mutual deterrence, reflecting the condition of parity in destructive capabilities, in place of the psychology of unilateral deterrence, which had reflected America's monopoly of terror. The credibility of a first-strike strategy is bound to wither in an atmosphere of mutual deterrence.

Moreover, the unqualified manner in which the Eisenhower administration endorsed the virtues of military disclosure as an instrument of negative deterrence suggested that it might not have reconciled its arms control policy with its military strategy of passive deterrence. For while President Eisenhower was telling Congress and the nation about the great advantages of invulnerability that the United States would derive from its Polaris submarine program, which capitalizes upon concealment, he was warning the United Nations General Assembly about the dangers of concealment. "In an age of rapidly developing technology," he declared in his September 22 address in 1960, "secrecy is not only an anachronism—it is downright dangerous.

To seek to maintain a society in which a military move can be taken in complete secrecy, while professing a desire to reduce the risk of war through arms control, is a contradiction."

THE RELATION OF THE MILITARY
TO THE POLITICAL ENVIRONMENT

These contradictions in armament and disarmament policy indicate that at the end of the Eisenhower administration the United States lacked and badly needed an overall strategy of stability in order to coordinate military strategy with arms control policy and one strategy of deterrence with another. The overriding task of the Kennedy administration would be to recognize the full implications of nuclear parity and build on the basis of this recognition an integrated, logically consistent set of military policies to stabilize the military environment.[27]

An overall strategy of stability, however, cannot properly be formulated merely in terms of the military environment; it must also take account of the relation of the military to the political environment. A central aspect of this relation concerns the Communist view of stability. Perhaps, in our conviction of the absurdity or "impossibility" of nuclear war, we have exaggerated the autonomous effect of a novel military technology in stabilizing—or, for that matter, destabilizing—the military environment. After all, military conflicts will still arise from *political* conflicts, most probably when general political conflicts are manifested in a local clash of will and power, as in Berlin. They will not be generated spontaneously by weapons technology and the configuration of military power alone. Therefore, we should not expect the wisest choice of military deterrents to eliminate all warfare from international relations, especially warfare that springs from political conflicts beyond the control of the major nuclear powers. And, by the same token, we should not expect a common Soviet and American interest in avoiding suicidal war and an unrestricted arms race to engender, by itself, much cooperation in alleviating the concrete political sources of tension and conflict. In short, we should not expect a re-

---

[27] For the author's subsequent views on post-Eisenhower developments in American military strategy, see Robert E. Osgood, NATO: *The Entangling Alliance*, University of Chicago Press, Chicago, 1962; *Nuclear Control in NATO*, Washington Center for Foreign Policy Research, Washington, D.C. 1962; "Nuclear Arms: Uses and Limits," *New Republic*, Vol. CXLVII, September 10, 1962, pp. 15–18. See also, Secretary of Defense McNamara's statement in February, 1963, on American strategic nuclear concepts and plans in *Hearings, Senate Committee on Armed Services, Military Procurement Authorization, FY 1964.*

versal of the historic relationship between arms and politics, which makes a stable political environment the condition, not merely the result, of a stable military environment.

To accept the complete stability of the whole military environment would mean to abandon even the threat of war as an instrument of policy; but to give up the threat of war would be to accept the political status quo or else to be content to alter it entirely by means unrelated to the configurations of military power. Whether or not the United States could afford to adhere to these policies of self-denial, they are certainly directly contrary to Communist doctrine and practice and to the Communists' currently announced expectations. Consequently, the Western powers should guard against repeating the previous confusion of democracies in mistaking their own longing for peace and order for the pacific intentions of a revolutionary power that is really bent upon exploiting their longing in order to weaken their will and ability to resist.

In what respects and on what terms, then, might the Communist powers accept the stabilization of the military environment? Temporarily, they would seem to have accepted stability to the extent of avoiding direct, overt military action, while they pursue their undeviating goal of political preponderance by non-military or paramilitary means, in the expectation that their sheer economic and scientific progress, combined with nationalist and anti-Western sentiment in the colonial and former colonial areas, will alter the world balance of power decisively in their favor. In this respect, the vulnerability of the "zone of peace" to Communist pressure and blandishments is the West's greatest deterrent to overt military aggression, but this is not a situation that should recommend itself to us as a policy.

On the other hand, neither the Soviet Union nor Communist China shows any interest in stabilizing the military environment as a general goal, and both are committed to overthrowing the political status quo. The Chinese continue to seek what they consider to be vital territorial interests, as in the Formosa Straits, by means that do not exclude open warfare and that certainly depend upon the indirect pressure of a huge and progressively more modern military establishment. And Soviet leaders manifest a disturbing new confidence in Russia's military ascendancy, which they seem eager to exploit for diplomatic and propagandistic purposes. Both declare that "national-liberation" wars are justified and inevitable and proclaim their duty to support them.

Neither Communist power is interested in mollifying the West's fears of nuclear war, which arise from the instabilities of the balance of terror combined with Communist-manufactured and Communist-supported crises. On the contrary, the Soviet Union, especially, shows considerable skill in playing upon these fears in order to divide the Western coalition, intimidate allies who provide strategic bases or receive military assistance, deter the West from intervening to support the victims of Communist subversion and guerilla warfare, undermine the uncertain *status quo* in the center of Europe, seize the propaganda initiative, and "mobilize the masses" under the "banner of peace." Perhaps the Russians are pleased to receive assurance against an American first strike through America's policies, actions, and statements as well as through the growth of Russia's own retaliatory strength; but they are evidently confident anyway that they can exploit international tensions without incurring much risk of war. At the same time, they remain determined to stress the dangers of catastrophic war arising from Western defense policies and Western resistance to Communist incursions; and they seem incapable of interpreting Western proposals for mutual assurance against surprise attack and the other hazards of contemporary weapons as anything but devices of propaganda and espionage.

The difference between the Soviet and American approaches to negative deterrence is political, not technical. For this reason it is unlikely that the Communist powers can ever go very far toward accepting an agreement that would formally acknowledge that their security depends upon military cooperation with non-Communist powers and a drastic curtailment of their secrecy, which is not only a military asset but an internal political imperative. Consequently, in the absence of a convincing posture of active deterrence based upon non-nuclear resistance, America's concern to allay mutual fears of surprise attack by international agreement is more apt to heighten Soviet distrust and encourage the Soviet Union to play an adventurous game than to induce her to cooperate in establishing safeguards against the hazards of the missile age.

This is not to say that there is no limited area of mutual interests within which the United States can secure Soviet cooperation in stabilizing the military environment. It is only to say that the Soviet appreciation of this ground and Soviet willingness to act upon it will depend not so much on American ingenuity in devising schemes of formal cooperation as, first, on American resolution in developing with her allies a consistent posture of active, passive, and negative deterrence that is credible without being provocative and, secondly, on American skill in utilizing this posture to achieve tacit and informal agreements and to consolidate the many existing mutual restraints on military power.

Chapter 6

The Nth Country Problem,

Mutual Deterrence,

and International Stability

ARTHUR L. BURNS

NUCLEAR WEAPONS DIFFUSION

The acquisition of nuclear weapons by nations other than those who possess them in 1963, the Nth country problem, will have effects on world military and political stability that can be assessed only within limiting assumptions of some sort. Here we assume that: (1) current ideological divisions will continue and some degree of world bipolarization will persist; (2) the Soviet Union will oppose proposals for policing a nuclear arms inspection program; (3) there will not be an all-out war; and (4) current economic growth patterns, including the postwar phenomenon of renewed growth in highly industrialized countries, will persist.

Given these assumptions, it can be postulated that several countries that equal or surpass Britain in potential, such as France or Western Germany, will be in a position by 1970 to acquire at least an equivalent of the British deterrent force of 1963. (Meanwhile, however, advances by the Soviet Union and the United States may render ineffectual any force on that scale.) Nuclear capabilities of somewhat lesser magnitude may come within range of other countries, for example, Communist China, Canada, perhaps India, and doubtfully some Scandinavian nations.

Observations concerning the types of nuclear capabilities that may be diffused must be limited to those produced by predictable technological developments, such as miniaturized nuclear explosives; more variety, range and navigability of missiles; advanced detection systems; more comprehensive civil defense programs; and nuclear submarines. Changes of status caused by innovation in military technology, that is, the qualitative arms race, cannot, of course, be predicted. Innovation may produce international instability by causing rapid changes in the balance-of-terror, as well as by accelerating or decelerating nuclear diffusion.[1]

However unpredictable the process of technological innovation may be, we may be sure that uncertainties about technological and scientific "breakthroughs" in weapon development will be a continuing aspect of the environment, as will political and military responses to such uncertainty. A likely continuing response is the acceleration of effort by all competitors to achieve such breakthroughs. As a consequence, non-nuclear countries and countries wanting no more than tactical atomic weapons may be restricted to the alternatives of large defense budgets or a tight alliance with a super power to offset the effects of innovation. In some cases a third alternative—of a small power providing conventional forces and a super-power sharing its nuclear weapons—may be possible. This alternative would accelerate the diffusion of nuclear capabilities.

The diffusion of nuclear weapons has been impeded somewhat through the 1963 treaty banning all but underground nuclear tests. However, we must seriously question how effectively this ban will be implemented particularly since neither France nor Communist China will agree to stop testing. Furthermore, agreements to refrain from atmospheric and underwater testing of nuclear devices is unlikely to inhibit many nations from engaging in research and developmental activities aimed at obtaining a nuclear capability, and from making underground tests of nuclear devices.

A more effective means for impeding nuclear diffusion could be

---

[1] The study from which this chapter derives was composed before the publication of *The Spread Of Nuclear Weapons,* by Leonard Beaton and John Maddox, but has been revised in its light, the writer having been convinced by the timetable for various nations' acquisition of options on and stockpiles of atomic weapons. It seems unlikely that innovation could in the near future speed up such a timetable.

achieved through direct arms control; but it appears that many nations, including the Soviet Union, are at present unwilling to accept the controls necessary to ensure the success of such a program. Furthermore, political and moral agreements that influence Western countries might have little effect on nations such as Communist China.

DETERRENCE POTENTIALS

In judging the implications of the diffusion of nuclear weapons, it is perhaps most important to consider the absolute and relative war potentials of current and future members of the nuclear "club," regardless of who they may be, in terms of three types of deterrents: independent, triggering, and minimum atomic.

Independent Deterrence

Independent deterrence refers to the ability to discourage a major nuclear power from launching an attack inimical to one's own interests because one has a sufficient nuclear capability to launch a massive retaliatory strike. There are a number of factors that will impede small nations from achieving the status of independent nuclear powers. First, a small nation's economy is hardly likely to be able to support the variety of facilities required for a significant nuclear force. Second, only the great powers may be able to achieve any considerable economy in the production and deployment of weapons. Third, small nations may be restricted, by the size of their territories, or by lack of access to the sea, in dispersing their retaliatory forces. Fourth, and most important, large and wealthy powers may have the means to price small nations out of the deterrence competition.

Triggering Deterrence

However, the deterrent balance among the very few leading countries may, even in the decade 1965–1975, allow a small nation to achieve a position of power with a triggering deterrent capability, which may be either "passive" or "active." A passive triggering deterrent capability would result from a small nation's having sufficient missiles or other deterrent forces to ensure that a large power could not knock out the small nation's retaliatory capability without leaving itself vulnerable to a first strike from another large power. Technologically, this assumes the dominance of the type of weapon-system that presents many weapon sites yet does not permit the launching of more than a few delivery-vehicles, on the average, from each site. It also requires that the large power, whose response is to be triggered, have the means of detection by which it can determine which of the other large power's launching sites have lost their attack capability as a consequence of having retaliated against the small power. It will be seen that a passive triggering deterrent is possible only in very restricted circumstances, namely, against a major power whose own deterrent would be only just invulnerable were there no power capable of a passive trigger.

Passive deterrence is also possible on a different basis, namely, when the deterrent balance between two super-powers is *just* stable, and when a first strike by one of them against a small power would be regarded by the other as a virtual early warning of a strike against itself. Thus, some commentators have suggested that the British nuclear force has possessed such a capability to deter Soviet attack during the late 1950's and early 1960's.

An active triggering capability would result from a small nation's manufacturing, buying, or being given control of enough nuclear forces to reduce, by a first strike, a given great power to a level whereby it could not retaliate against another first strike by a second great power that was disposed to attack it. An active triggering force thus requires a shaky balance-of-terror between major powers, and would be more threatening to international stability than a passive triggering force since it is more likely to be pursued by an adventurist nation as a means to power.

Minimum Atomic Deterrence

The third type of deterrent to be considered is the minimum atomic variety. Deterrence of this nature would depend technologically upon the possession of nuclear bombs and some relatively crude method of delivery. The basic assumption underlying minimum atomic deterrence is that small powers might deter attempts to conquer them by having an atomic arsenal sufficient to guarantee greater damage to the conqueror than successful conquest would be worth to him.

A minimum atomic deterrent might or might not be a successful deterrent. However, many small nations may soon be in a position to acquire such a strategic force. Even if it did not deter large powers, it would increase the small power's status among its peers. There are of course a number of inherent dangers to world stability in the development of such deterrents. Not only would there be a risk that endemic brush-fire wars with small-scale atomic weapons might at any time involve the great powers with each other; but also the possible occasions of accidental nuclear war might increase. Acquisition of minimum atomic deterrent, even in fairly large numbers, would hardly make a stable world situation unstable, unless the balance-of-terror between the two super-powers were very delicate indeed. Similarly, the general effect of this kind of nuclear diffusion is unlikely to be as important as changes of policy or balance between the two super-powers.

Thus, a full array of Nth country possibilities would include independent, triggering, and minimum atomic deterrents. All three kinds of deterrents may be evident by 1970 if no explicit arms control succeeds, or unless the weapons technology of the two super-powers freezes out all lesser states. As at present, it would seem that even an economy and technology of British dimensions can barely support a fully independent deterrent. Furthermore, while the Chinese Communist economy might by 1970 produce the basic materials, it is unlikely that it could develop, solely from its own resources, the vast array of scientific and technical workers needed to produce the delivery and detection systems that could match those of the United States and the Soviet Union.

Of course, a reasonably advanced country may be given or may have acquired for itself an adequate deterrent that it directly controls, and still lack the resources to *maintain* membership in the most exclusive of the nuclear clubs. Communist China and even a united Europe may not achieve by 1970 anything more than triggering deterrents. By then, many countries, for example, the Benelux nations, Japan, India, Italy, Israel, and some of the Scandinavian, British Dominion, South American, and Southeast Asian countries may possess triggering deterrents. However, most of the above are more likely to fall into the wide category of minimum atomic deterrents, the range or variety of which tends to invalidate any simple model of the Nth country world.

THE ROLE OF TECHNOLOGY

The course of weapons technology will strongly determine the degree and kind of nuclear diffusion. For example, the super-powers could develop anti-missile and anti-aircraft missiles to an effectiveness that left the deterrent balance stable between themselves, but ensured that no other power had a credible independent deterrent, or even perhaps a passive trigger against either of them. Lesser powers might nevertheless decide it would be worthwhile to acquire minimum atomic deterrents against each other, or as a possible way to achieve a higher rank in the nuclear club should technological innovations again favor an inexpensive and credible independent deterrent. A simple and inexpensive fusion weapon would make this prospect more inviting to lesser powers than it seems to be at present, especially as Communist China develops its nuclear armory.

In many of its aspects, the course of military technology is essentially unpredictable since it depends in turn upon the course of discovery. The relatively predictable aspects are in the engineering of a project where the component processes have all been discovered, and notably of course in production after the manufacture of a prototype. But now that such great sums are invested in weapons research and development, discovery has become an important and yet highly uncertain independent variable in the international situation. We cannot even say in advance whether nuclear diffusion will be furthered by simplification of nuclear techniques, or hindered by the super-powers' development of sophisticated delivery systems. Nor do we know how the technological process will affect negotiations for arms control that might inhibit diffusion.

If the major powers fail to agree on more substantial measures of arms control than the current test ban treaty, and if military technology does not develop predominantly to favor either attack or defense, the likeliest situation for 1970 will be a loose bipolar world with many small powers, some of which are not strongly identified with either of the major powers. The presence of a number of smaller nations with triggering or minimum atomic deterrents may act as a destabilizing force. But, contrary to almost universal opinion, not all situations produced by nuclear diffusion need be less stable than the current modified bipolar situation. For instance, a world comprising for the most part three, four, or five substantial independent deterrent nations or blocs might be more stable. But in any case, the balance-of-power and the conditions for stability will no longer be definable in terms of a classic nation-state model.

THE BALANCE-OF-TERROR
IN A FOUR-POWER WORLD

One of the most significant (if not most likely) possibilities mentioned above is the achievement of independent deterrent status during 1960–1970 by both Communist China and a close alliance centered about the European Economic Community. Let us examine in detail the implications of this possibility for international stability.

The 1970 International Climate

Once again we must make some regulating assumptions. We shall therefore suppose that in 1970 mainland China will have maintained its Communist regime. It is further assumed that some nuclear weapons will have been acquired by Communist China by the mid-1960's. It is also assumed that no large-scale limited wars involving both the United States and the U.S.S.R. will have altered the basic situation in the Far East and Southeast Asia, and that Tokyo and New Delhi are not particularly responsive to pressure from Peking.

With respect to Western Europe, it is assumed that the European Economic Community (Inner Six)[2] will have a successfully integrated economy. Britain and the other nations of the Outer Seven[3] may be more intimately associated with the Common Market; on the other hand, they may have either moved collectively closer to non-commitment or they may continue to pursue different foreign policies with Britain re-establishing a close relationship to the U.S., notably in Indian and Pacific Ocean affairs. Industrially, the EEC will be broadly comparable to the Soviet Union. The technical and scientific manpower of the Inner Six and those countries associated with it will have grown to absolute levels comparable to those of the United States and the U.S.S.R., and qualitatively will not be inferior to theirs. But the U.S.S.R., supported by its high annual rate of industrial growth, will make heavy inroads into markets in many underdeveloped countries previously enjoyed by the Western world and Japan, and can also sell consumer durables and capital goods to countries of high consumption.

Furthermore, it is assumed that in India, Latin America, and the Middle East, economic growth will have been maintained, but at a lower rate than in the four major areas, so that relative variations in economic potential and achievement will be more marked in 1970 than they are presently. Japan will have achieved a high growth rate, but will not be a major deterrent power.

As a military grouping, the EEC is assumed to have moved during the 1960's toward military independence from the United States, partly from a wish for autonomy and international prestige, but chiefly because of a decline in the credibility of the threat of United States intervention against Soviet incursion into Europe.

---

[2] Belgium, France, Germany, Netherlands, Italy, and Luxembourg.
[3] United Kingdom, Denmark, Norway, Sweden, Austria, Switzerland and Portugal.

Technological and Systemic Conditions of Stability

Many observers believe that in a multi-power international system, comparable to the one we have just depicted, the military and technological stabilizers operative in a bipolar world would be rendered ineffectual. However, it has also been argued that in a system of at least three independent nuclear powers, a second-order or systemic feature would reinforce mutual deterrence, that is, that even if a power were to contemplate a surprise counterforce attack on one of the others, it would be deterred by the realization that its force would consequently be so depleted as to be easily destroyed by a counterforce attack from the third power. This deterrent would, in the above case, operate only against the U.S.S.R.

In an attempt to examine whether a four-power world (the U.S., the U.S.S.R., Communist China and Europe) would increase or decrease international stability, let us survey the requirements for strategic and limited war capabilities, including research and development, which may operate upon the likelier aspirants to independent deterrent status in the 1970–1975 technological context.

Forces for Strategic War. It is assumed that by 1970–1975 any military establishment that can afford it will prefer a *mixture* of deterrent weapon systems in order to compound the enemy's problems of diversified attack and countermeasures. With or without a ban on nuclear tests, a spectrum of thermonuclear weapons should be available to the United States and the U.S.S.R.; while the United Kingdom, France, Communist China, and possibly others as well, are likely to have access to a lesser yet considerable range of nuclear weapons. There also may be deliverable warheads of many hundreds of megatons.

Fleets of nuclear submarines armed with thermonuclear missiles are likely to be used by all four major powers, until a thoroughly reliable submarine detector has been developed. In the long run the nuclear submarines alone would not be stabilizing weapons. Presumably they can hunt each other down, and they can also be destroyed by aircraft armed with air-to-sea missiles. They thus resemble other fleets, the classical objects of a quantitative exponential arms race.

Missiles employing terminal guidance may be available as part of an expensive system, but simpler forms such as the Minuteman should be quite inexpensive, although they will continue to require considerable depth for any useful deployment. Some stocks are likely to be kept hidden and highly protected by all powers as insurance against post-attack blackmail. Most operational missiles are likely to be mobile in order to frustrate an enemy's attempt to disarm an opponent. Whether there would be a case for greatly hardened and defended sites to absorb heavy and extensive attack is not easily predictable, although it seems unlikely in Europe because of the lack of sparsely populated areas.

By 1970, a nuclear bomber armed with stand-off air-to-ground missiles and defensive weapons could be in production by some of the major powers. Depending upon the state of detecting and tracking equipment, this weapon system might be as effective a deterrent as the nuclear submarine. But, employed by rival powers, the nuclear bomber also might (depending upon quite fine details of its performance) give rise to a classic exponential arms race. In view of the arms race's course in 1961–1964, however, it would appear that the U.S.S.R. has tacitly accepted a long-term inferiority in potential for defense production, which makes the foregoing weapon-developments less likely.

If the United States and/or the Soviet Union have outer-space launching platforms and stations and orbiting missiles in position in 1970, they might well provide the most hopeful countermeasure to ICBM's and submarine-launched missiles. As United States negotiators implied in March 1960, outer space is a favorable location for beginning arms control. Short of internationally directed countermeasures against missiles, an international warning system might reduce the possibility of surprise attack with any airborne or space weapon. This type of arms control avoids or reduces the need for ground inspection. It could re-direct the course of strategic-weapons technology and would certainly bear upon the problems of diffusion and stability in the 1970's.

Ten years may not be too short a time for developing and deploying other types of strategic weapons, for example, unmanned underwater launchers, strategic chemical weapons, weather control, and still other methods of destruction not yet conceived. Such possibilities properly set studies such as this in a dubious light. However, since our review has been in terms of mixed deterrent weapon systems, the possibility of a given novelty having made obsolescent all of the types imagined above is somewhat reduced.

Forces for Limited War. In the world we have assumed, only the United States could possibly manage to rely almost wholly upon strategic and nuclear weapon systems. The three other major powers—China, Russia, and Europe—would need less-than-ultimate forces to deter or to meet less-than-ultimate aggression because of their extensive frontiers with each other or with important sub-deterrent states.

This contention derives from an assumption that the threat of total thermonuclear retaliation will not protect areas and interests not of ultimate concern to the threatener. To be more exact, the more stable the general balance-of-terror, that is, the more sure an opponent is of his second-strike capability, the less feasible a first-strike.

There are strong arguments to suggest that all four major powers of the 1970's will require forces capable of fighting non-nuclear wars. Malcolm Hoag[4] argues that in the current situation the United States should develop some "active" deterrent, that is, a first-strike capability, to back up a primarily non-nuclear European force for limited war. This contention presupposes that the present balance teeters between first- and second-strike potentials and that in any case, the United States must have as much second-strike capability as possible. In practice, a region such as Europe might be so near the potential aggressors, and have so few resources of geographical depth in which to locate retaliatory forces, that there would be no point in its having more than a "trip-wire" of conventional and nuclear forces, either to repel a minor conventional attack or probing action, or as a patently obvious device for initiating reciprocal destruction of cities if more than minimum conventional challenges were presented.

Europe and the United States would certainly need to raise the costs of any attempt by a potential enemy to attack or control certain areas (North Africa and the Middle East, Latin America and Pacific Asia) that might be classed as "eventually vital" to them. But how much risk of immediate total war the West should assume on behalf of interests possibly vital only in the long run is a moot question. It was recently fashionable to advocate the use of tactical nuclear weapons as the most evident and effective means of raising enemy costs of limited war. However, if we use nuclear weapons even when the enemy uses non-nuclear means to threaten parts of such areas, then we must be prepared to destroy friendly populations.

Perhaps an alternative is to apply "automation" to conventional warfare by partly replacing the large number of troops usually assumed necessary for limited campaigns with engines of war. Such weapons as the "neutron bomb," the biological and chemical weapons—especially those designed to disorganize and unhinge military forces—and the new sensors and guidance equipment might within ten years thin out the combatants required on both the non-nuclear and the tactical-nuclear battlefields.

[4] M. W. Hoag, "NATO Strategy and Limited War," in NATO and American Security, K. Knorr, ed., Princeton University Press, Princeton, N.J., 1959, pp. 123 et seq.; and "What Interdependence for NATO?", World Politics, Vol. XII, No. 3, April 1960, p. 381,

Military authorities, both Soviet and Western, appear now to hold that the presence of tactical nuclear forces is needed even in conventional war, where they have the valuable functions of "deterring" the enemy from exceedingly large concentrations of conventional weapons, and of inhibiting his movements of forces and supplies. More obviously, the possession of tactical nuclear weapons may in a conventional war deter an enemy from initiating the employment of tactical nuclear weapons. To carry this line of thought to a logical conclusion one would advocate a strategy of graduated deterrence. Thus, if all went well, the only wars ever fought would be non-nuclear wars with limited forces and for limited objectives because of the belief by both sides that a conflict utilizing nuclear weapons could never pay.

Nevertheless, we cannot, unfortunately, rule out the possibility that there will be limited wars or even lesser incidents in which tactical nuclear weapons can be used to military advantage without serious danger of escalation to central war, for example, against an invasion fleet or the bases of non-nuclear bombers that are set to attack highly populated areas. Though the presence of nuclear weapons will usually deter a probing action, there are likely to be some non-nuclear probes that cannot be deterred. This alone should be enough to induce all major deterrent powers to maintain capabilities for fighting, and not merely deterring, tactical nuclear wars.

In summary, it seems highly probable that major strategic deterrent powers of the 1970's should and will likely maintain substantial and complex forces for limited war, both nuclear and non-nuclear. This will make major deterrent status very expensive indeed, even for powers that depend upon an ally for research and development.

Capability for Research and Development. Russia and America have developed virtually all modern weapon systems. Britain and France have unsurpassed records of inventiveness and of brilliance in fundamental research, but together cannot match the budgetary allocations, the number of engineers and technologists, or (in some fields) the attractive facilities and opportunities found in the United States.

If Britain and the EEC were, by 1970, to have been pooling defense resources for several years, the evidence suggests that ideally, the resultant coalition would quickly take its place among the pioneers of military technology. However, there obviously would be many concrete hindrances such as language barriers, conflict of interest over location of facilities for research and production of prototypes, and difficulties in resolving disputes about research strategy. But the principal objection would likely spring from the fact that the new economic organism, upon which the military coalition was based, might feel it more gainful to use its scientists and engineers in civilian rather than military research. For these reasons, and because serious, avoidable waste presently arises from autarchical trends in NATO defense production, the argument for greater efficiency weighs heavily in favor of Europe's leaving the principal jobs of military research and development to the United States.

However, even if Britain and the Inner Six nations chose to save most of their military research and development expenditures by purchasing or bartering for the latest strategic deterrent systems produced in United States, serious difficulties would still remain. Productive facilities otherwise created for or expanded by programs of research and development would for the most part be lost. Having second priority for United States weapons, the Europeans would be forced to accept long delivery times. Above all, they would be accepting something less than complete independence and autonomy in defense. The supplying power could to some extent regulate the Europeans' international behavior by threatening not to supply new weapon systems, or replacements, spare parts, training units, etc., for the existing systems. The United States could hardly relinquish such a political lever. Indeed it can be argued that it would be impolitic for the United States to do so.

There would thus be disadvantages to supplying Europe with weapon systems from the United States' viewpoint. One would be that by freeing Western Europe of military research and development commitments, the United States would be helping to build up the scientific and technological base of an economic competitor. Another is that there might be security risks and leakage of intelligence. Furthermore, the example might help Communist China to pressure the U.S.S.R. into arming the Chinese.

The advantage to the United States might not be obvious or immediate. The chief benefit would be to stabilize European power by providing the most adequate deterrent possible and, in particular, to reduce European propensities for triggering the strategic forces of the United States.

Similar considerations apply to relationships between Communist China and the U.S.S.R. In fact, Russia might be in much more danger of being triggered or catalyzed into war by China than would the United States by Europe. However, if Moscow could give Peking a safe, invulnerable system *restricted* to a second-strike capability, the Russians as well as the Westerners might breathe a sigh of relief. But this, even technically, seems impossible.

Despite the foregoing disadvantages, we should rather expect that in our four-power world of 1970 the United States will still be supplier to Europe of new deterrent systems; much less certainly, the U.S.S.R. to Communist China. This, of course, means that in one military sense the world would still be bipolarized, because (along with other political and ideological tendencies) the new major powers' continued dependence on military technology would set a limit to the logic of "power diffusion."

STABILITY IN A MULTI-POWER WORLD

Given the preceding characterization of a four-power world in 1970, it is now possible to draw some conclusions about systemic stability within the international system, that is, the propensity for the total international system to preserve itself without disappearance of or loss to any but small powers or groupings, without basic changes in the nature of interstate relationships, and therefore without wars of such a scale as to produce such changes. In viewing systemic stability two problems will be discussed in detail—the stability of alternative United States-European alliances and potential alliances in South and Southeast Asia.

Stability of Alternative United States-European Alliances

The stability of a number of alternative United States-European alliances will be considered within the following five limiting assumptions:

1. There will be no wars between the United States and the transatlantic West, that is, the Inner Six, the Outer Seven, the European neutrals, or any new blocs that may have formed by 1970.

2. The European powers and Communist China will have little opportunity and less motive to attack each other by 1970.

3. The Chinese will not have an "active" trigger for sending Russian strategic and retaliatory forces against the United States or Europe; and they are quite unlikely to be able to catalyze a war between Russia and North America. China could actively trigger a Russian strike against the United States only through a surprise Chinese attack against the U.S. that would leave the U.S. with so little strategic retaliatory force that Russia could initiate, survive and win a central war. China is not likely to have weapons by 1970 that would overcome the problems of distance and accuracy in such an attack against the U.S. Similarly, it is not then likely to possess the highly varied and sophisticated devices that would seem necessary to catalyze, with safety to itself, a central war between the United States and the U.S.S.R.

4. China will not have a passive trigger adequate to stimulate Russia

to attack the United States if the latter can maintain two distinct and adequate strategic forces or allocations of force, one earmarked for China and the other for the U.S.S.R. China would have a passive trigger only if a United States counterforce strike against China were likely to expend so much of America's (and possibly Europe's) retaliatory forces that it would pay Russia to initiate a counterforce strike against North America (and Europe). The Western world might before 1970 encourage such an attack by maintaining only a minimal deterrent force, but this does not seem a serious possibility.

5. The U.S.S.R. may need and can probably maintain up to three distinct strategic retaliatory forces or their combined equivalents. China may wish to do the same but may not be able to as early as 1970. This is because both the U.S.S.R. and Communist China may need to contemplate the possibility of receiving three combined or successive counterforce attacks—from the United States, from Western Europe, and from each other.

Limiting condition (4) must be qualified by stating that Communist China may not behave as predicted. For example, China might very well contemplate using the nuclear capability for destroying cities which it could easily command by 1970. China's strategists have not yet participated in the convergence of strategic military doctrine recently noticeable among American, European, and Russian analysts. Thus, a modern education for Peking in the facts of life and death is probably essential to world stability.

Having stated the limitations that are likely to apply in the 1970's, regardless of the direction that United States-European alliances may take, let us now examine some organizational alternatives for Western deterrent strategy. These include:

1. Fragmented, independent, transatlantic NATO.
2. Separate strategic deterrents with combined forces for limited war.
3. European limited war forces with a United States active deterrent force.
4. European community deterrence:
   a. Self-supplied deterrence;
   b. Deterrence systems supplied by the United States.

Fragmented, Independent, Transatlantic NATO. In this situation we assume that the United States and the Soviet Union both have invulnerable second-strike capabilities, so that the United States' strategic umbrella obviously does not cover Europe. Britain and France are assumed to have reasonably invulnerable second-strike forces, Britain's seaborne, while the Benelux nations and Italy have "low-confidence" capabilities of the same sort. It is postulated that there is some joint conventional and nuclear tactical force for Britain plus Western Europe, but chiefly on paper, and that Western Germany has excellent conventional and nuclear tactical forces of its own, a number of nuclear submarines, and probably a large number of medium-range ballistic missiles (MRBM) on its own soil. The Scandinavian and Eastern Mediterranean flanks of Europe are ill-protected.

Militarily this is one of the least stable of our organizational alternatives, though at the political level it may be quite static. The U.S.S.R. can capture or subvert successive countries of Europe and North Africa. Western Germany relies on a combination of low-confidence deterrent considerations, and her MRBM's are a standing incitement to Soviet strategic assault or conventional capture. If a Russian conventional attack appears to have a significant probability of penetrating Western Germany or escalating into tactical nuclear war, Germany can deliver a counterforce attack against Russia severe enough to trigger parts of the strategic forces belonging to some or all of the other transatlantic powers. The Soviet Union, for its part, would likely hope to turn these other powers and the United States against Germany.

Separate Strategic Deterrents with Combined Forces for Limited War. The United States is assumed to supply each NATO power (or viable grouping) with the best available second-strike deterrent, upon condition that jointly they maintain the forces needed to defend the Western European region in limited war.

Provided that separate second-strike deterrents are at that stage credible, this alternative has a considerable potential for stability, even as late as 1970. Admittedly, many of the current difficulties of limited conventional defense of Europe would still remain, but the limited war capability would be complemented by strategic deterrents.

European Limited War Forces with a United States Active Deterrent Force. The proposal of Europe's possessing limited war forces and the United States' assuming responsibility for an active deterrent force has been advanced by Malcolm Hoag.[5] Transposing it to 1970 seems to present two difficulties:

1. It absolutely requires the United States to have some capacity for active deterrence (a first strike) against Russia, and the technological conditions of the time may not permit this.

2. Even if technologically feasible, the efficacy of an active deterrent

---

[5] *Ibid.,* p. 13.

will depend upon somewhat subtle considerations of psychology and bargaining theory. The Russians, for example, might not share (in its entirety) the West's conception of rational behavior.

European Community Deterrence. In the section on research and development, the alternative of self-supplied deterrence was regarded as inadvisable for the West as a whole. However, if it comes about there would appear to be two major consequences.

First, if Europe developed its own deterrent, North America could confine its attention, broadly speaking, to the Western Hemisphere, the Arctic, and the world of the Pacific; but only so long as Europe's situation vis-à-vis the Soviet bloc remained stable. Suppose that, in particular, Europe were driven by technological considerations to develop a formidable first-strike capability. Such an event might affect North America's military involvement in Europe in several alternative ways: (1) it might be triggered by Europe, actively or passively, into a nuclear strike against Russia; (2) a total conflict might reduce both the Soviet and the European bloc, leaving North America to consider whether Communist China should be brought to submission before the remains of Europe and Russia could be reconstructed; or (3) Europe might suddenly capitulate to Soviet blackmail or conventional attack, thus drastically upsetting the world's balance-of-power.

Second, British and European military technology might not be far enough advanced by 1970 to provide adequate and invulnerable deterrent forces. Providing such forces is far more difficult in Europe than in Russia, China, or North America because of the lack of continental depth, and proximity to the Soviet bloc. By the same token, however, Europe's land-based first-strike potential against Russia is perhaps fiercer than North America's. It might therefore be expected that self-supplied weapon systems would destabilize Europe-Soviet bloc relations precisely as outlined in the preceding paragraph. In general, then, we can conclude that self-supplied European deterrence does not suggest a very stable world.

The alternative of deterrent systems supplied by the United States avoids one of the possible sources of instability in the previous alternative; that is, it would be more likely that Europe's strategic deterrent force would be invulnerable and efficient. And, like the alternative of imported national deterrents which has been previously discussed, the present alternative would allow the United States a voice in the type of strategic force employed by Europeans. For example, the United States could discourage vulnerable and provocative first-strike systems.

The chief source of instability under this alternative would be the possibility of limited war, which the joint European deterrent may not be able in all cases to deter, and for which the Europeans may lack other adequate capabilities. United States assistance for Europe may be desirable in combating this, for example, it might be helpful if there were Western cooperation in producing conventional and tactical nuclear weapons. The United States might also maintain an alliance with Europe against limited aggression in the Middle East and Africa.

In return for the latter, however, the United States might wish for the support of the Europeans and the British in, say, Southeast Asia. However, if relationships developed along such lines, this would negate the original idea of relieving the United States of responsibilities for Europe and would in fact all but restore a united Western Alliance and a loose bipolar world.

Potential Alliances in South and Southeast Asia

The South and Southeast Asia region are currently so unsettled that by 1970 instability in other regions may by comparison seem quite unimportant. For this reason, it is a daunting task to take account of influences possibly emanating from these regions in 1970, since so many different sorts of change are possible during the 1960's. But if we list some of the possible changes, a pattern, of sorts, may emerge.

Soviet Expansion toward the Indian Ocean. The U.S.S.R. is now recognized as having achieved a most favorable position in Afghanistan. On one shore of the Arabian Sea, Iran, the Trucial States, and Oman might fall under Soviet influence or control in the next decade. On the other shore, India's responses to Communist activity from within and Russian power or friendship from without were a matter of concern to the West until Communist China's unlooked-for incursions against India exposed Russia's inability to assist her. Indian authorities, for their part, recognize that the Indian Ocean region (which includes Eastern African countries, Pakistan, Ceylon, and, marginally, Indonesia and Australia, as well as the states already mentioned) is a power vacuum in which only the United States is currently deploying, through Pakistan, a military force with modern armament. On the other hand, the United Kingdom's renewed committment to Malaysia may betoken a revival of British influence in the Indian Ocean.

A Soviet breakthrough, perhaps by seaboard stepping-stones into North Africa, could establish the U.S.S.R. as an Indian Ocean power, thus posing for India alternatives of cooperation with Russia or active resistance to further encroachment.

The Sino-Indian conflict has, on the other hand, enabled the Western Alliance to demonstrate its potentiality for military support against

Chinese incursions, and seems to have evoked in India a ready resistance to Communism of either the Chinese or the Russian brand. But there was no response from India's neighbors against the Chinese. Pakistan, indeed, responded favorably to the Chinese action. Though without regional support, India remains the cornerstone of Southern Asia, so that the power structure of the whole region would be transformed were India to join either the Russian or Chinese camp, whether through sheer external pressure, subversion, or popular disenchantment with those forms of Western democracy to which India's elite still strongly adheres.

Fluidity in East and Southeast Asia. With few exceptions, the countries bordering Communist China, from Nepal to Korea, are a mosaic of slowly developing, politically fragile successor-states of the British, French, Dutch, American, Japanese, and other empires. If for a decade these states manage to maintain the international status quo, their grouping as an economic and defense community sponsored by India and Japan may become an aspiration of the 1970's. A problem for the United States then, would be whether to foster or to check this presumably neutral grouping and, if fostering it, to find the right tempo and limits for reducing Western commitments in parts of the area. Meanwhile, the most likely power to be projected in this region is American, even though Malaysia, designed to liquidate British responsibilities, has reactivated them, and though General de Gaulle is trying to re-establish a French sphere of influence in the Far East. Political change in Washington itself, furthermore, could lead to a thinning-out of the currently heavy American expenditure of money and resources in Southeast Asia. Congressional opinion could well find support for the view that Communist Chinese expansion southward might be resisted wholly by the deployment there of the U.S. nuclear strategic forces.

It seems likely that fallout would blow back from short range attacks launched westward against the Chinese mainland from Japan, Taiwan, and perhaps Korea. Thus for military, as well as for political reasons, the United States may tacitly designate these three countries as non-nuclear zones. On the other hand, it may prove necessary to deploy tactical nuclear weapons in mainland countries that are members or protocol-states of the Southeast Asia Treaty Organization. The Philippines and perhaps Sabah (formerly North Borneo) would be suitable locations for land-based strategic missiles, except for possible dangers of conventional attack or sabotage. In general, however, it would be no safer in Southeast Asia than in Europe to dispense with a conventional military, naval, and airborne capability.

If states in Southeast Asia were to fall to conquest or subversion by Communist China (or by the U.S.S.R., which still extends influence in the Communist parties of the region), then India and the others might be driven much closer to the Western alliance and Japan might develop warmer feelings toward its treaty with the United States. But if that does not happen, and the Chinese develop a nuclear arm sufficiently strong to make doubtful a first-strike victory for the United States, there might be a clamor among some of the Asian SEATO members for more direct control of atomic weapons than SEATO presently gives them. But this seems unlikely by 1975.

East and Southeast Asia with a Triggering Deterrent. Either through SEATO and other alliances or by acquisition from more advanced nations of the area such as India and Japan, countries of East and Southeast Asia may within a decade come into possession of atomic weapons and more or less crude means of delivery. This would give them a low-confidence method of directly deterring Chinese Communist expansion; alternatively, a somewhat uncertain trigger for sending Western strategic nuclear weapons in a counterforce first-strike against Communist China; or, yet again, a general-purpose lever against Western Powers and against each other.

The trigger might work as follows: the possibility that atomic weapons might be used against Chinese personnel in Asian wars could easily provoke the Chinese into threats of punishing such users of atomic weapons by striking at their cities or those of their allies. The threats might even be carried out, so that something like Kaplan's strategy of limited retaliation[6] would come to be practiced by the Chinese. (Kaplan envisages a "teaching" strategy, by which the retaliatory power demonstrates its resolve, thereby making a long-term gain at the expense of severe short-term costs to itself.) At that point, or even earlier if it were foreseen, the United States or other Western powers might decide that China's ability to mete out punishment had become intolerable, and that a disarming counterforce attack should be launched against her. Whether or not the U.S.S.R. would then decide to begin a third world war would likely depend upon the relative second-strike capabilities of Russia, Europe, and the United States.

CONCLUSIONS

In conclusion, the following forces should be emphasized as major sources of systemic instability in the 1970's. First, atomic armories of

---

[6] M. A. Kaplan, *The Strategy of Limited Retaliation*, Policy Memorandum No. 19, Center of International Studies, Princeton University Press, Princeton, N.J., 1959.

more than nuisance value may be available to several countries in Asia, the Middle East, and South America. The effects of this type of nuclear diffusion would be much less predictable than, for instance, the acquisition of more formidable second-strike systems by states of the European economic community because the military positions of Asia and the Middle East are much less defined than in Europe. Second, Communist China may pose a serious threat to international stability by 1970. And third, the qualitative arms race between two or more super-powers will provide a source of instability at least as serious as any nuclear diffusion.

The analysis suggests two alternative "worlds" for 1970–1975: one, a bipolar world with Southern and Eastern Asia either absorbed into the Soviet camp or having become a semi-independent protectorate of the Western alliance; the other, a world of four or five strategic nuclear blocs (the U.S.S.R., Communist China, the United States, Europe—including the UK, and possibly an Asian bloc), all independent but for the fact that the Asian and the European groups import their advanced weapons from the United States.

Chapter 7

European Community Deterrence:

Its Organization, Utility,

and Political and Economic Feasibility

CHARLES G. McCLINTOCK and DALE J. HEKHUIS[1]

This chapter examines the utility and political feasibility of establishing an effective, credible, and efficient strategic deterrent for Western Europe.[2,3] Two major hypotheses are advanced: (1) the current deterrent strategy of NATO based solely upon the nuclear retaliatory capability of the United States is inadequate and inappropriate for the strategic defense of Europe, and (2) the formation of a European Community organization with an independent strategic force is both desirable and feasible. In examining these hypotheses, environmental trends that contribute to the inadequacy of current Western deterrent

---

Part of this chapter appeared originally in the September 1961 issue of the Journal of Conflict Resolution.

[1] The authors are particularly indebted to Paul Ginberg, George Mandanis, and Arthur L. Burns for their insightful criticisms of this chapter.

[2] See Herman Kahn, "The Nature and Feasibility of War and Deterrence," Stanford Research Institute Journal, Vol. 4 (1959).

[3] Effectiveness denotes a sufficiently strong capability to inflict unacceptable damage. Credibility denotes an unmistakable intent to "make good" on the threat of nuclear retaliation. Efficiency denotes a minimum duplication of effort among countries.

134

strategy are reviewed, the utility of alternative organizational means for alleviating this inadequacy is assessed, and the poltical feasibility of a European Community Deterrent (ECD) is appraised.

ENVIRONMENTAL TRENDS

The most important environmental trend of consequence for Western deterrent strategy is the increasing Soviet capability to inflict catastrophic damage upon the United States. During the early years of NATO, the Soviets were confronted with a powerful Western deterrent composed of two elements: the NATO tactical forces on the continent, and the American Strategic Air Command. At that time, the U.S.S.R. did not possess operational nuclear weapons. In recent years, however, Russia has rapidly improved her military-technological capabilities, and in the near future will be able to launch large-scale nuclear attacks upon the United States.

One major implication of this growing Soviet capability is an increased likelihood that the United States could be "blackmailed" into abandoning the defense of Europe, although the number of United States casualties that the Soviets would have to threaten to inflict to discourage United States strategic retaliation to a Soviet attack upon Europe is unknown. The difficulty of assessing the susceptibility of the United States to nuclear blackmail has been noted by Kahn:

If the Soviets and the Europeans would not believe we would honor our commitments to our allies if it means 177 million American casualties, what level of casualties do they believe we would accept? How many, indeed, if the decision were yours, would you accept? 100 million? 50 million? 10 million? 1 million? It's a hard question.

I have discussed this question with some Europeans, asking them to guess how the American President would act. I have found no European who believed we would initiate a war if the casualties would be much over 20,000,000 and some believed we would be deterred at less than 2,000,000.[4]

The Soviets will soon have the capability to inflict substantially more than 20,000,000 casualties in a nuclear attack upon United States population centers. The credibility of NATO's current deterrent policy in Europe is based almost solely upon the intent of the United States to employ its nuclear retaliatory force. Thus, the increasing Soviet nuclear capability—accompanied by the growing belief that the United States is vulnerable to "nuclear blackmail"—has produced and will continue to produce a substantial weakening of the collective defense posture of the Western alliance.

---

[4] Kahn, op. cit., p. 129.

The European concern with the decreasing credibility of the willingness of the United States to employ nuclear weapons in the defense of Europe is reflected in the actions of Franz Strauss, Germany's Minister of Defense. At the December 14, 1961 meetings of the allied foreign ministers in Paris, he was successful in persuading this group to begin to examine the question of forming a NATO-controlled deterrent. In connection with this action, the *Economist* notes the obvious military advantages of the proposal in face of the growing problem in credibility. However, they also note the "political disadvantages that spring from the extraordinary difficulty in defining 'joint control'—that is, who gives the order to fire the missiles." [5]

A second major environmental trend is the increasing number of countries with independent nuclear weapon capabilities.[6] Within the NATO alliance, this development is serving to fragment the West's deterrent posture into a number of independent deterrents. Such independent deterrents are grossly inefficient in terms of duplication of effort. Furthermore, single European nations are incapable of allocating sufficient resources to the development of an effective deterrent, that is, one which is sufficiently strong to inflict unacceptable damage upon a potential aggressor.

A third environmental trend which has implications for Western deterrent strategy is the current movement toward the unification of Europe. It is not within the scope of this chapter to give a detailed analysis of the trend towards European union.[7] However, several important conclusions can be drawn from the variety of postwar attempts toward political, economic, and military integration in Europe: (1) whereas the supranational economic and scientific programs—European Coal and Steel Community (ECSC), European Economic Community (EEC), and European Atomic Energy Community (EURATOM)—have brought about a significant measure of economic integration among the Inner Six (France, West Germany, Italy, the Benelux na-

---

[5] "Europe's Deterrent," *Economist*, December 30, 1961, pp. 1266–1267.

[6] As noted in a recent study by the Academy of Arts and Sciences, twelve countries already have a sufficient technical and industrial base to embark upon successful nuclear weapons programs in the near future. These countries, most of which are highly industrialized and currently possess operating reactors or have arrangements for obtaining reactors are: Belgium, Canada, China, Czechoslovakia, France, East Germany, West Germany, India, Italy, Japan, Sweden and Switzerland. See W. Davidson, M. Kalkstein, C. Hohenemser, *The Nth Country Problem and Arms Control*, National Planning Association, Pamphlet 108, 1960.

[7] For a comprehensive review of the post-war movement toward European union, see M. Margaret Ball, *NATO and the European Union Movement*, New York: Praeger, 1959.

tions), attempts at military integration, for example, Western Union (WU) and the European Defense Community (EDC); and at political union, European Political Community (EPC), have thus far been unsuccessful; (2) there have been marked interdependencies among the efforts to integrate Europe economically, politically, and militarily; and (3) although De Gaulle refused in early 1963 to permit British entry into the EEC, the eventual participation of Britain as a full member of the European community movement is not unlikely.

The success of the European union movement to date—particularly in the economic sphere—is likely to have two major effects. First, a more favorable environment will exist for the consideration of proposals for additional forms of community activity. Second, the decline in the economic and political dependence of Europe upon the United States will continue, and consequently one of the major forces that has contributed to the past cohesion of the NATO alliance will be weakened.

A final environmental trend is the emergence of new weapons technologies. The development of long-range missile systems and the advent of the Polaris submarine markedly reduce United States dependence upon European military bases. Therefore, it will become increasingly difficult for the United States policy-makers to rationalize overseas bases to economy-minded Congressmen, and to Europeans who wish to be independent from both the United States and the U.S.S.R. Should the United States continue to withdraw from its overseas bases,[8] the likelihood of rapid and effective employment of United States deterrent forces in response to overt Soviet military action in Europe would be further reduced—if credibility is viewed as a function of not only a formal commitment (for example, a treaty obligation), but also an operative commitment (for example, the physical presence of U.S. forces in allied countries).

Thus, the decreasing credibility of the United States threat to invoke its deterrent capability on behalf of Western Europe, the diffusion of nuclear weapons, the diminishing United States dependence on foreign bases, and the increasing political and economic unity of the Inner Six will contribute to a reduction in the military interdependence between Western Europe and the United States. Such reduced interdependence adversely affects both the cohesion of the NATO alliance and the credibility of current nuclear defense strategy in Western Europe.

One alternative Western strategy that would take into account these

---

[8] In late 1962 and 1963 the U.S. negotiated with Turkey to remove U.S. missile bases from its territory.

environmental trends is advocated by George Kennan[9] and others. It involves a withdrawal of United States and Russian forces from Germany or Europe. The policy of disengagement is based upon two fundamental assumptions: (1) that Europe does not possess the capability to deter the Russians militarily; and (2) that Russia, for political reasons, would not take military advantage of the situation. The possible consequences of this policy include reunification of Germany and the growth of governments independent of Soviet and United States influence.

However, one may question the validity of the two assumptions underlying a policy of disengagement. The assumption that an effective and credible European deterrent would be too costly neglects the possible willingness of the United States, in its own interest, to supply technical and financial assistance. The assumption that Russia would be deterred from direct military intervention in Europe for political reasons is highly tenuous.

ORGANIZATIONAL PROTOTYPES

Three alternative organizational frameworks exist for implementing a strategy of nuclear deterrence in Western Europe: (a) fragmented, (b) alliance, and (c) community. Fragmented deterrence exists when the decision to develop and/or employ strategic nuclear weapons is made independently by sovereign nations. Alliance deterrence is operative when the decision to develop and/or employ strategic nuclear weapons is made by individual nations in the light of a formal pact or treaty agreement in a manner consistent with their sovereign interests. Community deterrence is conditional upon individual nations agreeing in advance to accept the decisions of a supranational institution relative to the development and/or employment of strategic nuclear weapons.

Fragmented Deterrence

The current trend in Western Europe is toward fragmented deterrence. The principle motives for independent acquisition of nuclear weapons by sovereign powers include the fear that the United States will not employ its deterrent forces if the Soviets attack Western Europe; the pursuit of national prestige; greater diplomatic leverage; and protection against nuclear blackmail.

Although these are legitimate motives, it is difficult to make a

---

[9] George Kennan, *Russia, the Atom and the West*, Harper, New York, 1959.

convincing case for fragmented deterrence as an effective, efficient and credible means for implementing Western deterrent strategy in Europe.

Its inadequacy stems partly from the economic and technological inability of any of the countries of Western Europe to sustain the development, production, and maintenance of a modern, complex strategic capability. The British experience with the Blue Streak missile has amply demonstrated that an independent missile development program on a relatively small scale cannot hope to outpace technological obsolescence.

There is also considerable doubt as to the credibility of national deterrents, that is, whether an individual nation would possess sufficient resolve to employ its capability in the face of an all-out Soviet threat. In this circumstance, a strategy of piecemeal attack and nuclear blackmail would have considerable appeal and potential for the U.S.S.R.

From the point of view of Western Europe as a whole, national policies of fragmented deterrence are grossly inefficient in the sense of duplication of effort. Finally, fragmented deterrence increases the probability of accidental war and of irresponsible employment of nuclear weapons and further complicates the problem of negotiating arms control agreements.

Alliance Deterrence

Alliance deterrence, as distinct from fragmented deterrence, is based upon a formal treaty or pact founded upon a set of common interests. In the case of NATO, the treaty consists basically of a statement of common interests, an agreement to consult in the event of a threat to the security of any one of the parties, and a commitment by each member to take "such action as it deems necessary" in the event of an attack upon any one of them. Thus each party, although committing itself to act, has reserved for its own determination the specific type of action to be taken.

At the inception of NATO, the members recognized that the strength of the alliance would be fundamentally dependent upon a U.S. commitment to defend Europe. As Osgood points out, "The founders of the Treaty, conscious of America's history of isolation, believed that a truly entangling multilateral alliance, embodying explicit binding obligations, was essential to make this commitment convincing to the nations of Western Europe as well as to the Soviet Union." [10] This en-

---

[10] Robert Osgood, "NATO: Problems of Security and Collaboration," *American Political Science Review*, Vol. 54, 1960.

tanglement has been operationally accomplished primarily through the extension of SAC's nuclear umbrella to Western Europe, the stationing of United States troops and the establishment of aircraft and missile bases in Europe, the assumption of leadership of SHAPE, and military and economic assistance.

However, a number of areas remain where both the United States and the Western European nations are relatively free of entanglement. The SAC and Polaris systems are under national, not NATO, control. The United States "guarantee" to invoke its deterrent capability in behalf of Western Europe is verbal, not written. The nuclear warheads at European IRBM bases are under United States ownership, their use being subject to veto by either the U.S. or the host country. Although Article 2 of the NATO Treaty provides for nuclear sharing,[11] very little has been accomplished.

Several proposals for nuclear sharing have been advanced, however, for the purpose of strengthening overall Western deterrent capabilities. One would have the United States sell or give nuclear weapons to individual allies. Other schemes would involve delegating control of portions of the strategic capabilities of SAC, Polaris, and/or Bomber Command to joint NATO or European deterrent forces, coupled with United States assistance in the development and procurement of solid-fueled IRBM's.[12] A more recent proposal is for a seaborne, nuclear weapons fleet manned by multi-nation crews.[13]

Programs for sharing nuclear weapons, other than on a nation-by-nation basis, would provide a greater overall nuclear deterrent capability for the same expenditure of resources, and probably would involve less risk with respect to the dangers of accidental war. A major weakness remains, however. In the framework of an alliance, individual nations would still remain the focus of decision-making, for as Knorr observes, each member country would want "its finger on both the trigger and the safety catch." [14]

---

[11] ". . . The Parties, separately and jointly, by means of continuous and effective self-help and mutual aid, will maintain and develop their individual and collective capacity to resist armed attack." (The NATO Treaty was signed in 1949).

[12] See Alastair Bucham, NATO in the 1960's, Weidenfield and Nicholson, New York, 1960 (especially pp. 57–82) for arguments for a joint NATO nuclear deterrent.

[13] See "Splitting NATO's Atoms," The Economist, Dec. 8, 1962, pp. 991–992.

[14] Klaus Knorr, "Aspects of NATO Strategy: A Conference Report," in K. Knorr, ed., NATO and American Security, Princeton University Press, Princeton, N.J., 1959.

Community Deterrence[15]

The strategy advocated in this chapter would involve creating a community deterrent[16] in which a group of European nations would agree in advance to accept the decisions of a supranational institution for developing and employing strategic weapons. Through a community effort, sufficient resources would be available, with some United States aid, to build and maintain an effective deterrent. Also, since strategic decisions would be made by predesignated representatives and would not require the approval of sovereign nations, a community organization could meet a variety of environmental contingencies with speed and flexibility. Furthermore, such an organization would provide a more stable basis, that is, one with less error, and less likelihood of irresponsible employment, for the control of nuclear weapons in Europe than would an alliance or a fragmented deterrence system in which each sovereign nation would possess more-or-less independent control over its own strategic weapon force.

A major drawback to a policy of community deterrence would be a risk of excessive reliance on nuclear deterrence for the military defense of Europe. In order to forestall this risk, it would be advisable that United States technological and financial assistance for a European deterrent capability be predicated on the condition that West European countries devote additional resources to the strengthening of NATO's limited war capability.

Several other objections to community deterrence have been advanced by Buchan in his analysis of NATO defense strategy. Buchan maintains, contrary to a basic premise of this proposal, that the U.S. threat to invoke massive retaliation as a response to a Soviet attack on Europe is indeed credible. He argues that a review of international military crises over the past ten years reveals that the United States, far from being a conservative actor, has actually had to be restrained by her NATO allies from taking too hasty action in Korea, Indochina, Quemoy, and Lebanon. He further adduces that American public opinion

---

[15] A community deterrent would not necessarily replace the NATO alliance. The relationship between community deterrence and NATO is discussed in the next section of this chapter.

[16] The idea of a European Community deterrent has been proposed by others. For example, Ben T. Moore, in his book *NATO and the Future of Europe*, Harper, New York, 1958, suggests a European Nuclear Defense Union as a possible solution for the strategic defense of Europe.

is convinced both of the vital United States interest in the integrity of Europe and of the improbability that "capitalism" in one country could survive. Consequently, he concludes that "the fact that the defense of Europe might now invoke great damage for the United States is most unlikely to inhibit her from action." [17]

However, Buchan's parallel between past United States actions in the Middle and Far Eastern areas of the world and the current West European defense situations seems inappropriate. The threat of United States massive retaliation as a means for defending the Middle and Far East had not been publicly enunciated as United States doctrine nor was it seriously considered by United States strategists to be a usable alternative. Further, the United States probably perceived that there was little risk of nuclear reprisal for her actions in these areas. Finally, one must question whether American opinion on the vital significance of Western Europe is insensitive to a mounting Soviet nuclear capability.

The remaining objections advanced by Buchan against community deterrence include the following: (1) a community deterrent based on the Inner Six or the WEU countries comprises only a part of Europe and would "cut across the command structures and political arrangements in NATO which have been built up with so much effort over the last ten years"; (2) the effectiveness of a community deterrent would depend heavily on British participation; (3) many years would be required to build a credible deterrent from scratch; and (4) most importantly, "it would strike at the heart of the whole concept of interdependence, and fulfill one cherished Soviet ambition—that of dividing Europe from America." [18]

In contrast to these objections this chapter argues: (1) that NATO command structures and political arrangements are no longer appropriate for the strategic defense of Europe; (2) that British and French participation would be favorably influenced by a firm United States position in support of ECD; (3) that it would not be necessary to build from scratch in the event of United States technical assistance; and (4) that European-American strategic interdependence in the framework of an alliance is operationally untenable.

---

[17] Buchan, *op. cit.*, p. 45.
[18] *Ibid.*, p. 70.

THE ROLE OF COMMUNITY DETERRENCE IN WESTERN DEFENSE STRATEGY

The principal objective of a European Community Deterrent would be to convince any would-be aggressor that an all-out attack upon any member nation would bring immediate nuclear retaliation. To be effective and credible, ECD would have to possess not only sufficient nuclear retaliatory weapons that could survive an initial attack, but also the necessary organizational machinery and resolve to act.

A secondary objective of ECD would be to discourage and contain limited aggression against Western Europe. That is, should limited warfare involving a Western European nation and a Communist nation occur, the presence of ECD would help to contain the action within a minimum geographical area, limit the number of nations involved, and discourage the use of high-yield nuclear weapons. An aggressor awareness that the extension of a localized fighting zone, either by purposeful action or by carelessness, could trigger ECD would act as a cogent restraint.

In relation to other Western defense establishments, ECD would play a complementary role. For instance, NATO would continue to assume primary responsibility in situations where member nations experienced aggressive violation of national boundaries of either an ambiguous or a forthright nature. In these instances, the tactical forces of NATO would act quickly to contain the attack. Where limited tactical aggression occurred against a neighboring non-NATO nation, the deployment of NATO forces would tend to confine the action, preventing its spread to NATO nations. However, in either situation, the alerted community deterrent force would act as an added constraint on the enlargement of the conflict.

Because of this complementary relationship between NATO and ECD, a high degree of coordination between the two would be necessary, particularly in delineating those situations calling for strategic use of the community deterrent force and those requiring tactical action by NATO. In order to achieve continuous coordination, perhaps some sharing of military equipments would be desirable—particularly information gathering and communication systems.

The relationship of ECD to United States strategic forces would be one of complete independence of weapon activation. No definitive pre-attack commitment would be made regarding the employment of U.S. strategic forces in the event of a nuclear attack on Western Europe. Such a commitment would merely indicate to a potential aggressor those conditions that would govern a United States reprisal. And this predictability of response by United States deterrent forces would decrease their value in discouraging the initiation of all forms of military aggression against Europe.

A second disadvantage of a United States pre-attack commitment would be the confusion that could ensue from an ambiguous attack situation. For example, should the Soviet employ an offense in such a way that the intent could not be clearly ascertained, the resulting delay and controversy in interpreting United States strategic obligations could result in a decay of U.S.-ECD relations, and a lessening of their combined effectiveness. Conversely, if the United States were attacked and not Western Europe, the ECD would have the option of retaliating in support of American strategic forces.

There would be no formal relationship between the ECD and non-European nations. The strategic defense of such nations would fall outside the responsibilities of ECD. However, individual ECD nations could exercise relative freedom in committing their own tactical forces to the defense of non-European nations. Thus, the existence of ECD would not preclude the use of national tactical forces by individual member nations to fulfill unilateral obligations.

In summary, the creation of a European Community deterrent would provide the West with two independent strategic deterrent forces in addition to NATO. The redundancy provided by two such strategic forces would significantly strengthen the West's deterrent position. An attack upon one force would serve to warn the other, and would probably stimulate either a passive or an active response. The ambiguity of not knowing the exact conditions under which the second deterrent forces would make an active response would serve to deter enemy aggression against the first. Also, the task of neutralizing both deterrent forces would be substantially greater than neutralizing one.

THE FORMATION OF A COMMUNITY —AN ANALYTIC APPROACH

Prior to examining the political and economic feasibility of a European Community Deterrent, a general conceptual approach for evaluating the political feasibility of community-type organizations will be presented. This analytic approach will then serve as a structure for the examination of the political feasibility of ECD in particular.

The formation of a community-type organization can be depicted as an evolutionary process consisting of a sequence of steps. Each step represents a necessary but not a sufficient condition for the next. For convenience, the process may be broadly divided into three stages: (1) initiation—the commitment by political units to participate in a community-type organization; (2) institutionalization—a consensus on a formal institutional basis for a community-type organization; and (3) integration—the development of loyalty to the organization.

Initiation

In analyzing the initiation stage, situational (background) and motivational variables are critical. Situational variables represent the objective or perceived environment of potential participants and include the sociocultural linkages and communication patterns between members, their economic and political environment, etc. Motivational variables refer to the incentives (both positive and negative) which members perceive to be associated with participation or non-participation in the organization. These motives may be divided for analytic purposes into three categories: (1) inter-country shared motives—those incentives for participation that are held in common by all potential participants; (2) idiosyncratic—those incentives for inclusion that are peculiar to individual nations; and (3) negative motives—all negative incentives relative to participation.[19]

The initiation stage can also be conceptualized in terms of March and Simon's model of organizational equilibrium[20] in the following manner:

1. Potential members consider joining an organization in terms of perceived inducements. These inducements, representing rewards for membership, have two potential sources:
   (a) External: Rewards which are generated from outside the organization. Thus, the United States provided economic rewards, through the Marshall Plan, that acted as external inducements for the formation of European economic community-type organizations.
   (b) Internal: Rewards that are generated by the organization itself. Thus, EEC has provided its members with a number of direct economic rewards.

---

[19] E. Haas speaks of "identical aims" and "converging aims," which correspond to the first two of the preceding motives. See Ernst Haas, "The Challenge of Regionalism," in S. Hoffman, ed., *Contemporary Theory in International Relations*, Prentice-Hall, New York, 1960.

[20] J. March and H. Simon, *Organizations*, John Wiley, New York, 1958.

2. Potential members of an organization consider joining in terms of the contributions (costs) they expect membership to entail.
3. Nations will participate in an organization when the perceived inducements are as great as or greater, in terms of a nation's own values and the alternatives open to it, than the perceived contributions they are required to make.

Given an analysis of background variables and their relative importance, the motives of potential participants, and the interaction between background conditions and motivations relative to the balance between contributions and inducements, the probability that a community-type organization could be initiated can be assessed.

Institutionalization

An agreement by political units, that is, nations, to participate in a community-type organization is a necessary precondition to the second stage of community evolution. This second stage, institutionalization, involves the achievement of a consensus among the potential participants as to the appropriate formal basis of the organization. That is, in order to function, an organization requires a more-or-less formalized set of expectations defining the relationships among and responsibilities of its members, both to one another and to the organization itself. The assignment of these responsibilities—the rights and obligations of membership—enables the organization to develop procedures for making and implementing decisions. Although the emergence of a system of expectations which characterizes an organization is a continuing process throughout the organization's life, a more or less formal framework, for example, a constitution, a charter, a general agreement, is necessary early in the evolutionary process. Such a framework specifies (institutionalizes) among other things, (1) the membership base, (2) the scope of the organization's task, (3) the distribution of responsibilities among members, (4) the procedures for decision-making, and (5) the distribution of burden-sharing.

Integration

It is the third stage of community evolution, integration, that has received the bulk of theoretical analysis to date. Haas, in his work on the uniting of Europe, focuses upon the process of integration at the community level. He notes, "As the process of integration proceeds, it is assumed that values will undergo change, that interests will be redefined in terms of regional rather than purely national orientation, and that the erstwhile separation of national group values will gradually be superseded by a new and geographically larger set of beliefs." [21] Thus, the integrative process is described in terms of a shift in values or in loyalties.

The problem of the formation of new loyalties, particularly as they relate to the evolution of supranational organizations, has been considered by Guetzkow.[22] He describes the process of forming loyalty as one in which an individual simultaneously develops loyalty to a new object and modifies the "exclusiveness" norms attached to existing loyalties. This process does not necessitate the dropping of old loyalties, but rather their generalization to new objects. Thus, to form a new loyalty to a supranational organization does not always involve abandonment of national loyalties, although it is possible that the new object (supranational) may replace the old object (national) as a means to the participant's goals. At the same time, a quasi-identity between the two objects may be established so that loyalty to both may be held simultaneously.

POLITICAL FEASIBILITY OF A EUROPEAN COMMUNITY DETERRENT

In order to ensure the credibility of ECD against piecemeal blackmail on the part of the Soviets, it is essential that the organization be composed of nations willing to accept decisions made at a supranational level. With this prerequisite in mind, a logical nucleus for such an organization would include those nations constituting the European Economic Community, that is, France, Germany, Italy, and the Benelux nations. Britain should also be included because of her critical role —political, military, and economic—in European defense strategy. Given this nucleus of nations, ECD could then establish a strategic deterrent that would have the capability and the resolve to inflict unacceptable damage in response to an all-out military attack upon one or more member nations.

In this section, an attempt is made to determine the political feasibility of establishing a community deterrent in Europe. Consideration is first given to some of the factors that contributed to the failure of the European Defense Community, as well as some of the lessons to be learned from its defeat. Secondly, an evaluation of the political

---

[21] E. Haas, *The Uniting of Europe*, Stevens and Sons, London, 1958, pp. 13–14.
[22] H. Guetzkow, *Multiple Loyalties*, Princeton University Press, Princeton, N.J., 1955.

feasibility of ECD is made relative to the participation of the EEC countries. Background or situational conditions which would promote or impede the initiation process are assessed. Then, intercountry and idiosyncratic motives that would favor initiation are examined. And, finally, motives that would operate against the formation of ECD are identified.

The third part of the analysis focuses on British motives for and against participation. The feasibility of British participation in ECD is examined independently from that of the EEC countries because of a number of historical and contemporary factors that would make British participation in ECD unique.

The Defeat of EDC

A proposal for military supranationalism is not unfamiliar to Western Europe. An abortive attempt to establish a European Defense Community (EDC) was undertaken during 1950–1954. Consequently, prior to assessing the political feasibility of a new proposal for a supranational military force, it is pertinent to assess the factors underlying the failure of the former.

The EDC Treaty, as formulated at the Lisbon Conference of the North Atlantic Council in February 1952, derived from an informal plan advanced by M. Pleven, Prime Minister of France, in September 1950. The proposed draft treaty as agreed upon by the six participating nations[23]—France, West Germany, Italy, and the Benelux nations—specified an integrated European army and air force, excluding naval and overseas defense forces. The integrated forces were to be controlled by a Board of Commissioners consisting of nine members whose actions were subject to review by a Council of Ministers. There was to be a common budget, contributed to by member countries in proportion to their national income, and a common armaments program.

The treaty was ratified by West Germany and the Benelux nations, but was rejected by the French National Assembly in August 1954. It is difficult to identify, let alone weigh the relative importance of, those factors that contributed to France's defeat of EDC. The French parliamentary debates evoked a miasma of emotional and ideological controversy that all but obscured the real issue of EDC—the military defense of Europe. However, certain of the more apparent contributory factors can be noted.

Time was one of the critical variables contributing to the defeat of

---

[23] Britain declined participation in EDC shortly after the initial Pleven proposal.

EDC. Four years elapsed from Pleven's initial proposal to its final rejection by the National Assembly. During this period, France underwent five changes in prime ministers, Stalin died (March, 1953), Dien Bien Phu had fallen, the Soviet military threat appeared to have abated noticeably, and NATO had become a strong military force. Thus, the international political and military environment of 1954 had changed substantially from that of 1950, which saw the outbreak of the Korean War.

It is also clear that much of the anti-EDC argument derived from an obsession with German rearmament. EDC opponents had good reason to believe that the defeat of EDC would forestall any type of German rearmament.[24] Preoccupation with national greatness was a further impediment. In this respect EDC was viewed by its detractors as an institution that would denationalize France's army, merge her into a continental union, and thus deprive her of military means for maintaining the French Union.

Still another contributory factor was the protection afforded Europe by the American nuclear umbrella. As Lerner points out, the "nationalist" as opposed to the "European" view in France on EDC derived its vitality from a single fact: ". . . . that so long as they were living under an American guarantee, the French faced no urgent practical need to expand their resources on defense." [25] Finally, the American threat of an agonizing reappraisal of defense strategy in the event that France failed to ratify EDC, helped to assure EDC's defeat. Not only did it provoke French hostility to the United States, but it also led some EDC opponents to react with a counterthreat of a *rapprochement* with the Soviet Union.[26]

What then, are the lessons to be learned from the failure of EDC for a proposal for a European Community Deterrent? First of all, consideration of ECD could not be permitted to persist over the excessively long period of time accorded EDC. Having advanced ECD as a serious proposal for European defense, it would be necessary to ascertain quickly the positions and attitudes of the EEC nations and Britain. In the event that the overall response of these countries was negative or lukewarm, the United States should not attempt to employ threats to force acceptance of ECD. It is clear from the EDC experience that

---

[24] R. Aron, "Historical Sketch of the Great Debate," in D. Lerner and R. Aron, eds., *France Defeats EDC*, Praeger, New York, 1957, p. 11.

[25] D. Lerner, "Reflections on France in the World Arena," in D. Lerner and R. Aron, eds., *France Defeats EDC*, Praeger, New York, 1957, p. 215.

[26] D. Lerner, *op. cit.*, p. 219.

threats are not an effective means of influence—particularly when it is apparent that they will not be invoked.

Current and past French preoccupation with national greatness suggests that it would be prudent to advance a supranational organization as only a partial measure for European defense, leaving the commitment of tactical military forces subject to national control. In addition, a strong effort would have to be made to secure British participation. In the case of EDC, it was obviously difficult for France to consider renouncing her Big Three status, while Britain was determined to maintain hers.

The emotional content of France's opposition to German rearmament is no longer as intense as during the 1950–1954 period. During this interval, the recency of World War II contributed strongly to French obsessions with German rearmament. Furthermore, the issue at that time involved permitting Germany to proceed from a zero level of armament to a significant military capability. Since then, Germany has established a strong tactical capability and has become a full member of NATO, although possession of nuclear arms is still precluded by the Western European Union (WEU). Thus, although French fears of German militarism continue to exist, the argument of complete denial of weapons to Germany is no longer relevant.

Finally, with respect to the credibility problem, United States policymakers should exercise particular care to stress objectively the inherent riskiness of extreme European dependence on the United States nuclear deterrent capability. Simultaneously, they should scrupulously avoid any actions which might be interpreted by the Europeans as a threat to abandon the defense of Europe. Such an approach, when coupled with United States offers of technical and financial assistance, should provide a more favorable climate for European consideration of ECD than was the case for EDC.

Community Deterrence among the EEC Countries

The following analysis concentrates on the political feasibility of French and German participation in ECD. The successful initiation of a community deterrent would demand the participation of both. Furthermore, given French and German support for ECD there would be a strong likelihood of concurrence among the remaining EEC countries, that is, Italy and the Benelux nations.

Background Conditions. Deutsch *et al.,* in a study of ten cases of successful and unsuccessful unions of states in Europe and North America during the 1485–1918 period, enumerate a number of background conditions, which they describe as essential to the formation of an amalgamated security community, that is, an organization in which a governmental structure is created providing for supranational decision-making.[27]

These conditions include: (1) the presence of a distinctive way of life; (2) the existence of a strong core area made up of one or more nations that have the resources to act and direct the other participating nations; (3) a recent history of superior economic growth among some, if not all, of the participating nations; (4) the expectation of joint economic rewards; (5) a wide range of mutual transactions; (6) the broadening of the power base within participating nations to include more elites, that is, a wider distribution of rewards among elite groups; (7) communication between elites across nations, and (8) a high mobility of persons from one nation to another.

The study also lists four conditions which were found helpful but not essential to the establishment of an amalgamated security community: (1) the reluctance to wage "fratricidal" war; (2) the existence of an external military threat; (3) strong economic interdependencies among participants; and (4) ethnic and linguistic assimilation.

Haas in an intensive study of the economic integration of the EEC countries[28] concludes that most of the conditions cited in the Deutsch study were a consequence of, rather than a prerequisite for, community formation. In either case, many of these conditions currently prevail within the EEC area, and can be appropriately considered as background conditions for the initiation of a community deterrent.

For analytic purposes, background conditions that have particular relevance to the formation of a community deterrent within the EEC countries will be divided into two classes: ideological and institutional. Three ideologies, that is, organized sets of values and beliefs, that have particular significance are "Europeanism," "provincialism," and "historical antagonism."

---

[27] Deutsch, et al., qualify their analysis in two respects. First, with respect to the use of historical cases as a base for generalization, they note, "Past examples are suggestive, not conclusive. They point in a general direction, but not toward a specific destination." Secondly, in their definition of essential and helpful conditions, they state, "When we call conditions 'essential,' we mean that success seems to us extremely improbable in their absence. Though essential, they seem to us insufficient. . . . A similar consideration applies to those conditions we called helpful but not essential: we found that integration occurred in their absence, and might well recur in this way in future cases." See K. Deutsch et al., Political Community and the North Atlantic Area, Princeton University Press, Princeton, N.J., 1957.
[28] Haas, op. cit., p. 20.

"Europeanism" denotes an identification of diverse groups of Europeans with a common cultural heritage. In reviewing the strength of this identification Haas observes: "United Europe seems to be a remarkably resilient and adaptable symbol: individuals of Conservative, Liberal, and Socialist leanings have no difficulty in embracing it. Political parties in all countries contain adherents as well as opponents of the symbol. And the heterogeneity of movements specifically devoted to the realization of the symbol in fact is equally impressive." [29]

The ideology of Europeanism appears strongest among the EEC countries. The historical interdependencies among them, strongly reinforced by the existence of community-type economic and scientific organizations, and by common identification with a democratic form of government, contribute to the strength of this ideology. Thus, when UNESCO's Institute for Social Science[30] interviewed a representative sample of Belgians (Flemish and Walloons), French, Germans, and Hollanders in 1956 and asked the question, "Are you, in general, favorable to the efforts being made to establish a united Western Europe?" a strong affirmative response was obtained. (See Table 9.)

The expression of a particular belief, however, does not preclude the presence of a contradictory one. Psychologists refer to this phenomenon when describing ideology or attitudes as "compartmentalization," that is, the ability to maintain logically inconsistent beliefs simultaneously. Thus, even though a large number of persons believe in Europeanism, and in the advisability of a European Union, they simultaneously maintain strong provincial values that are reinforced by historical differences in language and custom.

TABLE 9. *European Attitudes toward European Union*

Opinion	Flemish	Walloons	French	Germans	Hollanders
Favorable	61%	70%	74%	72%	79%
Opposed	9%	4%	9%	5%	7%
No opinion	30%	26%	17%	23%	14%

For example, Deutsch and Edinger report the following in their study on West Germany: "The favorable attitude towards European integration is subject, however, to two qualifications: though not necessarily impractical, European union seems remote, and it must not take

---

[29] *Ibid.*, p. 20.
[30] N. Anderson, "Opinion in Europe," in *European Yearbook*, Vol. 5, 1959, p. 155.

away from Germany the sovereign right of ultimate decision." [31] In public opinion polls conducted in December 1956, only 34 per cent of the interviewees believed that they would live to see the Western European countries unite to form the United States of Europe. In polls held in September, 1955, only 25 per cent and 32 per cent, depending on the phrasing of the question, would grant to a European parliament the right of ultimate decision in questions involving important German interests, while between 42 per cent and 46 per cent maintained that the ultimate decisions must remain with the national government of Germany.

The strength of provincial attitudes in France is reported by the French public opinion journal *Sondages*. According to this source: "European union is perhaps a distant vision, corresponding to the dormant aspirations of a large section of public opinion. However, this vision does not occupy the first place in the public conscience. As we have seen (through public opinion data), the realization of this union has never emerged as the most urgent or most important goal which the 'French' government had to face. A spontaneous hierarchy established itself where economic and financial preoccupations predominate. Since 1954 the troubles of North Africa and Algeria dominate over all others." [32] Thus, the French also appear to be preoccupied with national or provincial problems.

Furthermore, although 55 per cent of a representative sample of Frenchmen polled in 1957 approved of efforts toward West European Union, only 35 per cent of the sample agreed that France should participate within a political federation of West Europe in which the power of decision is delegated to a common government and not to the governments of participating countries.[33]

In a recent study by Daniel Lerner and Morton Gorden,[34] there is evidence of significant changes in the attitudes of European elites towards supranational and international decision-making. Lerner conducted a series of sequential surveys within elite groups in France, Britain, and Germany defining elites as leaders in government, politics, business, labor, military, church, and the "intelligentsia." He asked

---

[31] K. Deutsch and L. Edinger, *Germany Rejoins the Powers*, Stanford University Press, Stanford, Calif., 1958, p. 28.

[32] *Sondages*, "La politique étrangère de la France et Opinion publique, 1954–57," Numbers 1 and 2 (1958).

[33] *Ibid.*, p. 164.

[34] Daniel Lerner and Morton Gorden, *European Leaders Look at World Security*, Center for International Studies, Massachusetts Institute of Technology, Cambridge, 1960.

questions concerning various political, economic, and military matters of national and international significance, and his results are of interest both in terms of differences between the elite groups of the three nations studied, and the changes in attitudes within given leadership groups through time.

In the 1959 survey, Lerner found that 85 per cent of the German, 80 per cent of the British, and 65 per cent of the French samples preferred a supranationalistic or an internationalistic basis for taking action to a nationalistic one. Lerner distinguishes a supranationalist who prefers the Europe of Six from an internationalist who prefers a larger Europe or the United Nations as the focus of decision-making, particularly within the economic and military sector. As one might expect, the British were found preponderantly to be internationalists, with only 15 per cent preferring a supranationalistic approach; whereas among the French elites, 35 per cent expressed a supranationalistic orientation; and among the Germans 48 per cent chose this mode of organization.

As noted by Lerner, the strong supranationalistic orientation of France and Germany was illustrated in their responses to a number of items, for example, an almost complete support of the European Community, and a willingness to establish a European armaments pool and a permanent supranational army under European command. In contrast, Britain preferred the Atlantic and larger communities (international) for collective matters. They supported the OEEC over the EEC, placed heavy emphasis on the United Nations as a major factor in international affairs, and preferred an international to a supranational army.

The 1959 survey also indicated that whereas France and Germany viewed the EEC and the OEEC as preferred means for achieving economic and social development, the problem of military security was seen primarily in terms of the Atlantic community, and NATO in particular. Thus, NATO was perceived to be a very important instrumentality for assuring military security and the respondents in these two countries saw no contradiction in the formation of a supranational armed force and the existence of NATO. The British, on the other hand, endorsed an even wider based organization for economic and social development as well as for military integration.

In terms of the shifts in attitudes from 1956 to 1959 a number of important trends emerge. In general the elite groups of all these nations in 1959 appeared to be less inclined towards neutralism, more strongly committed to the West, and they more strongly supported pooling of military weapons and forces. As Lerner notes, an interesting psychological index of this change is the fact that a sizably greater proportion of respondents in 1959 reported themselves as having been in favor of the EDC than in 1956.

Sharp increases in support for the EEC were observed in France and Germany. In 1959 respondents in these two nations were considerably more willing to support both the European and the Atlantic Communities than they had been in 1956, assigning to the first the area of economic decision-making and to the latter, problems of military or collective security. In Britain, there were some divergences from the above trends. Britain from 1956 to 1959 showed a decline in confidence in NATO, and increased their endorsement of a wider organization of collective security. They favored integration of their military, but at a level beyond Europe and NATO. Regarding other issues, Britain's elites showed a decline in their perception of the importance of the Commonwealth, an increase in their estimate of the economic advantages of membership in the EEC, and a strong feeling that economic union with Europe would not hurt political ties with the Commonwealth. Thus, in general the British elites were less optimistic in 1959 than in 1956 concerning current forms of European and Atlantic community organizations, and seemed, perhaps as a result, to favor more internationalistic solutions, particularly in the area of military security.

Thus, although NATO was very strongly supported in 1959, it is apparent that among European elite groups, there is a growing predisposition to work towards supranational, integrated solutions to economic, social, and military problems. The initiation of a European community deterrent would seem congruent with these developing attitudes.

Thus, from an ideological standpoint, there exist within the EEC countries organized sets of values and beliefs that tend both to support and to impede the initiation of community-type organizations. The strength of provincial attitudes contributed to the defeat of the European Defense Community (EDC) by France in August, 1954. On the other hand, the strength of Europeanism helped to provide a climate in which EDC was at least seriously considered and in which the European Economic Community (EEC), European Coal and Steel Community (ECSC), and EURATOM were ratified.

The second class of background variables, institutions, may be defined as ordered sets of relationships, whether formal or informal, that exist among individuals relative to the pursuit of some common goal. The types of institutions, their structure, and the manner in which they function, as well as their goals, are important determinants of the behavior of nations. Certain of these institutional variables would facilitate the initiation of a community deterrent, whereas others would inhibit its formation.

The rapid growth in recent years of the national economies of the EEC countries should facilitate the formation of a community deterrent. The importance of economic growth to community formation has been noted in the Deutsch study: "Another of these conditions [for promoting community formation] we found to be markedly superior economic growth . . . [whereas] prolonged economic decline or stagnation, leading to economic conditions comparing unfavorably with those in neighboring areas, was found to be a disintegrative condition." [35]

Furthermore, the very existence of successful supranational institutions—EEC, ECSC, EURATOM—should contribute to the formation of other supranational organizations. The presence of these institutions has created an environment in which a great deal of formal and informal communication exists between elite groups within the EEC countries. Thus, European supranationalism has led to an increase in interaction not only between governmental officials but between industrial concerns, labor federations, political parties, and various other groups.

The major institutional factor that might impede the development of a community deterrent is the existence of sovereign states, which historically have defended the right to determine their own national policy. These institutions, through custom and self-interest, have usually resisted encroachments on any aspect of their sovereignty. Many groups that operate within the framework of these sovereign states resist change because they maintain an emotional identification with the state, and because they fear losing certain vested interests that are guaranteed by the national state. For instance, national military institutions might strongly resist the formation of a community nuclear deterrent because it would threaten a number of their historic prerogatives.

In summary, background conditions that would operate to support the initiation of a community deterrent include the ideology of Europeanism, the success of EEC, a rapid economic growth, a commonality in democratic forms of government, and the high level of intercommunication between the elites of the EEC countries fostered by the existence of supranational economic and scientific organizations. Background conditions operating against community formation would include the ideology of provincialism, the existence of historical antagonisms, and the presence of sovereign institutions.

---

[35] Deutsch, et al., op. cit., p. 41.

Inter-Country Shared Motives. A number of incentives for initiating a community deterrent are shared by all of the EEC countries. The most basic of these is the belief that Europe must be able to deter possible Soviet aggression. Such an incentive does not imply that the defense of Europe must necessarily be predicated upon a community deterrent. However, it is a prerequisite for the initiation of any military establishment—whether it be organized on the basis of an individual nation, an alliance, or a community.

Recent defense policies of several European nations would indicate the existence of the premise that Soviet military strength will continue to pose a significant threat to the military and political security of Western Europe. British, French, and West German defense budgets for fiscal 1960–1961 all showed modest increases over fiscal 1959–1960. The 1960–1961 French budget allocated 85 million dollars to initiate production of atomic bombs, 81 million dollars to initiate production of fifty Dassault Mirage IV Mach-2 plus bombers, and 20 million dollars for research and development of a 1250-mile-range ballistic missile. Germany, on March 5, 1960, signed an agreement with Belgium and the Netherlands to jointly produce at least 570 United States-designed Lockheed Starfighter aircraft in Dutch, Belgian, and West German factories. Furthermore, West Germany is showing increased interest in the procurement of American-manufactured armaments.

Another common incentive for the initiation of ECD stems from the growing doubts of Europeans that United States deterrent forces actually would be activated in response to Soviet aggression in Western Europe. This is forcing many Europeans to conclude that a necessary condition for an effective and credible European deterrent will be a deterrent capability independent of that of the United States.

The development of a community deterrent capability within the EEC countries would satisfy several other common motives. It would, for instance, permit Europe to exercise an increased influence on world affairs. It might also make it less likely that Europe would be drawn into a conflict between the United States and the U.S.S.R.

Relative to the latter motive (neutrality), public opinion in Europe has generally supported the position that Europe should maintain a somewhat independent position from both the U.S.S.R. and the United States. As noted in Table 10, in a series of public opinion polls conducted in Germany, responses were obtained that indicated that this sentiment was maintained by a sizable proportion of the population.[36] In France, similar results were obtained.[37] (See Table 11.)

---

[36] Ball, *op. cit.*, p. 12.
[37] *Sondages, op. cit.*, p. 130.

TABLE 10. *West German Responses to the Question:*
"What do you personally consider most important: That we Germans are on good terms with the Americans, on good terms with the Russians, or that we remain neutral between the two?"

Opinion	1951	1953	1955	October 1957	August 1959
Good Terms with U.S.	39%	46%	48%	42%	41%
Good Terms with U.S.S.R.	1%	1%	3%	3%	2%
Remain Neutral	48%	42%	45%	52%	54%
No Opinion	12%	11%	4%	3%	3%

TABLE 11. *French Responses to the Question:*
"Personally, do you think that France is currently in the Western Camp, in the Eastern Camp, or in neither of the two camps?"

	September 1952	November 1954	August 1955	December 1957
In Western Camp	42%	36%	23%	21%
In Eastern Camp	4%	2%	4%	3%
In Neither Camp	43%	39%	51%	51%
No Opinion	11%	23%	22%	25%

Idiosyncratic Motives. There are several motives for a community deterrent capability that operate within individual EEC nations, and that are not shared in common. Generally, these motives are associated with advantages that would accrue to one or more nations, but not to all, that is, motives of self-interest.

For instance, the Benelux countries and Italy have generally favored any move towards the integration of Western Europe because each feels that its status in the world, its own internal security, and its economic well-being are markedly enhanced by identification with one another, and with the more powerful nations of France and West Germany. Within these four nations, the inducements perceived in any responsible move towards federation exceed by a wide margin the contributions or costs of membership.

For France and West Germany, the inducements for integration do not compare so favorably with the costs. For this reason, one must specify in greater detail the idiosyncratic motives that exist within each of these two nations for and against a strategic defense community.

France, under the leadership of De Gaulle, has as its major political goal the restoration of France to the status of a great power. Consequently, it is probable that De Gaulle will commit France to a community deterrent system only if he perceives that such a move will be compatible with this drive for national status.

There can be little doubt that the French effort to develop a nuclear bomb was in part motivated by a desire to achieve the status of those influencial nations of the world which now make up the "nuclear club." Membership in this club serves a number of motives: (1) it increases France's ability to bargain with the United States and the U.S.S.R. on issues of world importance to France, such as the reunification of Germany; (2) it enables France to challenge Britain's role in world affairs and to demand equal treatment from the United States; and (3) it strengthens the French claim to leadership on the Continent.

Although France is now a nuclear power, the advantage so gained may be short-lived. It is doubtless recognized, though not publicly admitted by French leadership, that France does not possess the capability to develop a modern complex weapon-delivery system. A community organization would help make it technologically and economically feasible for France in combination with other nations to develop a truly effective and credible deterrent. Thus, it is likely that France would carefully weigh the advantages achieved by a community venture against the losses in national independence. If the French believed that they could maintain a position of European leadership, they probably would give serious consideration to participating in a community deterrent. This would coincide with De Gaulle's belief that Western Europe under French leadership can become a powerful Third Force between the Soviet Union and the United States.[38]

France may also in the future be motivated to initiate a community deterrent organization in order to exercise a measure of control over West Germany, particularly if it appears likely that the latter might develop its own nuclear weapons. Furthermore, the mere presence of West Germany in such an organization would markedly reduce the probability of unification of East and West Germany, and unification would seriously impede French aspirations for European leadership.

The idiosyncratic motives operative in West Germany are founded primarily upon the recognition by the ruling elite that the security of the Federal Republic depends upon outside military support, particularly that of the United States. Adenauer has long acknowledged that Germany does not have the capability or the desire to confront

---

[38] R. Macridis, "De Gaulle: The Vision and the Record," *Yale Review*, Vol. 50, Winter, 1960, pp. 172–187.

the Soviet bloc alone. As a consequence, Adenauer has been a strong supporter of close German-United States relations, a position not necessarily shared by a number of his countrymen. This divergence in viewpoint is suggested in the findings of the public opinion poll results reported earlier in which 41 per cent of the respondents felt that Germany should be on good terms with the United States, 2 per cent on good terms with the Russians, 54 per cent felt that Germany should be neutral, and 3 per cent had no opinion.[39]

A community deterrent organization would provide Adenauer and his supporters an opportunity to realize their goal of cooperating with other nations in the defense of Europe, that is, to avoid going it alone. Simultaneously, West Germany could maintain greater independence from both the United States and the U.S.S.R., a situation that would be more satisfying to the larger number of Germans who want to preserve a position of relative independence from the United States and the Soviet Union.

Since Germany is geographically in a highly vulnerable position for either limited or massive Soviet military attack, a community deterrent would also contribute to her feelings of internal security. Furthermore, the fact that Germany would not independently possess and control strategic nuclear weapons would reduce the strong fears engendered by this prospect both internally and among her eastern and western neighbors.

Finally, a community deterrent might help to forestall all-out competition between France and Germany for European leadership. That is, it would help create an environment in which "power would gravitate away from the national state and be shared equitably with the federation institution." [40] Although an equitable sharing of power is probably neither a basic motive of France nor of Germany, the creation of an additional supranational organization would contribute to such an eventuality.

Motivational Forces Against a Community Deterrent. There are a number of forces operating against a community deterrent among the EEC countries. A major obstacle to be overcome is the identification of both Europeans and Americans with NATO. Many persons have viewed NATO as a first step towards Atlantic unity, that is, the federation of Europe, Canada and the United States. Although it is objectively difficult to see how the NATO alliance has or would promote

---

[39] E. W. Schnitzer, "West European Opinion on Defense," Report T-123, The Rand Corporation, Santa Monica, Cal., 1960.
[40] Moore, *op. cit.*, p. 225.

organic unity among the Western nations, it still retains a symbolic value for many. And the replacement of NATO's strategic functions by ECD would substantially weaken this symbolism.

A second source of resistance would likely occur among those NATO nations that would not be included in ECD and that now enjoy the protection of United States strategic forces. It might prove difficult to convince these nations that a credible nuclear deterrent in Western Europe would afford them more security than a United States deterrent whose employment on their behalf is becoming increasingly less likely.[41]

A third motive against the formation of a community deterrent derives from the strong neutralist feelings which are found in the EEC countries. The mere suggestion that Europe should possess and possibly utilize nuclear weapons will intensify the activities of those neutralists who currently maintain a pacifist position—a position often based not so much upon Communist propaganda as upon the highly vulnerable position Europe would occupy in case of a nuclear war.

A fourth motive that might impede or defeat a proposal for an integrated nuclear deterrent is nationalism. As has already been noted, France, in particular, has the goal of elevating its own status and power in the world. To the extent that a community deterrent would be perceived by the French as threatening this goal, it would be resisted. Should France decide that ECD would promote its leadership in Europe, and should Germany and Italy perceive the situation similarly, the latter countries might well resist initiating a community deterrent.

Within countries there exists more specific motives that contribute to the strength of nationalism. For instance, nations that have overseas territories, France in particular, may feel that commitment to a common nuclear deterrent would weaken their position outside of Europe. Also, there are groups of individuals who, for reasons of power and economics, support the status quo within their own nations. Finally, others will protest ECD because they are emotionally tied to the values of nationalism: "When a nation is inserted into a group of powers, it should not be called upon to abdicate its moral and spiritual functions, for the benefit of an artificial legal arrangement, or of a uniform state without soul or conscience." [42]

A final motive against initiating a community deterrent is the anticipation of possible Russian counterstrategies. If it appeared that Russia

---

[41] The role of ECD relative to specific conflict situations in Europe is not examined in this paper. T. Schelling's work on "The Strategy of Conflict," *The Journal of Conflict Resolution*, Vol. 2, 1958, presents a conceptual approach to the problem.
[42] M. Juin and H. Massi, *"The Choice Before Europe,* Eyre and Spottiswoode, London, 1958.

might substantially strengthen the military capabilities of the satellite nations in response to the initiation of a community deterrent, the EEC countries might feel that the dangers here were greater than those of not having a credible deterrent. However, although the formation of ECD would undoubtedly pressure the Soviets into consolidating her East European satellites and strengthening the Warsaw Pact, it is very doubtful that the Soviets would react by creating an independent strategic deterrent in Eastern Europe. It would be dangerous for the Soviets to allow her satellite nations to control either nuclear weapons or substantial conventional forces. The satellite nations might "trigger" Russia into an unwanted war with ECD, or they might forcefully attempt to free themselves from Soviet control. Similarly, the presence of ECD might lead the Soviets to form a closer coalition with Red China. However, it would seem doubtful that the Soviets would provide extensive military aid to the Chinese—particularly not in nuclear weapons and technology. The Chinese represent not only a future military threat to the West, but possibly to the Soviets as well.

The Balancing of Forces. Consideration has been given to: (1) those background conditions that are relevant to the formation of a community nuclear deterrent among the EEC countries; (2) the motives held in common by the EEC countries for initiating a community deterrent; (3) certain idiosyncratic motives that support initiation; and (4) those motives that would operate against initiation.[43] An attempt now will be made to weigh these various forces and their interactions, and to balance the political incentives or inducements towards initiation against the political costs or contributions demanded.

In such an appraisal, certain of the variables that have been noted take on particular significance. First, the argument for ECD will be substantially weakened unless the Soviets continue to be viewed as a military threat by the EEC countries. Second, Europe would be hesitant to assume the costs—both economic and in terms of the loss of national sovereignty—of initiating a community deterrent unless there were substantial doubt about the willingness of the United States to assume responsibility for the strategic defense of Western Europe.

Furthermore, the awareness of a Soviet threat and the existence of

---

[43] In reviewing these motives, public opinion data have been cited to reflect relevant national attitudes. It must be noted that such data can only be suggestive of the support or opposition which might be given ECD. Public attitudes do not necessarily generalize from one issue to a related one. Nor do they reflect the highly influential role that political pressure groups play in opposing or supporting a given issue.

doubt concerning the use of the United States deterrent capability in the defense of Europe would not be sufficient inducements in themselves. There are numerous forces, particularly those arising from nationalistic self-interest and neutralism, that weigh heavily against the formation of a community deterrent. However, the sentiments that are generated by a strong emotional identification with a national state, that is, nationalism, are in part counterbalanced by the presence of the ideology of a united Europe. The latter has received substantial reinforcement from the activities of the European Economic Community, which has played an instrumental role in accelerating the economic growth of Western Europe. In the context of the ideology of a United Europe, ECD could be favorably viewed as a means for further elevating the status of EEC nations by enabling them to assume the position of the third most potent military force in the world. This would not only markedly increase the military security of Western Europe, but also would permit it to exercise greater political and economic influence upon world affairs. Even some of the neutralist forces in Europe might not strongly oppose the formation of a defense community that would afford the EEC nations greater independence from both the United States and the U.S.S.R. Finally, one additional force should be included in an assessment of the overall feasibility of ECD. A well-articulated United States policy decision to technically and financially support the initiation of ECD would provide a further impetus toward its formation.

The Prospects for British Participation in ECD

An assessment of British motives for and against community deterrence must necessarily take into account British post-war relationships with the Continental countries with respect to a variety of projects for economic, political, and military cooperation and integration. British policy during this period is of particular interest because of its clearcut distinction between relationships involving institutional arrangements based on consultation and cooperation versus arrangements founded on supranational considerations. Britain, until recently, consistently supported and joined organizations functioning principally on the basis of intergovernmental cooperation, including NATO, the Organization of European Economic Cooperation, the Council of Europe, the Western European Union, and the Free Trade Area. On the other hand, Britain vetoed her own membership in the European Coal and Steel Community, the European Defense Community, the European Political Community—all of which, being supranational organizations, would have demanded the surrender of a degree of national sovereignty. It was not until July, 1962 that Britain finally decided to negotiate for full membership in the European Economic Community.

Why were British policy-makers so consistently adamant against encroachments on national sovereignty? Three major considerations appear to have been operative: Britain's position in the Commonwealth, her "special relationship" with the United States, and her distrust of the Continental nations. Britain's ties with the Commonwealth nations and the commitment implications of these ties appear to have been the overriding motivation against past participation in supranational undertakings. Membership in both the Commonwealth, consisting solely of sovereign nations, and supranational organizations was viewed not only as logically inconsistent but also as impractical and unpatriotic, particularly from the viewpoint of special trading relationships with the Commonwealth countries and a requirement to honor defense commitments to these nations. Somewhat less important as a deterrent to participation in the European Union movement has been what the British regard as their special relationship with the United States, deriving in part from World War II relationships and post-war nuclear sharing arrangements. Closely allied with this special relationship has been the long-held Churchillian dream of an Anglo-Saxon Community. Aside from this dream, the British have felt that London enjoys a closer rapport and understanding with Washington than does Paris or Bonn, and that Continental relationships of the supranational variety would substantially impair this special position. However, the relevancy of this objection appears to have diminished, particularly since the EEC is fostering a close relationship of its own with the United States.

Britain has also demonstrated a historical reluctance to take part in supranational military undertakings and her rationalization of a policy of fragmented deterrence deserves special attention. Membership in the European Defense Community was rejected because the supranational Board of Commissioners of the Community would have exercised exclusive control over an integrated European army, a common defense budget, and a common armaments program. Such an arrangement, in British eyes, would have degraded British national sovereignty, restricted her ability to meet Commonwealth and colonial defense obligations, and impaired her control over national economic policy. It remains questionable, however, whether membership in the EDC would have seriously impaired British military obligations to the Commonwealth. As Baumann points out, "the prewar integrated strategic arrangements of the Commonwealth had largely ceased to exist." [44] Canada's defense has become more integrated with that of the United States than with Britain. And with the decline of British strength in the Pacific and the negotiation of the Anzus Pact, it is clear that both New Zealand and Australia have become more dependent on the United States than on Britain for their national security. Finally, the accession to national sovereignty of India, Pakistan, Ceylon, Malaya, and Ghana resulted in unequivocal assertions by these nations of their right and duty to assume their own defense obligations.

Britain's pursuit of an independent nuclear deterrent capability can only be explained by reference to the interplay of a complex of factors, including the declining credibility of the United States deterrent capability relative to the defense of Europe, budgetary limitations, national pride, and United States nuclear secrecy. The first two considerations appear to have had an overriding impact, however. Attitudes relative to the credibility of the United States nuclear guarantee evolved from more or less complete faith during the early post-war period to a growing feeling of uneasiness subsequent to the Korean War. The uneasiness was further intensified by the Suez incident. Similarly, the ever-mounting costs of maintaining a modern military establishment in the face of a strategic revolution brought about a re-orientation of British defense policy from a concept of "balanced forces" to "massive retaliation."

This re-orientation became evident in the 1954 White Paper on Defense which observed that "Clearly within a limited defense budget, we may not be able to afford both new weapons and conventional forces of the present size." [45] Further, as Healey points out, it was the concern of the Labor government for strengthening NATO's tactical forces "which led the Labor government to condemn itself to defeat in 1951 by undertaking to spend on defense an average of 10 per cent of the national income over the next three years. . . ." [46] Finally, in April 1960, the policy of independent deterrence itself came dramatically into question when, faced with the absurdity of developing a demonstrably obsolete strategic delivery system, the government cancelled the Blue Streak program. However, the logic of a strategy of fragmented deterrence appeared to die hard. As the *Economist* has pointed out in a summing up of Defense Minister Watkinson's state-

---

[44] C. Baumann, "Britain Faces Europe," *Political Science Quarterly*, Vol. 74, 1959, pp. 351–371.
[45] D. Healey, "Britain and NATO," in K. Knorr, ed., *NATO and American Security*, Princeton University Press, Princeton, N.J., 1959, p. 215.
[46] *Ibid.*, p. 213.

ment on the cancellation, "Blue Streak will not give us an independent power of retaliation, there is nothing really to take its place, but we must have independence, so somehow or other we will buy or make something that will do the trick." [47]

The outcome of the cancellation of Blue Streak was that Britain reached an agreement with the United States to purchase the Skybolt missile following its development by the United States. This nuclear missile, an airborne weapon with a thousand-mile range, was to provide Britain an effective independent deterrent force at a reasonable cost. However, the probability of Britain attaining an independent deterrent was again dealt a severe blow when the United States announced in December of 1962 that because of costs and potential obsolescence, it had decided to cancel the Skybolt program. The offer by Kennedy to provide Polaris missiles to defend Britain with submarines under a NATO nuclear command served to reduce the trauma of the cancellation somewhat. However, there can be little doubt that British aspiration of becoming an independent nuclear deterrent power had suffered a disastrous, if not an overwhelming setback.

In July 1962, some 5½ years after the formation of EEC on the Continent, Britain applied for full membership in EEC. Negotiations proceeded until January of 1963 when General De Gaulle declared unequivocally that Britain was not ready for membership. The near simultaneity of the United State's cancellation of the Skybolt program and the demise of Britain's hopes for an independent nuclear force, as well as the refusal of France to permit British entry into the Common Market has had several marked effects on Britain's orientation towards the United States and Europe. It has forced the British to recognize that they have lost any special relationship with the United States. It has resulted in a hard reappraisal of the feasibility of the doctrine of independent nuclear deterrence. And finally, it has transformed Britain from the role of the reluctant bride relative to membership in the EEC into a damsel who will employ every means to culminate the marriage vows.

The possible changes in British policy that may emerge from this series of traumatic events are reflected in the following comments by the *Economist*:[48]

Somehow an attempt has to be made to revive confidence that there is a future for a united Europe which would include Britain and which would act as an equal partner of the United States.

---

[47] "The Moral of Blue Streak," *Economist*, April 23, 1960.
[48] *Economist*, March 9, 1963, p. 872.

This can only be done in Europe, where the confusion is and probably the necessary point at which to start is defense, which has become the heart of the matter. General De Gaulle will not act to this end. Germany torn between France and America, cannot. Unfair as it may seem, the responsibility falls on Britain. . . .

It is hard to see how Britain can turn the adverse tide in European affairs without pocketing still more of its pride in strategic affairs and independence and committing itself, in a fuller sense than it has yet, to building up a mix-manned European nuclear force. Gradually, the scope of the common decisions needed to run such a force would tend to lead to political union in Europe and to partnership with America. This plan would not be subject to General De Gaulle's veto, as the common market negotiations were. It would carry conviction as a potentially effective defense policy in sharp contrast to the national deterrents—British, French and others to come.

ECONOMIC FEASIBILITY OF A EUROPEAN COMMUNITY DETERRENT

This section evaluates the economic feasibility of ECD. It presents illustrative estimates of the costs of alternative deterrent systems and undertakes an assessment of the economic capabilities of the EEC nations and the United Kingdom to sustain these costs.

Cost Estimates for Alternative Deterrent Systems

The following analysis of the costs of alternative deterrent systems will restrict itself to some typical estimates of the procurement and operating costs of the weapon forces.[49]

These costs are obviously a function of the size of the weapon force which, in this analysis, is dictated by the "level of urban blast damage" to be achieved in a retaliatory attack upon the U.S.S.R. Obviously, it is impossible to specify a single damage level that would constitute absolute deterrence. Rather, there are degrees of damage that an aggressor would be willing to risk depending upon the intensity of his attack motivation. This study assumes that the required potential damage to Soviet urban areas that would deter attack against the ECD nations is less than that required to deter attack against the United States, and that a reasonable design objective for ECD under this circumstance would be a 50 per cent level of urban blast damage.[50]

---

[49] These are rough estimates based on unclassified information. For a more comprehensive and precise development of system costs, recourse must be made to "sensitive" data.

[50] This argument is based on the assumption that the U.S.S.R. would stand to gain less in conquering the ECD nations than in conquering the United States.

Each of the following alternative deterrent systems is so designed as to approximate this requirement.[51] Accordingly, the total costs of each of the deterrent systems will be directly comparable.

It should also be pointed out that some of the necessary equipment components of a complete deterrent system appear readily amenable to sharing with United States deterrent forces, for example, information-warning systems, without sacrifice of decision-making independence by ECD. These components need not be duplicated by ECD, as they will be developed and employed by the U.S. irrespective of the existence of ECD. Since sharing could reduce the total cost of ECD, this analysis will consider only the costs directly associated with the retaliatory weapons, namely, weapons and spares, bases, support facilities, equipment and personnel. Furthermore, no research and development costs will be included in the cost estimates. Finally, no attempt will be made to estimate the costs of mixed deterrent systems, although it is likely that ECD would be composed of more than one system.

Nuclear Submarine System. Assuming an ECD weapon force made up entirely of Polaris weapon systems, the total investment cost, including required supporting facilities, would approach 3 billion dollars.[52] Operating costs each year, including personnel, would be about 0.4 billion dollars. Over a five-year operational life the average annual cost (investment plus operating costs) would approximate 1 billion dollars, while a ten-year operational life would imply an average annual cost of 0.70 billion dollars.

Land-Based Systems. Assuming that mobile land-based solid propellant missiles, generically similar to the Minuteman system, could survive an initial attack equally as well as the submarine-launched missile system, a total investment roughly one-third that for the Polaris nuclear submarine system, or about 1 billion dollars, would be required. The annual operating cost would be about one-half as large as that for the Polaris system. Therefore, over a five-year operational life, the average annual cost would approximate 0.4 billion dollars and over a ten-year life 0.3 billion dollars.

If these missiles were located at fixed bases, it would appear prudent to credit Soviet weaponry with sufficient impact accuracy to destroy them, even in the event of base hardening. Therefore, the actual num-

---

[51] The design studies were worked out for warheads of 5–10 megaton yield on the basis of typical values for mission reliability, kill probability, and CEP (Circular Error Probable) for each weapon system.

[52] All operating and investment costs for the deterrent systems cited in this section are in U.S. 1959 dollars. All operating costs are based on U.S. experience with no allowance for a U.S.-European cost differential.

ber of fixed base missiles required depends on the number of weapons launched by the Soviets against these bases. Assuming the initial Soviet attack numbered 2000 missiles of 5 to 10 megatons each, the resulting costs for a fixed land-based ECD weapon force would be equivalent to those for the Polaris submarine system.

EUROPEAN ECONOMIC CAPABILITY TO SUPPORT ECD

The previous section has indicated that average annual expenditures for a community deterrent force could range from 0.4 to 1.0 billion dollars assuming a weapon system operational life of five years. This section will demonstrate that expenditures of this magnitude are well within the overall economic capabilities of the EEC countries and Great Britain. This conclusion will be supported by: (1) citing dollar estimates of past defense expenditures; (2) analyzing the relative burden of defense expenditures on national economies; (3) examining budgetary allocations for nuclear weapons programs; and (4) assessing future economic growth prospects.

Dollar estimates of the gross national product and defense expenditures for the EEC countries, the United Kingdom, and the United States for 1955 are shown in Table 12. The aggregate GNP for the

TABLE 12. *Dollar Estimates of GNP and Defense Expenditures for 1955 for the EEC Countries, the United Kingdom, and the U.S.**

		(Billions of 1955 dollars)	
Country		GNP	Defense
United Kingdom		$ 66.3	$ 6.0
France		48.6	2.9
West Germany		57.6	2.4
Italy		31.5	1.6
Netherlands		11.4	0.8
Belgium		10.8	0.6
	Total	$226.2	$14.3
United States		$380.0	$40.8

* Milton Gilbert and Associates, *Comparative National Products and Price Levels*, Organization for European Economic Cooperation, Paris, 1958, p. 87. These estimates are geometric averages of estimates based on U.S. and European relative price weights.

EEC plus the United Kingdom approximates 226 billion dollars, or about 60 per cent of the United States GNP. The United Kingdom, France, and West Germany account for about 75 per cent of the aggregate GNP. On the other hand, defense expenditures of the EEC countries and the United Kingdom total about 14 billion dollars (16.5 billion dollars in 1959 dollars), or less than a third of United States expenditures, with the United Kingdom, France and West Germany accounting for approximately 80 per cent of the European total.

Since 1955, total defense expenditures for the Western European countries listed in Table 12 have remained fairly stable. Defense outlays for these nations in 1959 approximated 16–17 billion dollars (in 1959 dollars). Table 13 shows defense expenditures as a percentage of

TABLE 13. *Defense Expenditures as a Percentage of National Income**

Country	1955 %	1957 %	1958 %	1959 %	1960 %
United Kingdom	10.2	8.9	8.6	8.3	8.1
France	8.5	9.7	9.1	9.2	8.8
West Germany	5.4	5.4	3.9	5.8	5.6
Italy	5.1	4.9	4.8	4.7	4.6
Netherlands	6.9	6.4	5.6	4.7	5.0
United States	12.3	12.2	12.5	11.8	11.3
Belgium	4.6	4.5	4.4	4.4	4.3

* Percentages computed from total defense expenditures estimated by NATO Information Service, and from national income at current factor cost as reported in the 1961 UN *Yearbook of National Accounts Statistics.*

national income for selected years during the 1955–1960 period. These data indicate that the United States has consistently allocated a larger share of its national income for defense purposes than have the Western European countries.

The United Kingdom is reported to have expended about 180 million dollars on the development on the Blue Streak missile prior to its cancellation.[53] The 1960–1961 French budget allocates 85 million dollars for the production of atomic bombs, 81 million dollars to initiate production of fifty Dassault Mirage IV Mach 2-plus bombers, and 20 million dollars for research and development of a 1250-mile-range ballistic missile.[54] These expendtiure levels fall considerably short of that

---

[53] *Economist*, April 23, 1960, p. 307.
[54] *The New York Times*, November 19, 1959.

required for the annual support of ECD. Nevertheless, a redirection of these funds away from the development and procurement of already outdated weapon systems to the establishment of a modern deterrent system would be possible in a joint venture such as ECD.

There is no question, however, that annual expenditures of 1 billion dollars per year for an ECD force could be sustained simply by increasing the current aggregate defense budget of the EEC countries and the United Kingdom at a rate consistent with annual economic growth, which is anticipated to approximate an overall rate of 5 per cent. Thus, a five per cent increase in aggregate defense spending over the 1959 level—16 to 17 million dollars—would bring about an additional increment of 800 million to 900 million dollars. Nevertheless, it must be recognized that if (as is recommended by this study) the ECD countries were to substantially increase their limited war capabilities simultaneously with the formation of ECD, an increase in the proportion of national income allocated to defense would be required. In this circumstance, depending upon the extent to which the ECD nations were willing and able to expand their limited war forces, it would be appropriate for the United States to seriously consider providing financial assistance for the procurement of ECD deterrent systems.

It is clear, however, that most of the European countries, particularly West Germany, allocate a significantly smaller proportion of their annual income to defense than does the United States. This may have been due in part to the past willingness of the United States to assume the responsibility for the strategic defense of Europe.

West Germany, of course, has been restricted in its defense program under the weapons limitations imposed by the Western European Union (WEU). Still, the German government and parliament have viewed rearmament less enthusiastically than have several American policy-makers and military spokesmen. This moderation reflected the principal priority of the Adenauer administration—namely, the rebuilding of a vigorous, internationally competitive economy. There is little doubt that the rapid pace of West German economic growth during the 1950's was due in part to the absence of a necessity to devote substantial resources to a defense establishment. However, a strong, efficient industrial base has now been re-established, and the West German economy is among the healthiest in Western Europe. Hence, there can be little question that West Germany can now "afford" an expanded defense program.

In summary, the costs of establishing ECD are not of such a magnitude as to seriously impede its implementation. Although it appears that a European effort to establish both ECD and a stronger limited war capability would require a modest increase in the proportion of the national income devoted to defense, the proposed ECD nations, as a consequence of their vigorous post-World War II economic expansion, currently possess the economic capability to support such an increase. Furthermore, the United States should seriously consider providing a measure of financial assistance for the establishment of ECD contingent on the willingness of the ECD nations to strengthen their limited war capabilities.

THE ROLE OF U.S. POLICY IN THE INITIATION OF A COMMUNITY DETERRENT

Perhaps the most critical determinant of the political feasibility of ECD would be a United States policy decision to strongly support its formation. Support of ECD would be consistent with previous United States policy regarding the formation of supranational organizations in Europe. Since the end of World War II, the United States has strongly backed most moves toward the economic and political unification of Europe. Secretary of State George C. Marshall first set forth this policy on June 5, 1947, in an address at Harvard. As a condition for receiving U.S. economic aid, he held that Europe should take the lead in outlining a joint program for post-war recovery, agreed to by a number of, if not all, European nations.

However, a United States decision to support the initiation of ECD would require substantial revisions in current United States defense policy. First, it would demand new legislation to amend the current Atomic Energy Act, which prohibits transmittal of atomic weapons or production technology to other countries. Traditionally, Congress has been reluctant to have nuclear weapon secrets pass out of the hands of the United States for fear they would be obtained by the Soviets, or result in the diffusion of atomic weapons among additional countries. Furthermore, it has been argued by Congressman Holifield [55] and others that the Soviets might retaliate by giving atomic weapons to Red China and other Communist countries.

The fear that the Soviets might obtain United States' weapon secrets is currently less significant than formerly. Soviet technological progress has obviously overcome its one-time inferior position in weapons development. Furthermore, the Nth country problem will continue to persist irrespective of the United States' nuclear sharing policy. Consequently, it would seem more in United States interest to support a

---

[55] *The New York Times*, Feb. 10, 1960.

program that would ensure the control of nuclear weapons by a supranational organization composed of a number of states, than to witness passively each European nation develop and control its own individual deterrent. Finally, Holifield's concern that the Soviets might provide nuclear weapons to her allies in response to a United States nuclear sharing program for Europe appears unwarranted. It does not seem likely that the Soviets would have sufficient faith in her allies—particularly China—to provide them with nuclear arms. Furthermore, in the case of China, the question may soon be academic, for she is rapidly developing her own nuclear capability.

A second major policy change would involve United States recognition and acceptance of the fact that it can no longer exercise predominant control of the Western alliance. As Europe becomes economically and politically stronger, the United States will be increasingly forced to recognize that the Western alliance is made up of "peers."

In supporting the formation of ECD, the United States would have to acknowledge the possibility that Europe might not use its deterrent force or its increased political power in a manner totally consistent with United States objectives. Although this could constitute a substantial military and political risk to the United States it seems highly probable that the long-range goals of a supranational organization made up of seven European democracies, not subject to the idiosyncratic behavior of one member, should not be markedly discordant with those of the United States. Furthermore, a militarily or politically weak Western Europe is certainly a greater danger to United States interests than one that is strong—even though its policies may not be identical with those of the United States.

A third United States policy requirement would be to provide technical and financial assistance to the community deterrent organization. The nature of this support, both in degree and in kind, would be predicated upon: (1) the economic and technical resources required for establishing a credible deterrent in Europe, and (2) the relative capability through time of the European community to support its own strategic deterrent.

Chapter 8

What Constitutes
Effective U.S. Deterrence

THOMAS W. MILBURN

The strategy of deterrence, that is, the threatening of an adversary with some dire consequence should he behave in a manner inconsistent with one's own interests, continues to be a major instrument of United States foreign policy, particularly in its relations with the Soviet Union. It is generally viewed as a less costly way of obtaining United States goals and preventing Soviet aggression than fighting World War III. In implementing a policy of deterrence the United States has relied primarily on *negative deterrence*, that is, on the threat characteristics possessed by its strategic nuclear forces including the Strategic Air Command and Polaris systems.

As long as deterrence, strategic or otherwise, continues to form a major part of United States foreign policy, it would seem appropriate to determine what factors contribute to its success, what criteria should be employed to determine its efficacy, and how it might be modified to meet United States policy goals better. If such a determination can

An earlier version of this chapter appeared in the Journal of Conflict Resolution.

be made, it is then possible to decide what proportion of our resources should be allocated to the general area of deterrence, and how expenditures should be apportioned among the various programs that fall within the framework of deterrence. It is obvious, given limited resources in money, time, and manpower, that inappropriate allocations can not only reduce the effectiveness of our deterrent, but can also deprive other United States domestic and foreign programs of needed resources.

The problem of determining what represents an effective deterrent system is extremely difficult. Environmental conditions such as technology, the intentions of our adversaries, and the nature of alliances change continuously. Yet policy makers must deal with such problems even though the kind of action needed to deter an adversary must necessarily fluctuate through time with changes in the environment. Since deterrence in the current environment is a mutual process, that is, since it represents a major strategy for both the Soviet Union and the United States, both parties can affect the environment that they share in common. Thus, they, as well as we, can influence the nature of the situations which we both face. Furthermore, as in any system of interaction, the choices made by a first party affect those of the second, which in turn affect those of the first, and so forth. The problem of assessing first-, second-, and third-order responses to a given action, as well as their unexpected or improbable consequences, both on the future actions of the enemy and oneself, make the task of the policy maker extremely precarious.

And even if the policy maker is able to judge validly the effects of given actions by himself or an opponent and the appropriate allocation of resources needed to effectively initiate or counter these actions, there remains the difficult problem of defining what more or less specific goals one is attempting to achieve, and how one's limited resources should be distributed to achieve these goals. Even though it is unlikely that one can arrive at precise answers to the preceding problems, that is, what are one's goals, what are their relative importance, how should one allocate one's resources between them, what are the effects of this resource allocation upon one's actions, what consequences do one's actions have on an opponent and oneself, etc., the initiation of studies in this area can be valuable. They can, for instance, demonstrate to the policy maker the complexity of the factors that are involved in decision-making; they can perhaps provide him with additional alternatives to consider; and they can help him determine, given a decision regarding a particular action, what are the most economically and perhaps the most psychologically appropriate steps to take in implementing it. The major purpose of the present chapter is to explore some of the assumptions underlying deterrence, particularly the psychological assumptions, and to introduce an additional class of action alternatives that can be employed within the general framework of deterrence, namely, deterring an enemy from making certain responses contrary to one's own interests by taking actions which reward him for making alternative responses consistent with one's goals. We shall call this form of deterrence, *positive deterrence*.

HOW DETERRENCE WORKS

One can seek rationally to deter a potential aggressor from initiating large-scale violence in several ways. First, one may try to increase an aggressor's cost for achieving his objective. Such cost may derive both from the effort the aggressor must put forth to achieve a given result and/or from the loss he supposes he might sustain from some form of retaliation made against entities or relationships that he himself values.

In the case of the Soviets, it is conceivable that their basic goal is domination of the world. At the same time, there is considerable evidence that several other goals such as self-preservation, national security, prestige, and obtaining a high level of industrial production are important to the Soviet elites. Thus, in pursuing a goal of world domination, the Soviets must take into consideration the possible costs to other goals that this policy might produce. Similarly, in evaluating possible actions the Soviets might initiate, the United States must recognize that Soviet actions are in part defined and constrained by a concern for a multiplicity of goals. The conception of an individual or nation with but a single goal is a dangerous fiction.

Second, one can seek to deter a potential adversary from taking certain actions by decreasing the likelihood that he will be successful in achieving his objectives. For instance, if it is perceived that the adversary's instruments of retaliation are widely dispersed, effectively hidden, and well protected, the estimate of the military advantage of an overt attack would be more conservative than if his weapons were highly vulnerable to attack. Similarly, the likelihood of an opponent's successfully stimulating a revolution in a given nation to obtain a regime more favorable to his own interests can be reduced by taking actions that increase the economic, political, and social stability of an existing regime.

Third, one can seek to decrease the extent or quality of the rewards available to an adversary, that is, to decrease the expected utility of his efforts. If an adversary aims to conquer one, and you threaten to destroy all the resources which he is attempting to gain, then his expected utility for an attack should be markedly reduced.

POSITIVE DETERRENCE

The fourth way in which one may deter an adversary from pursuing a course of action that one views as unfavorable to one's own interests is to reward the adversary for selecting other actions that do not have unfavorable consequences for one's own interests. Thus, in everyday life, one often attempts to change the actions of another individual by offering him behavioral alternatives that may turn out to be both more satisfying to him than those he originally contemplated, and less inimical to one's own interests. For instance, delinquents can be provided opportunities to aggress harmlessly, to achieve, and to win prestige and influence through organized athletics rather than antisocial behaviors.

Internationally, one can supply a potential aggressor with rewards and satisfactions of various sorts, not for abstaining from aggression per se, but for moving in directions consonant with the goals of one's own long-range national policy. Rewards might range from public congratulations, through trade concessions, to treaties. They might be given in response to any behavioral steps, however tentative, in directions consonant with the values of the deterrer. Thus, in the case of the Soviet Union, the United States might offer as rewards for non-aggressive activities reductions in U.S. weapon forces, increases in the sharing of scientific knowledge, trade concessions, or economic loans. Such forms of positive influence may be more powerful, that is, enduring and efficacious, in changing the behavior of an adversary than the more conventional forms of negative influence that are based solely on the psychological mechanism of threat. One advantage of positive influence is that it does not evoke as rapid, often ill-considered, responses as do threats, that is, negative influence.

The employment of positive influence is not simple. Only the rewarded can know whether the "rewards" are indeed rewarding. One may hate the giver of gifts who in giving condescends or imposes obligations. We may infer that rewards are successful when the desired behavioral changes result, that is, when the intensity or frequency of such behavior increases. This may take considerable time, but it still remains easier to make judgments about the effects of positive than of negative influence. In the case of the latter, one can never know whether an adversary has not taken some detrimental action against one because of the threats one has imposed, or because of a number of other reasons which may not be related in any way to one's capacity for hurting or punishing him.

In the application of positive rewards or incentives, most psychological research indicates that durable behavior changes are produced more rapidly when one successively rewards small changes of behavior in a desired direction than when one demands some ultimate level or standard of performance to be achieved before giving a reward. The extension of this observation as a hypothesis for the U.S.'s relations with the Soviet Union would suggest that the use of positive deterrence as an influence process should be most successful if the U.S. would reward all Soviet moves that are consistent with U.S. goals, no matter how tentative or small they are.

It is conceivable that the Soviets upon occasion might reward American leaders for actions that they perceived as being in harmony with Soviet goals. There is evidence in the psychological literature to indicate that it is possible under certain conditions to initiate a process of reciprocal rewarding. A sequence of such interactions would resemble the reciprocal tension-reducing process described by Charles E. Osgood [1] wherein the Soviets and the U.S. might compete in the most effective use of positive deterrents, that is, rewards, rather than of negative deterrents, that is, weapon systems.

Finally, one can deter by employing a combination of both positive and negative incentives at the same time. That is, one may deter an adversary from taking actions inimical with one's own interests by threatening to punish an adversary for moving in one direction while simultaneously proffering rewards, that is, some prospect for gain, for moving in another direction.

THE PSYCHOLOGY OF THREAT AND REWARD

Both the United States and the Soviet Union seek to influence each other's behavior with threats of retaliatory punishment. To the extent that either party utilizes the threat of punishment as the only or strongly predominant method of influencing the other's behavior, they ignore the empirical findings of psychologists and other social scientists regarding the functioning of both individuals and groups. Wolfenstein [2]

---

[1] C. E. Osgood, *Graduated Reciprocation in Tension-Reduction: a Key to Initiative in Foreign Policy*, unpublished manuscript, Institute of Communications Research, University of Illinois, Urbana, Illinois, 1960.

[2] Martha Wolfenstein, *Disaster: A Psychological Essay*, Free Press, Glencoe, Illinois, 1957.

and Leites,[3] for instance, have observed marked similarities in behavioral reactions of individuals and groups to disasters and other aversive stimuli, such as punishment. Their findings indicate that an external threat initially tends to increase the cohesiveness, purposefulness, and threat consciousness of a group. To the degree that this principle is applicable to international relations, it may well be that expanded threats to the Soviet Union or Communist China may tend to strengthen the Sino-Soviet block as well as their separate governments. As noted in Chapter 7 of this book, there can be little doubt that the post-World War II threat of the Soviet in Europe markedly contributed to the underlying motives for European integration, and the development of NATO.

Further empirical observations indicate that threats of punishment produce marked differences in behavior from promises of reward, at least in the behavior of individuals. Threats generally suppress the expression of a particular behavior, and do little to change the underlying motives of the organism involved. Rewards, on the other hand, permit the organism not only to behave, but also to change its underlying motivational structure, that is, its goals. Thus, punishments or threats of punishment are generally viewed as less than ideal means for producing behavioral changes. When used alone, threats are likely to produce anxiety and hostility, which are sometimes expressed in unexpected and irrational ways. Changes in behavior (and in the goals of an organism) are probably accomplished most effectively through a combination of rewards and punishments, by discouraging one set of behaviors through threat of punishment, while providing the organism with, and rewarding him for performing, other activities. Although most evidence in this area derives from research on individual organisms, the principles involved do not seem remote from the actions of nations.

The application of a mixture of negative and positive incentives to influence an adversary's choices among various behavioral alternatives assumes rationality on the part of the aggressor. A psychotic leader could precipitate a conflict out of an enormous drive for self-destruction, or he could attack for pre-emptive revenge (as homicidal paranoids do) when he was "certain" that he was about to be attacked. Aggressive responses, even to threats of overwhelming force, have occurred throughout history. While systematic data collection on such topics is scanty, the historian Harold Lamb[4] has described cities that refused to

---

[3] Nathan Leites, A *Study of Bolshevism*, Free Press, Glencoe, Illinois, 1953.
[4] Harold Lamb, *Tamerlane: Conqueror of the Earth*, Doubleday, New York, 1928.

surrender to Tamerlane even though they knew that non-surrender meant the death of all their citizens.

There is also some evidence that the environment, including the threats that an opponent presents, evokes different behaviors in crises of which one is not initiator or master. North's systematic analysis[5] from archival documents of events leading to World War I and the decision of the Japanese to enter World War II suggests that Austria-Hungary prior to World War I and Japan prior to its entry into World War II were unable to discriminate and distinguish real from fictitious threats in the environment. In both instances, it is apparent that unrealistic perceptions of threat contributed to the decision to go to war. Thus the historical examples studied by North suggest that misperceptions of environmental events have led to war. In planning a strategy of deterrence, it is important to recognize the possible role of such fictitious perceptions and the resulting irrational behaviors on the part of one's adversary, and to attempt to define those situations under which such behavior is most likely to occur.

DEFINING "WIN"

If one assumes that a conflict situation, for instance the Cold War, exists and that one's objective or goal is to "win" or to resolve the conflict in one's favor, then it is necessary to define what one means by "win." More specifically one might ask what win means for the U.S. relative to the Soviet Union? To develop a useful concept of win it is necessary to realize that the U.S. is engaged with the Soviets in a non-terminal, and a non-constant sum game; a relationship having both competitive and cooperative aspects, where gains (or losses) by one side do not imply reciprocal losses (or gains) by the other. In such a relationship what does it mean to win? To deter the Soviets from aggressive behavior in certain situations may be a kind of win in that it permits the U.S. to work relatively surely and inexpensively (compared to the uncertainties and costs of a nuclear holocaust) toward acquiring the loyalties of men to democratic institutions. Winning for the U.S. may also mean the achievement of social reforms and economic development for the more impoverished half of the world under non-Communistic regimes, or it may mean the continuance and strengthening of our alliances with other nations. If the U.S. achieves limited goals of this type or increases the probability of their occurrence,

---

[5] R. C. North, *Studies in International Conflict and Integration*, Stanford University, unpublished report to the Ford Foundation for academic year 1960–1961.

it succeeds and wins within a limited context in a game of indefinite duration.

The use of the term "win" in the field of deterrence is thus generally stated in terms of the success of prohibiting the Soviets from employing military force against other nations and/or restricting their political, economic, and social influence. In addition, many persons have expressed concern for the need of a strategic military capability for winning if deterrence should fail. In the latter context it is not altogether clear what "win" means. It could conceivably mean achieving some payoff significantly larger than the cost paid to achieve it. Such a win is sometimes defined as the post-conflict ability to dictate terms to one's opponent. Given this definition, it might be hard for either side to attain a win in a major nuclear conflict. Win in the post-war context is also defined as not losing, that is, retaining one's autonomy by not having to accept terms from the other party to the conflict. In this sense, it is conceivable that both sides could win because each felt that the task of controlling the other after a nuclear war was too difficult, too unpleasant, or simply unnecessary. Thus the term "win," although often cited as a major goal in a conflict situation, takes on a myriad of meanings according to the values or sub-goals of the parties involved in a conflict. Prior to establishing an effective strategy of deterrence, both positive and negative, it would seem essential to clearly specify what one means by winning in the context of a non-terminal, non-constant sum game. It also seems that it is highly problematic as to whether the term "win" would have meaning following an all-out nuclear war.

THE PROBLEM OF COST

One of the fundamental premises in the strategy of deterrence is that the likelihood that an adversary will take an action inimical to one's own interests is decreased to the degree that one is able to increase the adversary's costs (as perceived by him) of such action. Thus, in order to launch a nuclear attack, the initiator, if operating within a rational framework, must expect with reasonable probability to gain significantly more than he can conservatively expect to lose. To launch an attack rationally, an adversary must be able to estimate both potential gains (rewards) and losses (costs). Furthermore, in order to develop a strategy of deterrence, it is essential that the deterrer also make estimates of what forces he needs to raise the aggressor's costs of aggression to a point where he is discouraged from such actions.

There is evidence to indicate that it is increasingly difficult to discriminate psychologically between added units at the extreme ends of any judgmental scale.[6] In the present instance, this would imply that substantial increases in one's nuclear capability would have to be made, once a high level had been achieved, to produce minor increases in an adversary's perception of the magnitude of one's nuclear retaliatory capability. Thus, after one is perceived by an adversary to have a high destructive capability, it would seem likely that the economic costs of additional weapon systems would not justify the small gains achieved in one's perceived capability to deter. Furthermore, the establishment of a moderate deterrent force, employed in a sophisticated way, would likely be perceived to be as great a deterrent by an adversary as a massive force employed in an unsophisticated manner. Similarly, a moderate sophisticated deterrent would likely be perceived as less subject to error, machine or human, and thus would be less likely to provoke irrational behavior on the part of an adversary (and oneself) under tension than a massive unsophisticated system.

In terms of the foregoing analysis, the costs to the Soviet Union of overt aggression might be increased by making it clear that not one or two entities (that is, people or military equipment), but a variety of entities, relations, and even ideas of value to the Soviet decision-making elite would suffer damage. Soviet probability estimates that she could be successful in aggression against U.S. interests might be also decreased by increasing the invulnerability rather than the absolute size of our retaliatory force, perhaps through having it hidden, mobile, and widely dispersed. In both cases, the Soviet's expected probability of a significant net payoff—that is, that her potential gains would markedly outweigh her costs—would be decreased.

Let us examine some of the likely consequences (as costs to the Soviets) of the military use of even a moderate retaliatory attack by the U.S., one which the U.S. could deliver with a small, sophisticated retaliatory capability. Suppose that every major Russian city, through nuclear retaliation, were to have 20 per cent of its population killed, 20 per cent severely injured, and 40 per cent of its industrial plants severely damaged or destroyed. Ordinarily it is assumed that it takes more than two able-bodied people to care for every individual severely injured, if a program of treatment is well organized; if it is not, the ratio of able-bodied to injured must be larger. Normally, help is easily obtained from nearby urban areas in time of disaster; but if these have also been hit, or communication systems are disabled, this source of help is limited.

---

[6] See Smith Stevens, "To Honor Fechner and Repeal His Law," *Science*, Vol. 133, pp. 80–86.

Also, many uninjured people cannot be helpful because they are too old, too young, or otherwise lacking in disaster competencies; they require care themselves. Thus, following an attack in which 20 per cent of one's population is killed, and 20 per cent are seriously injured, a major proportion of the survivors must be used to render aid to the injured.

Furthermore, some people can be expected to leave any disaster area for presumably safer outlying areas. Thus, the effective labor force is depleted even more. Oskar Morgenstern[7] has pointed out that certain necessary societal maintenance and survival activities reduce the "compressibility" of any social system. That is, a certain proportion of people in any society must be in activities which guarantee the functioning of that social system as an organized entity. The proportion of people needed to operate a society at any substantial level of effectiveness after a major disaster will increase substantially. The amount of increase will, of course, vary according to the remaining patterns and levels of skill available, the quality of leadership, and the forms of organization available to obtain and distribute food, water, medical and other equipment.

The complexity of social organization in an urban environment indicates that each city sustaining the damage noted above is likely to experience major difficulty in fulfilling even its basic needs, for example, food, water, and medical care, for a matter of from several months to a year after the attack. Cities are basic organizational and communication entities in the functioning of any predominantly urban society. If many difficulties occur at the city level, they multiply for the country as a whole, since the latter functions as an even more complex entity. Certainly, difficulties in the functioning of cities must be expected to yield vast discontinuities in many areas of national life, if, indeed, the nation is able to function as a nation. Difficulties in national functioning are likely to be increased by the fact that far higher proportions of leaders with technological, scientific, and managerial skills live in cities, and when urban areas experience disaster, a disproportionate number of leaders tend to be at least partially and temporarily lost to society.

While World War II lasted longer than would the relatively light retaliatory nuclear attack described above, the damage of World War II to the organizational functioning of the Soviet Union was considerably less than the damage that would be produced by a nuclear attack. Yet,

---

[7] Oskar Morgenstern, *The Compressibility of Organizations and Economic Systems,* Research Memorandum No. 1325, The Rand Corporation, Santa Monica, Cal.

even during World War II, the Soviet population did not increase significantly, and her gross national product also showed no growth. Because skill levels, population, and education are currently higher than in World War II, the Soviets could now lose a far larger investment of effort, people, and material than they lost in World War II. The major point is that if one's forces are invulnerable, a large deterrent force is not necessary to threaten the Soviet Union since even a moderate retaliatory attack would cause substantial damage that would be highly costly in terms of a number of Soviet goals.

Most of the cost considerations mentioned thus far are in a sense logical or rational ones. Non-rational considerations, however, may operate as powerfully to influence the definition of cost. Those who have known disaster may perceive the costs of disaster to be very high and make determined efforts to avoid experiencing it again. Punishments or disasters, once experienced, have different meanings than before. In fact, unexperienced disaster may have only cognitive and no affective or emotional meaning.

People who have lived through and experienced the effects of a disastrous flood are less likely to invite death in an approaching one; those who have never known flood may even refuse to take defensive steps until they are in mortal danger.[8] Threats of disaster simply compel far greater respect and exert more of an emotional impact upon those who have had analogous experiences. Most living Soviet citizens have had some experience with military-wrought disasters; some 20 million Russians died during World War II. Americans have not had a similar experience for a long time, if at all. So on an emotional level, the impact of destruction, the perceived costs, ought to be greater within the Soviet Union than within the United States.

Moreover, there is still another reason why we may overestimate the size of the deterrent force needed to deter a Soviet attack on the West, namely, a Soviet tendency to move cautiously along paths of action that involve much uncertainty. Studies of people in the United States, who range from high to low in need for achievement, suggest that persons with high needs to achieve prefer fairly moderate odds unless they also fear failure, in which case they tend to avoid risks even more by seeking especially favorable odds.[9] High achievers tend also to avoid risky situations with large stakes. They would prefer to be successful in small increments over a long period rather than to gain or lose a

---

[8] Wolfenstein, op. cit.
[9] J. W. Atkinson, Motives in Fantasy, Action, and Society, Van Nostrand, Princeton, N.J., 1958.

great deal quickly. While this achievement or work ethic might be thought to be associated exclusively with the Protestant ethic rather than with Communism, it may be an important aspect of the "new look" that the Soviet leadership has made an integral part of Soviet Communism.

Considerable evidence exists to suggest that the Soviet leaders have strong needs for achievement as indicated by their emphasis on the future. Their five- and seven-year plans, their boasting of past and future accomplishments, their emphasis on a very high rate of capital formation at the expense of the consumer, and their emphasis on science and education all point to such a conclusion.

Recently, McClelland has analyzed fourth-grade primers for a number of countries as one way of determining the strength of the needs to achieve in these countries.[10] He found that textbooks in both the United States and the Soviet Union give substantial evidence of strong needs to achieve. An achievement orientation is also shown by the Russians' strong emphasis upon the important role of education in national planning, evidenced among other things by the high salaries paid teachers, the universalization of education, and by the fact that the Soviet Union is willing to spend 10 per cent of its gross national product for education.

No one who works hard will walk lightly into situations that permit the results of his efforts to be destroyed. The psychological costs would be very high. Thus, it does not appear very likely that the Soviet leadership would easily plunge into war other than through inadvertence or miscalculation, if they were to imagine that they would lose much of what they are committed to in terms of present and planned effort. The recent withdrawal of missiles in Cuba and the Soviet emphasis upon co-existence seem to substantiate this thesis. While few Americans knowledgeable about Russia doubt that she would like to dominate the earth, at least economically and politically, a war could materially lessen her chances for achieving such domination. Although the evidence of the Soviet leaders' needs to achieve and to control their environment is primarily inferential, there is evidence concerning its importance within Communist ideology itself. Leites[11] and Schramm,[12] for instance, have observed that there is a strong Soviet tendency to

---

[10] D. C. McClelland, *The Achieving Society*, Van Nostrand, Princeton, N.J., 1961.
[11] Nathan Leites, *A Study of Bolshevism*, Free Press, Glencoe, Illinois, 1953.
[12] Wilbur Schramm, "The Soviet Concept of 'Psychological' Warfare," *Four Working Papers on Propaganda Theory* (USIA Contract with the Institute of Communications Research), University of Illinois, Urbana, January 1955, pp. 101–143.

assume that history is on their side, that only small risks need be taken, although they should always be active and achieving.

A major war would involve many large risks and potentially high costs for the Soviets. For example, if the Soviet Union were to function industrially at a much lower level while she attempted to recover from the loss of significant elements of the population, she might well invite trespass by the land-hungry Chinese. Indeed, many Russians fear just that possibility should they have a war with the United States.[13] But, even if China were not to move into Russia, a severe economic, political, and population setback for Russia might permit some other nation to replace the Soviet Union as a major world power—a most disheartening prospect for patriotic, nationalistic Russians such as those who presumably make up the Soviet leadership.

Thus, the Soviet leaders could lose much that they value through initiating World War III, a possibility to which they can be expected to be alert. Beside the costs of losing leaders, resources (including people and machinery), progress, prestige, and power, they would risk discontinuity in the operation of the nation. Even if the Soviet Union were to recover, it could scarcely be without increased consumer belt-tightening, since any rapid degree of recovery would require an accelerated rate of capital formation. This is hardly an appetizing prospect for the Soviet citizen.

SUMMARY

The present chapter suggests that principles of human behavior derived from psychological and scientific social theory indicate that reward or a combination of reward and threat is a more effective means of influencing behavior than threat alone. To the extent that United States policy makers might seek to influence Soviet decision-making through the use of deterrent threat alone, our weapon systems and strategy are being utilized unimaginatively. A maximally-effective United States deterrent strategy would be modified to employ positive deterrence as well as negative deterrence. Along with the threat of nuclear retaliation, we would use a system of rewards or encouragement for actions which are consistent with, or at least certainly not detrimental to, United States goals. In addition, it is suggested here that the costs to Soviet goals of even a moderate United States retaliatory attack would be extremely high; hence, the United States may have less need for massive retaliatory forces than for smaller, and invulnerable ones which are capable of employment in sophisticated strategies.

---

[13] R. C. North, *op. cit.*

PART IV

DISARMAMENT,
ARMS CONTROL,
AND INTERNATIONAL
STABILITY

Chapter 9

Problems of Disarmament

ARTHUR L. BURNS

There never has been a successful agreement for complete disarmament. At most, limited arms control (for example, the recent nuclear test ban agreement, and the 1920's naval agreement between Britain, Japan and the United States) and limited imposed disarmament (for example, that inflicted upon Japan and Western Germany after World War II, and upon Germany after the First World War), have been achieved. In the latter case, clandestine arms production was organized in the Weimar Republic, despite the efforts of the Inter-Allied Control Commission.[1] Failure was not for want of trying. The League of Nations[2] produced volumes of negotiation. The historical contrast of un-

This chapter is a revision of a speech of the same title delivered at the University of Melbourne, and sponsored by the Melbourne University Australian Labor Party Club, in September 1960, in the series of Chifley Memorial Lectures, and published by the Club in the same year, National Press, Melbourne, Australia.
[1] E. J. Cumbel, in *Inspection for Disarmament*, S. Melman, ed., Columbia University Press, New York, 1958, pp. 203–214.
[2] Philip Noel-Baker, *The Arms Race*, Stevens and Sons, New York and London, 1958, pp. 387–392.

successful disarmament efforts with gradually successful reforms in internal politics, economics, and social life is marked.

TECHNOLOGICAL FACTORS IN DISARMAMENT

The political reasons for a lack of progress in complete disarmament are peculiarly deep-rooted, but there are also independent technological reasons. Since the great nuclear revolution, the tempo of weapons technology has risen until we expect a weapons revolution about once every four years.[3]

"Weapons revolution" means the production of a new type of armed force that can make obsolete a previously dominant type. The several major Powers begin a usually brief production-race until each has a "sufficiency," or until the new weapon-system is itself obsolete. Each sub-race, unlike pre-war weapons races, is expected to be non-exponential.

Weapons technology is a part of, and a pacemaker in, the great technological revolution of the mid-twentieth century—a revolution distinguished from previous technological revolutions by the greatly quickened interaction between basic scientific research and its technological application in agriculture, industry and military forces. An index of this feature is the increased proportion of a characteristic military budget (itself tending to run at a much higher proportion of the Gross National Product than in most former peacetime eras) allocated to research and development of new weapons. In 1958, for instance, the United States military budget of about 40 billion dollars represented just over 11 per cent of the national income, and about 14 per cent of this military budget was spent in one way or another upon research and development. Furthermore, there have been considerable side-payments to sub-atomic physics, to space research, to cybernetics and electronics, and to other related fields.

Motives are obvious enough for continuing the ever more successful search for new weapons—the "qualitative arms-race." As each new post in the qualitative race is reached, a separate "quantitative" race, or production race, is set off, for example, the ballistic-missile race which followed upon the Russians' and then the Americans' inventing long-range liquid-fuelled missiles.

Even in the nineteenth century there was a slow and reluctant quali-

---

[3] Ellis H. Johnson, "The Crisis in Science and Technology and Its Effects on Military Development," *Operations Research* 6/1, January-February, 1958, pp. 19 *et seq.*

tative race in naval armoring and armament.[4] Before World War II, revolutions in weapons technology succeeded one another slowly enough to permit long and finally disastrous quantitative races. These races in fighter planes, bombers, tanks, etc., in fact continued for many years before they exploded into war. Yet, the sheer importance of having predominance in numbers made these earlier quantitative races more likely to produce war than today's races for nuclear weapons and missiles. However, control over present stockpiles, though more important, is also harder, for a "nominal" nuclear weapon equals a thousand tons of TNT in a small parcel. So disarmament is today many times more difficult than before World War II. Under "complete disarmament," approximately fifty nuclear weapons, clandestinely stored or manufactured, loaded in civilian aircraft, could possibly force surrender on powerful nations. A cheating first-rank power could probably retain enough warheads by evasion to achieve this, though clandestine manufacture would as yet be much less profitable.[5] Even in a totally disarmed and well-inspected world, therefore, it might be necessary to maintain an International Police Force with a small and well-guarded stockpile of nuclear weapons, and elsewhere, a ready system of delivery vehicles.

POLITICAL AND ECONOMIC PROBLEMS

Quite apart from the dangers of evasion, the concept of disarmament merely as an administrative, economic, and political enterprise is staggering to contemplate. Demobilization after World War II, when there appeared to be no immediate military threat and when there was little question of needing secure forces at every stage of the operation, called for a major governmental effort. In negotiated disarmament these difficulties would be compounded. J. Nogee has formulated an interpretation of disarmament negotiations which construes them as "gamesmanship":

A cardinal feature of this game has been to reject the proposals of the other side without appearing to sabotage the discussions. . . . Every plan offered by either side has contained a set of proposals calculated to have wide popular appeal. Every such set has included at least one feature that the other side could not possibly accept, thus forcing a rejection. Then the proposing side has been able to claim that the rejector is opposed to the

---

[4] S. P. Huntington, "Arms Races: Prerequisites and Results," *Public Policy: Yearbook of the Graduate School of Public Administration*, Cambridge, Mass., 1958, pp. 55–59.
[5] Cumbel, *op. cit.*, p. 279.

idea of disarmament *in toto*. The objectionable feature may be thought of as the "joker" in every series of proposals.[6]

This interpretation is probably borne out by the story of the disarmament negotiations, but I am not sure that it makes enough of the situation's irreducible dilemma. To use Professor Nogee's analogy, the jokers may be in the hands of both parties, and not deliberately inserted by the players. It is easy enough for us to understand the dilemma from our side's viewpoint, but we can also see something of the other side's difficulties as well.

The Soviet Union has genuine difficulties about disarmament. She possesses a great one-sided advantage in intelligence, that is, information concerning the military posture of the West is more available to the Soviets than vice-versa. While the NATO and other Western alliances remain intact, she is at a one-sided disadvantage geographically. Even in 1964, the "unsolved problem" of Germany presses harder upon her than upon the West. The structure of Communist society, Chinese even more than Russian, would be subjected to great strain by international inspectors passing everywhere.

The difficulties in disarmament from the various Western points of view are in part the obverse of the Russian dilemma. But there are many other elements that are peculiar to the West's dilemma.

Some of these elements arise from implicit comparisons between the opportunities to exploit a disarmament agreement that might be more open to totalitarian than to Western societies. First, evasion of inspection would be easier in a totalitarian than in a liberal democratic society. Secondly, Soviet States might enjoy a military advantage if only nuclear weapons were to be banned: in terms of sheer manpower, the Western alliance is as well off as the Eastern bloc; but most Western societies cannot politically afford to maintain the conscription necessary nowadays for an adequate conventional defense.[7]

Other Western difficulties are concerned with the West's weaker bargaining situation in negotiating any disarmament agreement; for though Russian-Chinese disagreements appear to be serious, those of the Western alliance are more in evidence. Furthermore, Western positions appear the more rigid, since they have to be a matter of prior

[6] Joseph Nogee, "The Diplomacy of Disarmament," *International Conciliation* (*Carnegie Endowment for International Peace*), No. 526, January 1960, pp. 282–283.

[7] Denis Healey, "The Race Against the H-Bombs," *Fabian Tract* 322, Fabian International Bureau, London, 1960. Note, however, U.S. Defense Department statements to the contrary, 1963–1964.

agreement amongst many Powers with somewhat differing interests. Again, their habit of partial disagreement amongst themselves makes them less optimistic about getting agreement across the Iron Curtain.

Communist China provides another Western concern about the possibility of a universal ban on nuclear weapons, since such a ban could hardly be enforced without a broader recognition of Communist China than some Western Powers would be willing to grant. If Communist China were not party to the ban, the Soviet States might be able to store weapons and to conduct clandestine tests in China.

Politically, a disarmament agreement might seem to favor Communist plans for world domination, since it would presumably leave arms in the hands of internal police forces and militia.

One type of difficulty attributed peculiarly to Western Powers is, however, probably unreal. It is sometimes said that the United States in particular could not afford the *economic* consequences of disarmament. But, in fact, American defense buying declined in 1946 by 57 billion dollars and remained at about 14 billion dollars for the rest of the decade. During that time the national income rose considerably; there was of course a backlog of unsatisfied wartime demand. In 1954 and 1955, however, after the Korean War, the military budget of 50 billion dollars declined by 20 per cent. Three quarters of this decrease was released in a tax cut, but there was a slight and brief recession. Economists explain this on the view that tax cuts alone cannot by themselves make up for an equivalent or larger reduction in government spending since some of the tax relief will be saved and will not immediately call for a new supply of consumer goods. Part of any defense cut, then, should be used in other governmental or governmentally inspired expenditure if recession is to be avoided. Furthermore, there should be schemes for retraining and re-employment of the specialized parts of the defense labor force.

THE DETERRENCE ARGUMENT

Perhaps the most powerful of all forces in Western countries working against disarmament derive from the arguments of research workers and strategic analysts who honestly believe that difficulties in the way of inspection and control make disarmament impossible, while on the other hand the fortunate accident of a stable deterrent system or "balance of terror" makes disarmament undesirable. Certain striking facts of recent history support this belief. World opinion seems to regard the danger of total war as having receded because both the United States and the Soviet Union have developed the H-bomb. In relation to the GNP of most of the larger countries deploying extensive armed forces, the levels of military budgets have actually declined since the end of the Korean War.[8]

Furthermore, practices have been tolerated by the international system which, in a truly precarious military situation, would have been very likely to lead to total war; or, simply because they would have appeared so dangerous, they would not have been allowed to occur in less stable situations: for example, the shooting down of United States' planes flying near the Russo-Turkish border, the Suez crisis, the revolution in Hungary, the Berlin threat of 1959, the U-2 incident, the conflict in the Congo, the Cuban crisis, and all those threats by Khrushchev from Suez to the present day to use rockets against the allies of the United States. Proponents of the theory of mutual deterrence can claim that, even when strategic forces were very vulnerable, total war was averted in the way that their theory would suggest, while in an era of less vulnerable strategic forces the "balance of terror" will be much more stable.

Proposals for arms control are therefore directed to such measures as reducing the vulnerability and increasing the deployment of "sufficient" forces on *both sides*,[9] reducing the likelihood of surprise attack and slowing down the spread of nuclear weapons to small countries that do not have them at present and which may not ever be in a position to support sufficiently invulnerable strategic forces. But I know of no plan for limited arms control that is designed to stop the "qualitative arms race"—that is, the competition in research and development of new weapons.

THE CASE FOR DETERRENCE

The case for a "balance of terror" against total disarmament, and against gradual reduction of nuclear forces, derives from the premise that in nuclear affairs too little is even more dangerous—that is, provocative—than too much. However, the implications of a "balance of terror strategy" are complex and frequently misunderstood by its advocates as well as by its detractors.

"One-Way" Deterrence. When H-bombs were first invented, and

---

[8] A. C. L. Day, "The Economics of Defense," *Political Quarterly*, No. 1, Vol. 31, January–March 1960, p. 59; and Alastair Buchan, *NATO in the 1960's*, Weidenfield and Nicolson, London, 1960, p. 39.

[9] Oskar Morgenstern, *The Question of National Defense*, Random House, New York, 1959, *passim*.

when long-range ballistic missiles were still in the course of development, the theory of deterrence was much more appropriately known by the phrase that Churchill coined for it, "the balance of terror." A very few hydrogen bombs would suffice to destroy a city. But an equally large allocation of force would often be needed to attempt to destroy a single airport and the bombers on it, some of which even then would be likely to get away. Bombing of military installations and centers of population would easily cause severe damage, but the attacker would be likely to find himself severely damaged by the "last-gasp" retaliatory strike of his victim.

Such was the original version of the theory of mutual deterrence, which, in the United States at any rate (belatedly followed by the United Kingdom in Sandys' White Papers of 1957 and 1958), grew out of a doctrine of *one-way* deterrence. That is, it was asserted that the Soviet Bloc would be deterred from using its conventional weapons not by the prospect of adequate conventional resistance from the West, but by the prospect of nuclear annihilation to which it could not reply. Both versions of the doctrine have been described by George Kennan and others as "the maintenance of peace by the threat of killing hostages." I believe that this approach is not only morally objectionable, as I shall explain later, but also has certain defects from a military or international policy standpoint.

A major defect of the "balance of terror" is that it deters only other great deterrents. The lesser forms of aggression, for example, the conventional or tactical nuclear forces, cannot be deterred by the strategic deterrent alone. Thus, this great deterrent needs to be flanked by ranges of lesser deterrents, that is, by tactical nuclear and conventional forces sufficient to prevent an aggressor from winning a conventional war without recourse to total nuclear war. The provision of such lesser deterrent forces is known as "graduated deterrence." [10] The apparent necessity for lesser deterrents removes one of the supporting arguments for the original version of the mutual-deterrent or "terror" doctrine, namely that money could actually be saved by relying chiefly on strategic nuclear forces.

"*Margin of Superiority*" *Deterrence*. With the advent of ICBM's, a new and quite distinct form of mutual deterrence became feasible. According to this second version, an aggressor would be deterred from launching a surprise attack not primarily by the fear of having his own cities destroyed, but by the knowledge that however effective his surprise and however concentrated his fire of ICBM's, he would succeed in dis-

---

[10] A coinage from a British study-group headed by Rear-Admiral Buzzard.

arming himself by such an attack, while many of his opponent's ICBM's, launching pads, nuclear submarines, and perhaps even bombers would survive the attack. The argument for this kind of deterrence can be stated in simple mathematics,[11] if artificially confined to the case of ICBM's on dispersed sites.

Suppose each side deploys no more than one missile per site, and that on the average more than one missile is required to destroy a site; that is, the "probability of kill" is perceptibly less than unity. Then it follows that the margin of superiority in numbers of missiles that the attacker would need in order to be sure that he had eliminated enough of the victim's sites to guarantee him victory *increases* with the *absolute numbers* of the victim's sites. The important consequences (see Table 14) are that the victim or defender is safe, above a certain

TABLE 14. *Required Ratios of ICBM Sites—*
*An approximation utilizing "expected values"**

Probability of kill = 0.5   Defender's sites required to survive = 250

If Attacker(s) Had	The Defender Would Need
500	500
2,000	1,000
6,000	2,000
16,000	4,000
40,000	8,000

* Consideration of variance would increase the disadvantage of surprise attack.

level of numbers, even though he is not matching the attacker one-for-one; and that this margin of safety increases with the absolute number of sites.

Thus, the higher the numbers of "vehicles" on *both* sides, the more stable the balance of deterrence—the reverse of the situation with pre-atomic explosives and, for instance, battleships.

It will have been noticed that this second version of stable deterrence is not as objectionable morally as the earlier version. There is no blatant threat of killing hostages, as in the first case. But since it depends on the invulnerability of strategic forces, it assumes a rather spe-

---

[11] T. C. Schelling, in *NATO and American Security*, Klaus Knorr, ed., Princeton University Press, Princeton, N.J., 1959, pp. 184–185; and Arthur L. Burns in "From Balance to Deterrence: A Theoretical Analysis," *World Politics*, Vol. IX, No. 4, July 1957.

cial kind of military technology will continue to predominate forever. However, this version can lead to a much less stable situation in which the balance of forces may seem to make it militarily desirable to launch the first strike. For *if* a military commander is convinced that there is going to be total nuclear war, he has overwhelmingly strong arguments for trying to attack first.

At the very best, of course, the initiating and therefore less damaged side will be very likely to have lost millions of people. Nevertheless, the losses would be much greater for the side that had suffered surprise attack or had been caught in the highly vulnerable position of preparing to launch a surprise attack itself. Basically, this is because of the great destructive power of the thermonuclear weapons. Though they can destroy cities more readily, they have hundreds of times more chance of knocking out bomber-bases, rocket-sites, and submarines than have ordinary high explosives. But that is not all. The side that suffers the first blow is likely to lose its warning system, to have its communications badly damaged, to have its slower-reacting forces (its medium-range bombers and so forth) reduced, and to lose or expend the anti-aircraft and anti-missile systems it possesses. And all this is likely to occur in an hour or two.

In contrast, the side that strikes first, so long as its strategic forces and the enemy's are in large measure vulnerable to attack, tends to reduce its population losses by hitting at the enemy's forces. It strikes, as it were, in peacetime, whereas the enemy has to strike back in wartime, with all the attendant disadvantages. And by hitting first, there is some remote chance of actually winning a total war, that is, of compelling the enemy to accept terms.

The preceding analysis depends upon a quantitative relationship between the two strategic forces concerned, together with their vulnerability to each other. When and if both East and West shall have made their forces so invulnerable that the side that strikes first will thereby disarm itself, or at best use up much more of its own forces than the enemy forces could hope to destroy, the balance of mutual deterrence will be much more stable than at present. Under these conditions, advantages of striking first will have been lost.

Deterrence through "Invulnerable Forces." The prospect of both United States and U.S.S.R. strategic forces becoming less vulnerable in two or three years has led some Western analysts to propose a policy of "peace by mutual deterrence." It is a matter of documentary evidence, however, that the Russians understand how advantageous it would be, under present conditions, to strike first if they have to strike at all. Soviet military periodicals provide evidence of a revolution in strategic thinking that, as I have suggested, parallels the change in Western doctrine.

In particular, Russian strategists now use the concept of a "preemptive blow," which, as stated by the Soviet Marshal, Rotmitsrov,[12] is ". . . the last-hour seizure of the initiative and surprise from the enemy whom the Soviets know (somehow) to be preparing an imminent surprise attack." On this level, Western thinking is more mature, skeptical, and responsible concerning the difficulties of "knowing," or of estimating whether the other fellow wrongly judges that you think you will be attacked and therefore intends to attack you first, so that *you* had better strike *him* first, and so on.

Authorities on both sides have at one time or another spoken of the dangers and uncertainties of mutual deterrence. Khrushchev has made much of the dangers of accident, of bomber-pilots going mad, and of mistaking of physical signs such as misread signals from warning systems. But this sort of problem, pertinent though it may be, can be met at a cost. Safety devices can be installed at the price of a higher military investment, and perhaps at the strategic expense of a less efficient warning system. These measures would improve, not abolish, mutual deterrence. But other doubts can be raised about the technological and political foundations of both margin-of-superiority, and invulnerable force deterrence. From these doubts, I believe we can rebuild a strong military argument for thoroughgoing disarmament.

THE INSTABILITY OF MUTUAL DETERRENCE

A defense policy built upon the theory of mutual deterrence and the possession of a physically invulnerable force (for instance, a fleet of nuclear submarines armed with Polaris rockets) works, if it works at all, quite differently from former defense policies. While Britain held naval supremacy during parts of the nineteenth century, it was possible for the Admiralty to *guarantee*, for the time being, that no foreign force could land on the soil of Great Britain in numbers sufficient to threaten her people. But nuclear deterrence depends absolutely upon the enemy's recognizing a nuclear threat and its significance. This means that *all practical strategic and political considerations* must weigh against attacking at all. That is, the enemy must be convinced that attack would be absurd unless he is sure that his own *population*, rather than his forces, is about to receive a nuclear attack—and there can be

---

[12] Quoted in Garthoff, R. L., *Soviet Strategy in the Nuclear Age*, Stevens and Sons, London, 1958, pp. 85–87.

no guarantee that any particular group of leaders will invariably interpret the strategic and political considerations in such a light.

National leaders can fail to understand the implications of weapon-
systems that they possess or covet. (The Communist Chinese leaders
may do so at present.[13]) They can make terrible mistakes, or be
tricked into making them, though these are perhaps the least likely
causes of a nuclear attack upon populations. They can be evil or insane,
as were the Nazi leaders of the last days. Against antagonists with any
such characteristics, the great deterrent can promise little.

Complete disarmament of nuclear and future equivalent means of
mass destruction can alone protect populations against the dupe, the
ignoramus, the lunatic, and the diabolist if, and only if, its enforcement is thoroughly adequate. The idea of a "perfect defense"—a
weapon-system or shelter which could exclude all of an enemy super-
power's thermonuclear explosives or equivalent instruments of destruction from thickly-populated areas—is hardly imaginable at present, and
may even be self-contradictory. It may turn out that there is no way of
arriving at stable disarmament. But if so, neither is there a substitute
for it.

Another common source of doubt about deterrent stability is the
"Nth-country problem," discussed elsewhere in this volume. In practice
this worry is somewhat exaggerated, as can be seen by a comparison of
the military potentials of the two super-powers with those of the rest
of the world.[14] For a while, at any rate, the rest of the world together
could make only a marginal difference to the actual numbers of effectively deliverable nuclear weapons. Nor do I think there is much
ground for a popular argument about the mathematical probability of
accident increasing with the number of weapons, for the same reasons.
A much more serious doubt arises from the likelihood that any new
members of the nuclear club can hope to acquire only second-rate
strategic forces. Even Britain has faced this problem in an acute form
over the cancellation of the Blue Streak, and the United States abandonment of the Skybolt missile.

Another difficulty in the Nth country problem concerns the acquisition of low-grade atomic weapons (or, if they can be developed,
fission-free fusion weapons) by quite small states. Whether or not
these small atomic powers would be severally a danger to each other,

---

[13] Alice Langley Hsieh, "Communist China and Nuclear Warfare," *The China Quarterly*, No. 2, April–June 1960, pp. 1 *et seq.*
[14] As a rough index, America's military budget in 1960 was more than three times that of all her allies together.

the conflagration that they might start could perhaps spread to the great Powers themselves.

Objections to even more eligible partners have been raised. Contemplating the dispersal of nuclear weapons to European members of NATO, one eminent authority[15] declared: "The idea of ten countries sending out planes on alert, nervously fingering the trigger missiles, and having submarines with Polaris-type missiles roaming the sea—this idea is intolerable."

On the other hand, I am inclined to think that a big and genuinely independent Third or Fourth Bloc might, within the terms of nuclear deterrence, provide some sort of stabilizer to the present bipolarity.

Another and a serious possibility of overthrowing the balance of terror consists in a limited war suddenly escalating into total war. Even small wars are unpredictable affairs that may quickly get out of control. This danger will be greatest when there is only *just* a balance of terror, so that a little more vulnerability in either side's forces would give the other a motive and opportunity for hitting first.

Gravest of all threats against the stability of mutual deterrence is the possibility that new weapons will be invented that do not have the convenient mathematical properties attributed to invulnerable missiles. It does not seem to be impossible that a weapon could become dominant that has something of the characteristics of the old-fashioned capital ship, which, when numerically predominant, was highly effective against smaller fleets of capital ships, and was for a while the only effective counter to them. The huge efforts at research and development of new weapons could, in principle, lead to this sort of situation, especially as all parties want a flexible multi-purpose vehicle for delivering H-bombs. It is to be feared that the development of manned and maneuverable space-vehicles may upset the stable balance of deterrence in some such fashion.

Even more perilous would be the case in which one of the competitors was known to be well ahead in the race for development of the new flexible weapon-system. It might even be clear that if he were allowed to retain his lead he could expect a relatively cheap victory against the suddenly obsolete forces of the rest of the world. In that case mutual deterrence during the interval would be severely strained, and those who were behind in the innovations race might have strong reasons for combining in surprise attack against the leader.

Since no one can make a complete picture of all the technological possibilities and since some of those that we can envisage lead to a

---

[15] T. C. Schelling, *op. cit.*, p. 319.

breakdown of deterrence, there is no way of confining the qualitative arms race to routes that will maintain the present state of balance or stability. This may help to explain why some Western strategic thinkers,[16] who oppose disarmament at the moment nevertheless advocate it strongly in the long run:

Arms control agreements are enormously dangerous for the United States. If partial arms control brings a substantial relaxation of international tensions, the NATO countries—easily given to wishful thinking in this matter—might suffer the fatal disadvantage of a drop in defense budgets, a drop in military performance, a drop in alertness. And, unless control is airtight, such agreements might reduce for the Soviets strategic uncertainties which are holding them back at present. On the other hand, without effective arms control, the world will be so unstable militarily that it may not live to 1970 or 1980 without a catastrophic explosion.

THE MORAL OBJECTIONS
TO NUCLEAR DETERRENCE

I have maintained above that mutual deterrence by threat of massive retaliation says, "You cannot destroy in one blow all my nuclear delivery-vehicles. If you succeed in destroying more than a few of them, I shall send the rest to kill as many millions of your people as possible. But unless you do so, you need not worry, since I know that you are in the same position with respect to attack from me." We also saw that there is a less objectionable version of deterrence by overwhelming invulnerability, which says, "My nuclear vehicles are all deployed well away from centers of population. By all means try to destroy them— you will merely use up the bulk of your nuclear forces and hardly touch mine. I shall then be in so strong a position that you will have to accept my terms for disarmament and a political settlement." But this position depends upon a rather fine technical adjustment, that is, the participants could be driven back to massive retaliation by a marginal increase in the vulnerability of their strategic forces. Furthermore, it is likely to be available only to the super-powers.

In short, the reciprocal balance of terror entails a dilemma. The peace it offers depends upon a threat that I do not think we have the moral right to make. It is a dilemma we are involved in at this moment. The allies of the United States derive their security, several times removed but none the less in actuality, from the partly vulnerable strategic nuclear forces of the United States, and have done so for several years. If they had their own long-range weapons for the

---

[16] T. C. Schelling, *op. cit.*, p. 330.

destruction of cities, I do not see that their position would be morally worse than at present—only, perhaps, more evident to them, as it appears to be at the moment to some people in the United Kingdom. Acquisition by the United States' allies of tactical nuclear weapons reserved solely for destroying missiles (or even aircraft and submarines) sent with nuclear explosives against the allies' cities, would be morally justified insofar as any armaments are justifiable. The one count against these tactical types of nuclear weapons is that, until much cleaner ones are developed, their explosion tends to spread round the world a fallout which will almost certainly be fatal to some people, born or unborn. This certainly sets a moral question-mark against such tactical anti-weapon nuclear weapons. To help save millions of people in its own cities, a small power may be able to make a case for indirectly killing thousands of persons by radiation elsewhere, as well as the crews of enemy submarines and aircraft. However, the charge against nuclear weapons consists only partly in their radioactivity. The great evil consists in the mass-killing use to which we might put *some* of them, and in the threat of that use which is involved in the strategy of massive retaliation.

It is not clear to me that the alternative of complete unilateral disarmament is necessarily a moral improvement upon the alternatives of nuclear deterrence, at least for a power involved with allies in any of the following ways:

1. If it has a more powerful ally which would defend it by threat of massive retaliation *whether or not* it were disarmed;
2. If its unilateral disarmament (and, as a possibly inevitable consequence, its withdrawal from the former alliance) would leave its former allies vulnerable to attack.

For a nation in neither of those situations, unilateral disarmament would carry an implicit declaration that a nuclear attack would not be resisted in any way other than by evacuation of the cities. By refusing to defend itself or to allow itself to be defended by threat of massive retaliation, such a nation may in fact be inviting an attack from either side by creating a power vacuum, and may even provoke a conflict between other nations.

This raises a question about the motivation of campaigns for disarmament, unilateral or otherwise. Fear alone cannot be an adequate motive. Rational fear for the safety of one's children and countrymen can just as reasonably predicate a policy of security by deterrent power. Fear of suffering a nuclear attack seems to arouse the desire to possess independent "national deterrents." But the attempt to make oneself secure by possession of nuclear arms may arouse a concern for our predicament serious enough to convert disarmament negotiations from their present role—the major competition of the Cold War—into a genuine political enterprise.

Surely all the great Powers, Communist, non-Communist, and un-committed, are or soon will be in the same predicament of having to choose between surrender, preparations for preventive war, or the policy of defense by threat of massive retaliation. In the longer run, as I argued in the preceding section, technological change could well elimi-nate the last alternative, for all Powers. It is even possible that the option of surrendering should disappear—secrecy, exclusiveness, and precautions against pre-attack blackmail ("turning off one's hearing-aid") might remove the means of demonstrating to an aggressor that one was indeed laying down one's arms. All this could come about without unusual malevolence on the part of any nation—the mixture of more-or-less enlightened self-interest and moderate idealism that has been the highest kind of motivation for past international affairs could do it. What hope, then, can there be that the powers will ever manage to negotiate a disarmament agreement?

WHAT DISARMAMENT MIGHT BE LIKE

The concrete measures for disarmament that seem practicable are mostly exemplifications of the principle that trust is created by taking measures which *assume* general mistrust and willingness to take ad-vantage of the other fellow. One can then reduce the grounds for mistrust by making malevolence unprofitable. But I should also rely upon the notion of developing an international organ, firstly perhaps for surveillance and only later for armed policing as an independent Third Force that might help stabilize the conflict of interest between the two great blocs.[17]

An inspected universal ban on nuclear tests must, it seems, be im-posed if negotiations for disarmament are to bear fruit within the next few years. Theoretically, disarmament could precede and subse-quently include a universal test ban with inspection. As a matter of practical politics, I think it would be out of the question. If the French and the Red Chinese are not willing to forego the improve-ments in weaponry that a ban would entail, and if the Russians con-tinue to resist inspections, they would hardly accept the much greater

---

[17] I have suggested such a measure in "Disarmament or the Balance of Terror," *World Politics*, No. 1, Vol. XII, October 1959, pp. 132–145.

limitations of general disarmament. If the Russians cannot tolerate a few inspections a year in conjunction with a nuclear test-ban, they certainly will not accept the much greater inspection that even their own disarmament proposals have sketched in. Failing a universal test ban which provides for inspection, some dramatic crisis of a magnitude even greater than occurred in Cuba will be needed to make arms control once more a serious topic.

France has refused to participate in the current limited test ban unless the three previous members of the nuclear club begin to eliminate their stockpiles. She might nevertheless comply if the others were to agree to a cut-off in production of nuclear weapons. The Russians might also see some point in this, especially if it were accompanied by a promise not to disperse nuclear weapons any further, for instance to Germany. But Communist China is likely to demand a much higher price.

Communist China has more telling reasons and stronger motives than any other power for acquiring a nuclear stockpile. It can more easily frustrate a ban to which it is not a party, for example, by offering to conduct tests on its own territory for the benefit of other Soviet bloc countries such as the U.S.S.R. Its passion for secrecy is even greater than the Soviet's. The price for Red Chinese adherence to a ban may go higher than Taiwan's seat on the Security Council.

A favorite argument for the banning of nuclear tests used to be that it would be the first step toward general disarmament, accustoming the Russians to a mild form of inspection so that they might accept the more drastic variety needed for thoroughgoing reduction of military resources. This was an unimaginative attitude for it failed to recognize either the advantages that the U.S.S.R. might seek by preparing to test while the ban was still nominally in force, or the grave vulnerabilities likely to have been revealed in Soviet strategic forces by the U-2 operation. Events have made it clear that Russia might manage with impunity to defy the test ban, while experiencing renewed pressure for general disarmament as a result of the United States' having developed a credible counterforce.

Supposing that Russia came in this way under pressure to take general disarmament seriously, what sort of measures should the West propose?

Let me first assume that by that time the United States, and even Russia, will have much less vulnerable strategic deterrents than at present. (It is quite possible that the West European and British wing of NATO may have developed a joint deterrent also.)

I also assume that the two super-powers will then have effective missile-warning systems, using both radar and satellites. In those circumstances, there should be some easing of the chief difficulties for the West in disarming: (1) how to persuade the Soviet states that disarmament without effective inspection and control would be dangerous, and (2) how to replace, for America's globally distributed allies, the foundations of their defenses against less-than-total assault. The old foundation, mutual deterrence between Russia and America, would be dismantled in general disarmament.

The procedure now to be suggested indicates an as-yet-unexplored possibility of reciprocal deterrence. The program would be for the West to indicate that it will strengthen the allies' defenses, if necessary with tactical nuclear forces, at the same time that it will reduce its own strategic forces by transferring out of its own forces-in-being, the material for a warning-system, a nuclear stockpile, and means of delivery by the United Nations or a group of volunteer neutrals from different countries. It would invite Russia, but not conditionally, to make a similar contribution to this Third Force, which would function under a military requirement quite different from those of the Soviet and Western blocs.

The Third Force, while able to receive and broadcast warning of any surprise attack anywhere, should have only a limited ability to launch an attack itself. Its strategic nuclear forces should be maintained as invulnerable as possible, with the loosest of coordination at this stage. The aim would be to guarantee to the super-powers that, if either of them should launch an all-out attack against the other, the Third Force would be alerted under a coordinating commander, and would be able to dictate terms of surrender to the attacker.

The super-powers could then in safety dismantle their strategic nuclear forces, and with a minimum of the pre-disarmament inspection (taking of inventories) to which the Soviet has so much objected as "control without disarmament." Each bloc even now has a rough idea of the outside limits to the size of its opponent's nuclear stockpile and delivery vehicles. The quantities of the latter actually handed over to an international inspectorate, at first for the Third Force and later for dismantling, would therefore leave both parties, and the Third Force officers, with some idea of what the other still retained. Furthermore, our assumption of decreased vulnerability should allow both the U.S. and the Soviets to rely on smaller deterrent forces than before. The Third Force itself would be, of course, a known quantity.

So far, disarmament would have chiefly involved the two super-powers. At the next stage, at least, all advanced nations would need to be brought in. The Western nations could well prepare for this stage by studies of the best means to convince suspicious Soviet leaders that the West at any rate would provide a completely honest inventory before the final stages of disarmament. Again, it will be of little help to protest our good intentions: just as arming and disarming are, alike, politico-military problems, so revealing one's forces is as much a problem in military and political intelligence as is concealing them. And provided the allies' defenses are by then strong enough to prevent Soviet forces from simply walking in, the United States could properly withdraw from overseas bases. In general, much can be done unilaterally by the West to ensure that, during a process of disarmament, the Soviet powers have as little to fear from surprise attack as they would have to gain from attempting it.

Once an international warning-system and stockpile exist, measures of disarmament and inspection could succeed each other progressively and quickly. The Third Force stockpile would itself be reduced as the evidence accumulated of reductions in other stockpiles, tactical as well as nuclear. Demobilization of conventional forces presents an easier problem for inspection, but is politically more difficult to achieve whether for powers holding down colonial empires or totalitarian states like Spain and China, and, much more difficult for totalitarian imperialisms like Russia.

Even when all admitted national stockpiles have been turned over to peaceful uses, a dispersed stockpile should probably be retained for some years by the fully internationalized Third Force. There is no way of disarming science. Atomic and perhaps cheap fission-free thermonuclear weapons will within the next decade be quite easy to make, and if terrorists or enterprising criminals were to succeed in doing so, nation-states might be driven into nuclear rearmament for sheer self-preservation. The international stockpile, on the other hand, must not be capturable by any group or nation. Perhaps the wisest arrangement would be for an unassembled thermonuclear weapon to be kept under seal in the capital of each nation, rather as the dies are kept at the Mint, in the joint charge of national and international officials, so that the civilized world would have a surety against criminals, and so that no nation could have any rational motive for rearmament.[19]

Technological change could easily make obsolete the suggestions I have just made (and some may think, as of 1963, that the United States' credible counterforce has already done so), except in their most

---

[19] See Arthur L. Burns, "Stabilizing Propensities of a Third Nuclear Force" in Two Essays on Deterrence, *Tempo* (General Electric), RM 60TMP-86, Santa Barbara, California, December 1960.

general feature—the need for a counter-balancing and dispersed international force. At this point it is impossible to say how later approaches might be made to disarmament. As a very much second-best alternative, I believe it would be wise of the leading Western Powers to ensure that, failing early general disarmament, nuclear weapons are passed on only to substantial powers and groupings of powers (for example, the European wing of NATO), and only in the least vulnerable, least provocative form available. Other second-best procedures are available, but they are not a necessary part of our present subject.

The greatest problem of general disarmament may arise in the final stages of a disarmament program. Mankind has no experience to guide it in a world both industrialized and totally disarmed. Political questions suggest themselves to which only Utopian answers, or no answers at all, have so far been given. How, in such a world, are the strains of differential growth in economy and population to be taken up? How is personal liberty to be preserved when national and international organizations combine to prevent the misuse of powers which science will always be increasing? How are inevitable conflicts of national interest to express themselves? These are not problems of technique, but issues which can be met, if at all, by a creative political wisdom that we look for in vain among current political philosophies. But the prospect of these intractable problems is at least preferable to that of an uncontrolled qualitative arms race.

Chapter 10

Arms Control: Proposal for

a Special Surveillance Force

THOMAS C. SCHELLING

This chapter proposes that there be discussed with the Russians the establishment (for the U.S.S.R. and the U.S., separately, and perhaps for other countries) of a *Special Surveillance Force*. Its function would be to observe the enemy's behavior, at the enemy's invitation, and to report home instantly through authentic channels. Its purpose is to help tranquilize crises that threaten to erupt into general war, particularly crises aggravated by the instability of strategic deterrence—by the urgency, if general war seems imminent, of starting it before the enemy does.

The special feature of such a force would be its readiness, through advance preparation, to take advantage of motives and political circumstances as they might occur in a sudden crisis, rather than as they are during the normal ups and downs of the Cold War. It should be prepared to do things, with the sudden acquiescence of the enemy (host), that the latter might never dream of permitting except in extraordinary circumstances, when some kind of arms control—even if

This chapter originally appeared in the October 1960 issue of World Politics.

only a temporary monitoring of some synchronized withdrawal or re-laxation—becomes urgently required as an alternative to war or to the rapid deterioration of a strategic crisis. The attributes of the force should be readiness, speed, reliability, self-sufficiency, versatility, and ability to improvise.

UNDERLYING PREMISES

This suggestion for establishing a special surveillance force rests on two premises. The first is that any real stimulus to arms-control or arms-tranquilization measures would likely come in an unforeseen crisis that developed rapidly. There is not now a powerful belief in arms control as a necessary alternative to general war; but events could occur—technological events or political events—that would make the balance of deterrence much more unstable than it is now, or that would cause a drastic reappraisal of the instability that has existed all along—events that would make "measures to safeguard against sur-prise attack" (to use the current terminology) needed instantly as an alternative to war. At such a moment of crisis the motives for arms control, the political feasibility of various control measures, the willing-ness to incur costs, to break precedent, and to infringe the rights of other countries, might be strikingly different than in the circumstances of the Cold War. In other words, the demand for disarmament may come suddenly when it comes, and not be able to wait. Advance intel-lectual preparation, and material and personnel preparation, may be essential to meet that contingency.

The second premise is that there are actions that the United States and the U.S.S.R. might take cooperatively in anticipation of a possible sudden need to meet unforeseen emergencies. In the course of such emergencies the ability of each side to see reliably, that is, clearly, with its own eyes, and with authentic capabilities for communicating home, the actions that either are being taken or are not being taken in the other country may be essential to the avoidance of misunderstanding or to the negotiation of practical arrangements—even very temporary arrangements—that would help to stabilize mutual deterrence. (The possibility of a nuclear accident, or of nuclear mischief by some third party, suggests one type of situation for which stand-by observation teams of a versatile and flexible sort could be useful in the process of mutual reassurance).

NATURE OF THE CONTINGENCY

In considering the crises that may arise, and how they may arise, we should distinguish between (1) the crises that we should anticipate unilaterally and (2) those whose possibility or likelihood we can acknowledge to the Russians and discuss with them as mutual problems susceptible of cooperative preparations.

For example, we can think unilaterally about the crises that would occur if we received evidence that the Russians were preparing to launch an attack on American strategic forces. Just what to do under the circumstances is not obvious, particularly if the evidence is ambiguous, and especially if our capability to forestall an attack by a surprise blow of our own is not terribly reassuring at the time. As an important possibility, one might consider some kind of disarmament ultimatum, a demand for "measures to safeguard against surprise attack" of a potency and rigor suggested by the term "preventive disarmament."

Whether there would be any military restraint or sacrifice that we and the Russians could undertake and that we could adequately monitor under the demanding time schedule, of a sufficiently irreversible and advantageous form to satisfy us and yet not intolerably susceptible of double cross from the Russian point of view, is a vital technical question. The answer will depend, among other things, on the facilities for monitoring Soviet and United States compliance with whatever arrangements can be negotiated. Facilities and personnel may be needed instantly and continuously so that there is no lapse, even a momentary one, in the synchronized process of withdrawal, tranquilization, redeployment, submission to inspection, or disarmament. This particular contingency, however, is not the kind that we would discuss with the Russians or make a basis for overt cooperation prior to the event.

In contrast, certain contingencies are suggested by the notion of "accidental war," particularly in its more mechanical and psychological connotations. This is the possibility of a war that might result from the triggering effect of an accident or error in the literal sense, or from electronic and other false alarms, or from the calculated mischief of a strategically irresponsible third party.[1] There may be a legitimate basis for considering with the Russians the possibility that we and they

---

[1] T. C. Schelling, "Meteors, Mischief, and War," *Bulletin of the Atomic Scientists,* XVI, No. 7, September 1960, pp. 292ff.

might want to respond cooperatively in the face of certain events, certain uncertainties, certain "crises." At least this may be true of those contingencies in which there is a strong presumption that neither side is on the verge of premeditated war. It may be important to each side to reassure itself of this fact and to provide reassurance to the other side, which might otherwise be tempted to respond explosively to the uncertain potentialities of the situation.

There are also crises of the kind that could occur in the course of a violent limited war, or in a political crisis where the piling up of strategic threats had got both sides so committed that withdrawal without submissiveness seemed impossible, and in which general war began to seem imminent. (An unimaginative way to project such a crisis may be to translate the Suez or Hungarian crises into the context of Berlin or Formosa.) If it were part of the strategy of each side to reassure the other that it was not about to launch all-out war momentarily, on condition that it could satisfy itself that the other was not about to do so either, it might be possible to specify a sufficient set of actions to be taken and actions to be abstained from to constitute such reassurance—on condition that they could be instantly, continuously, and reliably observed, with the observers reporting through channels known to be authentic. This might be the kind of crisis that, while not readily susceptible of overt acknowledgment and discussion between us and the Russians, could be in the backs of our minds as we talked or negotiated about some of the less sensitive contingencies.

PRE-EMPTIVE INSTABILITY

This whole notion rests on a single premise about the character of the strategic problem: that there is likely to be, during most of the foreseeable future, an enormous advantage in striking first in the event that war occurs, and that each side will not only be conscious of this but be conscious of the other's preoccupation with it. In any circumstances in which the likelihood of early or immediate war rises above a certain threshold, the urge to pre-empt, to pre-empt the other's pre-emption (and to pre-empt his attempt to pre-empt our pre-emption, and so on ad infinitum) may become a dominant motive. This implies that crises could develop very suddenly. And when they do, both sides may fervently wish that the premium on first strike did not exist; both sides may recognize that they are trapped by the unstable technology of attack and defense; both may recognize that each is, from its own point of view, tempted to attack first in "self-defense"; and both may wish that there were adequate cooperative measures to be taken ("measures to safeguard against surprise attack") to tranquilize the situation.

AGGRAVATING FACTORS

There are some special technical considerations here. One is that the things that each side does to make its own strategic force more secure—more alert, less vulnerable to surprise, and better able to strike quickly if that is the way the decision goes—are likely to be the kinds of actions that can be interpreted as preparations for attack. They are likely to be actions that increase the danger of "false alarm" on both sides and that could lead to a succession of decisions aggravating each side's perception of the need to pre-empt. Thus the things that each side does in the face of uncertainty and instability may, by mutual feedback, aggravate the instability.

A second consideration is that each side may take extraordinary measures in a crisis that could not be maintained indefinitely. Sooner or later there comes a need to withdraw, recuperate, disalert, or otherwise respond to the "fatigue" produced in the strategic force by the crisis itself. It may be that each side could much more readily relax into something like normal alert status if there were a means available for monitoring a synchronized relaxation on both sides. It would be exceedingly difficult to work out a reasonable plan for a synchronized relaxation of that sort; but it may be more than difficult—it may be impossible—to monitor compliance within the time available unless certain ingredients of the inspection system are prepared and prepositioned before the crisis.

IRREVERSIBLE DESTABILIZATION

Once we imagine crises that might require some kind of *temporary* strategic cooperation, it is not much farther to the notion of a crisis that *irreversibly* changes the basic political premise that we and the Russians work on. At the present time our mutual deterrence probably gets some stability from our both working on the premise that general war, though terribly possible, is rather unlikely; that we will both try hard to prevent it; that we are both deterred by the "mutual suicide" possibilities; and that neither of us has yet come demonstrably close to triggering the other's pre-emptive decision. It is possible, of course, that today's (relative) tranquility reflects only that the enemy has taken the decision to launch an attack, has computed that his advantage will be greatest at a date still in the future, and is lulling us in the interim. But the contrary judgment seems to prevail. If, however, we really get to the brink of all-out strategic war; if we display to ourselves and to the Russians our willingness to take extraordinary risks; if the Russians demonstrate the same; and particularly if the crisis is one that leads us to readjust our estimate of how likely general war has been all along, then we may at that point revise our basic operating premise and expect the Russians to do the same. We may have to stop relying on *inertia* as a supplement to mutual deterrence, and plan to live on the brink of general war. At such a point we might decide that nothing the Russians could ever do would reassure us, since efforts to reassure us would naturally be associated with definite plans to attack us; we might also conclude that no *moderate* arms-control measures could be of any significance. At that point drastic disarmament, negotiated under the threat of immediate general war, with drastic implications for the political balance of the world and without regard to the sensitivities of neutrals and allies, may suddenly be recognized as the alternative to war.

"CRASH DISARMAMENT"

It would be a shame if in such a contingency, in spite of powerful and unprecedented motives on both sides to negotiate drastic disarmament as an alternative to war, the possibility were precluded by the sheer technical inability of each side to monitor, instantly and continuously, the other side's compliance with whatever arrangement for synchronized crash disarmament could be worked out. It would be particularly disgraceful if the possibility were precluded by the failure of both sides to think seriously and imaginatively about such contingencies in advance and to make certain basic and flexible preparations for them, such as procurement, training, pre-positioning, and the establishment of a degree of coordination with each other.

The notion of "crash disarmament," suddenly motivated and demanding facilities for negotiation, observation, and communication on a time schedule wholly different from that of normal Cold-War disarmament discussions, may seem strange and unreal, implausible and unrealistic, unprecedented and improbable. But any idea of general war between the United States and the U.S.S.R. is somewhat strange and unreal, implausible and unprecedented; any idea of disarmament that goes beyond the most innocuous sort of diplomacy seems politically unrealistic. Perhaps a few concepts like massive retaliation or limited war have come to seem real, plausible, and consistent with the motives of one or both sides only because we have gained more familiarity with such ideas during the last several years. Thus the need for a technical capability to engage in sudden disarmament is not to be judged for its plausibility or probability in the ordinary sense of historical familiarity; it is to be judged for its relative likelihood in comparison with the drastic and unprecedented, strange, and unreal contingencies that are involved in any discussion of our strategic relation to the Russians in the years to come, such as war itself.

UNILATERAL ACTIONS

Unilaterally, there are a number of implications that flow from such a contingency if we take it seriously. One is to *design our own strategic forces,* and to deploy them and to control them, and to provide them with an operating doctrine, in a manner consistent with the *need to endure crises,* and with emphasis on their potential strategic role of *policing disarmament* (in addition to their strategic role of deterring attack or fighting a war). A second is the need to think about, to plan for, and to war-game in detail the question of what we should (could) demand of the Soviets if we did reach the point where, in the interest of averting imminent war, we were willing to use the threat of imminent war to support a disarmament ultimatum (including one that might put the Soviets at a real disadvantage). A third is to think about the problem of actually negotiating with the Russians in such a crisis, and making preparations for communication and inspection, not only so that we can monitor their compliance but so that—equally essential to the success of a negotiation—they can monitor ours. And a fourth is the question of what we might, in advance of any such crisis, talk about with the Russians, and do with them, either by way of reaching understandings with them or by way of exchanging facilities and practicing their use. It is mainly the fourth and, to a lesser extent the third, that relate to our bilateral negotiation with the Russians ahead of time.

THE POSITIVE-EVIDENCE CONCEPT

In considering the kind of surveillance scheme that could be mounted in a hurry, and especially in considering what could be accomplished by a small but adaptable elite group of potential inspectors and communicators, it is necessary to keep in mind the motives that would be brought to bear on the kind of crisis being discussed. There is only one premise about these motives that can make sense of the scheme discussed in this chapter: that is, that both sides would be emphatically eager, desperately eager, to convey the truth if in fact the truth were reassuring, and to behave in ways that facilitate observation of the truth. In a crash scheme of disarmament, or arms restraint, or mutual withdrawal and tranquilization, both sides would require *positive evidence* of compliance, rather than just an absence of evidence that the other is cheating. In these contingencies the inspectors would not look for evidence about what the other side was not doing; they would demand to see what it *was* doing.

As mentioned elsewhere,[2] there are two quite distinct criteria for judging an inspection system. One is how well the system gets at the truth in spite of the subject's best efforts to conceal it; the other is how well it helps the subject to display the truth when it is in his interest to do so. (The difference is a little like that between a scheme for discovering the guilty and a scheme for permitting the innocent to establish their innocence.)

To give an artificial illustration, if the Russians told us that a particular submarine was not within a thousand miles of the United States, and we did not know where the submarine was, it would be looking for a needle in a haystack to discover whether they were lying. But if *in fact* the submarine is not within a thousand miles of the United States and the Russians wish to prove it, they always have the option of producing the submarine for us to take a look at.

I am not trying to propose in a simple-minded way that the truth is easy to document if only the motive is there, or that in a crisis each side's sole interest will be to convey the truth and there is no need to worry about cheating. I am simply saying that while cheating and deception are problems even in the best of circumstances, and while authentic evidence of the truth may be difficult to convey even if one wants to, there is nevertheless an enormous difference between discovering the truth in spite of the enemy's best efforts to conceal it, and creating facilities for his provision of satisfactory evidence on the assumption that he is powerfully motivated to reassure us and knows that we can be reassured only if we are presented with overwhelming evidence that passes our most skeptical scrutiny.

Take a case that involves less military technology and tactics than the submarine, the question of where Khrushchev and other important members of the Russian government are at any moment. If they have

---

[2] T. C. Schelling, "Surprise Attack and Disarmament," in Klaus Knorr ed., *NATO and American Security*, Princeton University Press, Princeton, N.J., 1959, pp. 176–208.

just gone deep underground in Siberia, or on a sustained airborne alert or have taken some other action that might suggest they were preserving their command and saving their skins in preparation for general war, and if they alleged that they were doing no such thing but were minding their own ordinary business somewhere in the U.S.S.R., it could be nearly impossible to discover the truth. We could not know with certainty everywhere they were not, in order to deduce (or prove) where they momentarily were. But if in fact they have not absented themselves, and badly want to prove it, all they have to do is to produce Khrushchev—if we have somebody available who can recognize him on sight and report home instantly through authentic channels.

What I am trying to emphasize is that the ways they could prove to our complete satisfaction the *truth* about something they *are* doing, when in fact they are doing it and badly want us to know it, are much simpler than the ways that we would have to discover the falsehood of the same proposition if in fact it were false and we had to search for our own evidence. I emphasize this point not because it makes the problem easy, but because it may keep the problem from being utterly insoluble.

NATURE OF THE ARMS CONTROL

Ordinarily arms control is thought to depend on some minimum of mutual trust; and it could be argued that cooperation between enemies on the brink of war is out of the question because mutual trust would be nil. But any scheme of negotiated behavior would have to rest on the premise of absolute mistrust. In fact, it seems certain that unless thoroughgoing distrust were acknowledged on both sides, no understanding could be reached. The sheer intellectual clarity required to recognize the nature of the common interest would be incompatible with the pretense that there was any basis for mutual trust. Commitments would have to be entirely physical, not verbal or legal or moral. Each side must do things in an observable way, simultaneously with the other's doing corresponding things in an equally observable way, according to a sufficiently synchronized plan that neither acquires an attractive opportunity to double cross the other.

In the case for which I have used terms like "withdrawal from the brink," "relaxation," or other words suggesting return to the *status quo ante*, the negotiated scheme may have a limited horizon. The scheme succeeds in a matter of days, if not hours, or at most in a few weeks, or it fails altogether. But in the case of a crisis that irreversibly aggravates strategic instability, permanently changing each side's expectations about the other, and in which the *status quo ante* is militarily intolerable to both sides or at least to one of them, a more heroic negotiation is involved; and the requirements for surveillance are more varied.

To fix ideas, consider an extreme case. Suppose we get evidence that the Russians have decided to launch a surprise attack either when a good opportunity occurs or on some specified planning date. Suppose the circumstances—the ambiguity of the evidence, the motives we ascribe to the Russians (including their fear that we might attack first someday if they do not do it first), and the military balance between us—make it not only intolerable just to sit still and wait but unattractive to pre-empt ourselves, and not altogether satisfying just to announce to them that we know what they are up to and are prepared for it. It is conceivable that one alternative course available to us, one worth considering seriously, would be an ultimatum demanding that the Russians instantly begin to disarm themselves sufficiently, in conjunction with measures for our observation of what they are doing, so that they could not at any time (with good prospects of success) attack us by surprise. Suppose that, in the interest of making this course succeed, we consider certain similar (not necessarily equivalent) concessions that we might make in order to reduce Soviet vulnerability to a surprise attack by us while preserving or even enhancing the security and potency of our retaliatory forces. In other words, suppose that we decided that drastic and "permanent" disarmament of some sort (aimed mainly, but not necessarily exclusively, at the surprise-attack problem) would be our objective and that we would seek it through the threat of all-out war. ("Permanent" means, I suppose, not that we or they or both of us would be physically incapable of rearming, but that neither could take steps to rearm or to evade the scheme in other ways except through a time-consuming process that would give the other side sufficient warning for it to take heroic measures for the security of its own retaliatory forces or to initiate war quickly on terms corresponding to those existing under the disarmament scheme.)

Under these circumstances, it is apparently necessary to negotiate under extreme duress, and very quickly, a drastic permanent readjustment of the world military situation, of such a sort that both sides can move by stages from something exceedingly temporary to something slightly less temporary and so on by degrees into something reasonably durable. Presumably one adopts suddenly the most extraordinary alert and readiness posture, delivering the ultimatum that (hopefully) initiates negotiation; the enemy does the same as he sends his response; and what is now required is to withdraw from the very brink of general war by some synchronized process that not only avoids instant war but leads by degrees into a durable system, with each side recognizing that if the synchronized process fails to work, or if no satisfactory solution can be discovered, each side will be tempted to initiate war if only because it expects the other to do so. And all of this has to be monitored!

The near-hopelessness of such an attempt to divert the course of history might justify the reader's giving up the chapter at this point, if it were not for two attenuating considerations, one hopeful and the other not. The first is that the very gravity of the situation, the heroic nature of the accommodations required, and the unprecedented seriousness of the moment, might make certain courses of action feasible that ordinarily would not seem to be, by making leaders on both sides aware of the demands of the situation, of the risks in not trying as well as in trying, and of the enemy's seriousness in seeking a conservative outcome. The second consideration is that, however modest the prospects of finding a solution on the brink of war, the gravity of the problem suggests that we should do what we can to keep open the possibility.

THE SCHEME AND THE RESOURCES REQUIRED

If the philosophy is accepted, the next question is what can be done. The internal answer is, first of all, that we should think about it seriously; second, that we should work out articulate, detailed, sequential descriptions of such kinds of crises as we can imagine and experiment with them to see what personnel and material ingredients might be required ahead of time in the event that we wished, in a crisis, to pull out the plan and examine it as a basis for action. The most important preparation is intellectual; and if the things we might wish to do involve human and material prerequisites, and we can foresee to some extent what they are, we can begin to provide them. If in addition the likely success of any scheme would depend on some prior understanding, formal or informal, tacit or explicit, vague or precise, that we had worked out with our enemies, we should think about the best way to concert with them in advance at least on the kinds of communication that we might need for a sudden negotiation, and on some of the concepts and ideas that it would be good for us to share in the event we had to reach agreement on a crash scheme in a hurry. This is a tall order, and implies research within our own government, and, ultimately, some kind of formal or informal communication with the Russians.

There is then the question of what we might begin to do now, in cooperation with the Russians, to prepare for some of these eventualities, and particularly for those eventualities that can bear to be acknowledged and talked about. I suggest that we consider the general idea of two versatile, flexible, adaptable observation and communication forces, one for each side and each located in the other's country, whose main function is to be available to meet whatever demands are placed on them in a crisis—recognizing that in a crisis improvisation will be needed, and that improvisation may be enormously facilitated by the instant availability of some adaptable facilities physically located near the points on the earth where they will be required.[3]

In trying to imagine what would go into these versatile emergency forces, there are at least three lines of inquiry that may be helpful. One is to think about some of the *tasks* they might be called on to perform in an emergency. A second is to think about the *capabilities* they need, whatever their tasks may be. And a third is to think, in a practical way, about what they can be doing meanwhile, about what current excuses there are for bringing them into existence, about the tasks they could be used on *in the interim* for purposes of practice and as a means of supplementing the justification for their existence.

The last point is a sufficiently important one to deserve a moment's emphasis. If anything makes a force adaptable, resourceful, versatile, and so forth, it is probably exercise—doing novel jobs, meeting unforeseen situations, being continually tested and, most important of all, doing this as serious work and not in the form of make believe. Any inspection-observation-communication force that might be established with a view to its potential usefulness in unforeseeable contingencies should if possible have operating functions during the interim. Thus an important criterion, perhaps the most important in thinking about the creation of resourceful facilities, is what is currently going on, or can be initiated, that would yield as a by-product adaptable teams and facilities so located as to be useful in an emergency.

For example, in the event that there is some formal agreement on nuclear-test suspension or a jointly monitored nuclear-test program, there will be required teams of observers with equipment for inspection and for communication home, of a kind that could be exploited in an

---

[3] There is a prerequisite that, if not now provided, should come at the head of this proposal. It is that facilities and arrangements, of a mobile and versatile sort, for communication between the Soviet and American governments be worked out and in some way concerted on, and that each side have adequate communication and other arrangements within its own government and military services to make sudden negotiation possible in the circumstances that would surround a crisis of this sort.

emergency. Their location may be useful; some of their communication equipment may be useful; the transportation they have available may be useful; their mobility, their knowledge of the terrain, and the operating procedures they will have worked out for themselves and with the host country could be enormously helpful if they were called on to do something of an analogous sort in the approximate area where they were. Thus one promising line of approach is to inquire how we can design and deploy and operate our nuclear-test surveillance forces, and give them experience, and test their competence, and increase their resourcefulness, with the deliberate idea that they may, in unforeseen contingencies, be the best means we have for letting home governments see with their own eyes certain things that the host government may want them to see.

Take an example. To avoid technical or classified-information difficulties, consider a non-military aspect of an effort by the Russians to reassure us that they were not about to attack us, on an occasion when we thought (or they thought that we thought) that they might be about to. Suppose they wanted to claim (among other things) that they were not evacuating cities. How would we substantiate this claim?

The idea is that they might, in case of our attack, save lives by getting people out of the target area, particularly if fall-out protection were available in the countryside; so the people still in cities and unable to get out before our attack amount to "hostages" in our hands. Depending on the city, on whether the city would be attacked by aircraft or missiles, or other weapons, the time for evacuation might be anywhere from a fraction of an hour to a few hours. And we would like to know, to within the nearest fifteen minutes, whether or not the Russians had begun to evacuate most of their cities.

They say they have not; how do we find out? To make it interesting, suppose that the crisis is one in which both sides have taken security measures and ordinary communication is cut off between the United States and various newspaper correspondents and officials in Russia. In Moscow it may be only necessary for somebody in the Embassy to look out the window; but even he will not necessarily see all of Moscow, nor under the circumstances would he necessarily be permitted to travel around Moscow in a special car equipped with its own electric generator and transmitting equipment. Nor could he necessarily recognize evacuation if he saw a sample of it, given the confusion of the crisis already postulated. It may take some analysis and advance thinking to discern what is going on. Outside of Moscow, we might not have, on thirty-minute availability, observers who could authentically report reliable information about the evacuation of Soviet cities. But suppose we had mobile observers available at widely dispersed spots in Russia, whose loyalty and reliability to the United States were beyond question, who could communicate authentically to us, identifying themselves beyond question through cryptographic or other devices, who could in fact proceed to various Soviet cities and observe what was going on and let us know within a very few minutes. In that case, if the Russians in fact were not evacuating their cities and badly wanted us to know that they were not, they could take advantage of the resources we had available in Russia by asking us to dispatch our people to cities of our choice, providing our observers with police escort, helicopters or the right to use their own, and anything else that would facilitate the job.

(This illustration, incidentally, may be a good example of a principle that can often be applied to positive-evidence schemes—to schemes where there is a presumption that the enemy will comply or that his failure to comply settles the question—namely, the use of random sampling. Ordinary probability theory suggests that if the Russians tell us that they are not evacuating any of their cities, and out of 200 cities that we might be interested in we can select a dozen at random, and if we find that of the dozen we examine none shows signs of evacuation, the odds are exceedingly small that the Russians are evacuating more than an insignificant number of their cities; and the risks to the Russians of cheating are high.)

So much for the example, which the reader can elaborate from here as well as I. The example does help to identify a few of the characteristics that the force should have. Most important of all is that these versatile observers be able to establish *communication* with their own governments in ways that are quick and reliable, and in ways that are unquestionably authentic. They must, in other words, solve the problem of identifying themselves so that the enemy cannot intercept the messages and change them, or physically commandeer the facilities, without its becoming evident back home that something is amiss. (Whether the observers require privacy of communication, that is, cryptographic facilities, is a different question, to which the answer would depend on the job at hand.)

What they need by way of communication equipment—their own generators or access to electric power, transmitters, receivers, relay stations—is an interesting technical question, of which a part concerns the division of responsibility between themselves and their hosts. Probably, the more opportunity there is during normal times for these observers to simulate, in cooperation with their hosts, the kinds of things they would do in a crisis—or, better still, to engage in actual jobs that are similar to what they might be called on to do in a crisis—

the more opportunity there would be to work out routines and procedures and methods of coordination so that they could utilize the facilities of the host country. If instead there is little for them to do but sit in their shacks under blackout waiting for the great moment, they may have to rely more on working out procedures for self-contained and independent communication than on trying to improvise sudden collaboration with the host country at a critical moment.

In addition to communication, *mobility* is a prerequisite to an adequate surveillance force. Mobility has several dimensions. One is the ability to cover sizable distances fast, navigating and avoiding hindrances. Another is being located initially at strategic points, dispersed to keep portions of the force within quick travel time to the places where they might be demanded. A third dimension is fine-grain mobility —the ability to move about within a city, to pass check points, to avoid molestation, and to enjoy immunity—in short, to have the equivalent of police protection and political authority, immunity to language barriers and other nuisances, and good guidance, road maps, knowledge of vantage points and access to them, and whatever else is required. Additionally they need practice—practice not only in the functioning of their own equipment and in their own capabilities to navigate, but in coordinating with their hosts, in overcoming obstacles and nuisances, in recognizing the kinds of occurrences that are "normal" so that they can be distinguished from abnormal obstructions on those occasions when abnormal obstructions might have a strategic interpretation.

In looking about for other jobs that observation teams might perform, and that would consequently be an excuse for such teams and an opportunity to experiment with them, some of the suggestions for monitoring space activity may become relevant. Even a rather innocuous program for inviting each other's observers to attend launchings, particularly those involved in programs of a more scientific and less military sort, might provide an activity at which observation and communication techniques could be tested and developed. Considering, for example, how much the Russians can observe in this country without the help of formal invitations from our military establishment, there might not be a great deal to lose in inviting them to places like Cape Canaveral from time to time. So if we thought it might someday be useful to have in this country some Russian observers of undoubted loyalty to the U.S.S.R. whom we could call on to help Khrushchev see with his own eyes something that we wanted him to see, there may be several activities that are not so terribly sensitive or dramatic that they would provide the Soviets with significant military data, and that would give us a chance to see just how hard it might be, on a few minutes' notice, to get a Russian to a spot 1,000 miles from Washington to see something significant, establish an authentic line of communication home, and persuade his own government that he had seen it. A little practice may go a long way, at least in overcoming such simple things as language difficulties, traffic regulations, how to find the Russians on short notice, means of communication, and even the personal and emotional problems that bear on such questions as the size of a team and the kinds of escorts they need.

Perhaps the newly initiated multi-lateral agreement permitting the mutual surveillance in Antarctica provides, under interestingly rigorous climatic conditions, some opportunities for seeing what the problems are in looking over an enemy installation, at the enemy's invitation, and reporting home what is seen.

SOME RESERVATIONS

It may be difficult to persuade a reader that the concept of a Special Surveillance Force is valid and relevant, and nearly impossible to persuade him that there is anything to be done about it. Beyond that, it has to be admitted that even if something can be done, it is by no means obvious that we and the Russians both have an interest in it, or even that *we* do whether the Russians do or not. It may go without saying, for most of us, that if drastic disarmament should ever become the only alternative to imminent war, and the war that is imminent looks pretty unpromising, a scheme to facilitate disarmament efforts would be all to the good. But there are at least two kinds of problems that reduce the advantages of such a scheme and that have to be acknowledged even if we decide on reflection that they are not of controlling importance.

One is that measures to avert war and to facilitate disarmament, even measures to avert accidental war, may reduce the potency of some of our deterrent threats, may reduce the Russians' fears of the consequences of their own aggressive actions, may remove some of the inhibitions on limited war by suggesting that the likelihood of explosion into bigger war is not as serious as it might have been. An important deterrent to Soviet aggression may well be the fear of "accidental war," an unpremeditated war, a war that does not begin with a cold-blooded determination by the United States to retaliate massively but rather comes out of the complex interaction of the fears and commitments of both sides—a war that results from false alarm, panic, mischief, human error, or a dynamic process of decisions whose consequences cannot be entirely foretold even by those who make them.[4] Reduce the fear of all-out war, including the fear of inadvertent war—perhaps *especially* the fear of inadvertent war—and an important deterrent to Soviet or Chinese aggression may be gone. Provide facilities for avoiding war at the eleventh hour and the Soviets may enjoy increased confidence that, whatever they do beforehand, they can always be saved at the eleventh hour and that the eleventh hour will be recognizable when it comes. Establish procedures and facilities that suggest that, when we might have launched all-out war, we will launch all-out negotiations instead, and the Russians may enjoy a new sense of immunity to American retaliation.

These are reservations that attach to any of the so-called "measures to safeguard against surprise attack," and that may similarly apply to measures to forestall general war at the last minute. How important they are depends on whether one is mainly concerned with the consequences of general war and the probability that it will occur, or with the need to intimidate and inhibit and discipline an aggressive enemy in circumstances short of total war.

The second sort of considerations that give one pause are of a lesser order. A flexible and adaptable observation system of the kind hinted at so sketchily here could be abused if one side or the other wanted to abuse it. One can feign alarm and demand reassurance as a means of using an observation force to get information not intended under the scheme, either information about how the enemy responds to dramatic events or just snapshot information about his posture that might be obtained by putting an observation force in action. The enemy can "spoof"; he can engage in spectacular actions that activate the system and play on our nerves but that, because of the system, are less risky than they might have been. He can accuse us of abusing the system for purposes of espionage. It is even conceivable that if we had our own trusted observers in Soviet territory who could see things that we knew existed but preferred not to acknowledge, we would find it more difficult not to acknowledge them. (If, for example, either side occasionally intruded into the other's territory and pretended not to, or if either liked to accuse the other of engaging in activities whose occurrence would be embarrassing to the other, it might be difficult or equally embarrassing to continue this once one's own observers could be called on to witness the truth.) These are in addition to all the other diplomatic and propaganda dangers that can readily be imagined.

---

[4] T. C. Schelling, *The Strategy of Conflict*, Harvard University Press, Cambridge, Mass., 1960, Ch. 8.

HOW TO GET STARTED

If it is decided that there is something to this idea and that the dangers are outweighed by the advantages, and that there may be programs of action that allow us to give a stand-by scheme some exercise, the immediate question is how to open up the subject with the Russians and how to formulate the problem.

One possibility is to shift our approach to "safeguards against surprise attack." There are, broadly speaking, two different aspects to the surprise attack problem. One is premeditated surprise attack; the other is pre-emptive attack, false alarm, accidental war, and the like. The two are tied together, but in a rough way the distinction can be made. If one makes the distinction, it looks as though discussions and negotiations with the Russians on the subject of surprise-attack schemes have so far been oriented, at least implicitly, toward the problem of premeditated attack. I say "implicitly" because there has been no explicit agenda or agreement on the point; but what has been discussed seems to imply long-term surveillance rather than schemes to cope with crises. And the United States has generally deprecated discussion of "accidental war."

I imagine that some of our reluctance to talk to the Russians about measures to forestall "accidental war" stems from our sensitivity to public opinion, particularly opinion abroad, and an unwillingness to acknowledge that there could be any basis for the Soviet contention that "accidental war" (however it is defined) is a real possibility. But that phase of our public relations may be past, and maybe we need not be quite so defensive about it. Furthermore, there are special difficulties in discussing measures to safeguard against premeditated surprise attack; it must be a serious embarrassment to both sides to talk about the kinds of vulnerabilities they are most preoccupied with. The very information needed to make progress is the most sensitive kind.

One might say that the *presumption of mutual interest* is strong in the prevention of unpremeditated war (the so-called "accidental war"), and that one may possibly discuss the subject without getting too close to the touchy question of just where he is most vulnerable and just what kind of surprise he would least like his enemy to engage in.

If, then, we acknowledge that unpremeditated war, or inadvertent war, or accidental war, or war resulting from a crisis of some sort is a significant possibility, and that the existence of a premium on striking first aggravates the possibility, we can assimilate this possibility to the general problem of surprise attack; and there may be a basis for discussing fairly openly just what kinds of joint measures could be taken to reduce misunderstanding in those cases where war caused by misunderstanding is imminent. It may be possible to begin with a list of reasonably innocuous hypothetical occurrences that could lead to a misunderstanding of each other's strategic intentions, and to discuss the kinds of measures that might lead to mutual reassurance and improved understanding.[5]

If, to take an example, there were no propaganda disadvantages in adopting the hypothetical premise that an accidental nuclear-weapon detonation might occur somewhere on the face of the earth, and specifically in the United States or the U.S.S.R., it might be a useful exercise to think with the Russians about the way that each of us could reassure the other that we were not misinterpreting the event as the harbinger of general war, and were not so afraid of the other's misinterpretation as to feel obliged to initiate a pre-emptive attack. (Perhaps events attributable to mischievous third parties would be a non-committal way to begin discussions.) We could at least discuss such simple questions as how to establish a line of communication between Washington and Moscow, and how to get inspectors not only to the scene of the accident but to vantage points where they could see that the nation was calm rather than frenzied and that strategic forces were not being readied for attack.

At least it is worth thinking about.

Since this proposal was first published in 1960, there has been reduced emphasis on surprise attack, a test ban without local inspection, and the establishment of direct cable and radio teletype communications between Washington and Moscow. The latter now appears to provide the best basis for improvising something of the sort discussed in this chapter. There has been, at Geneva, some discussion of an exchange of special military missions; perhaps the "hot line" together with such missions could somewhat serve the purpose discussed above or at least be steps in that direction. The "hot line" is at least an acknowledgment that the problem exists and that concrete measures can be found to help deal with it.

---

[5] T. C. Schelling, "Reciprocal Measures for Arms Stabilization," *Daedalus,* Fall 1960, pp. 892–913.

PART V

INTERNATIONAL
INSTRUMENTALITIES
AND STABILITY

Chapter II

International Integration: The European and the Universal Process

ERNST B. HAAS

EUROPEAN AND UNIVERSAL INTEGRATION

The established nation-state is in full retreat in Europe while it is advancing voraciously in Africa and Asia. Integration among discrete political units is a historical fact in Europe, but distintegration seems to be the dominant motif elsewhere. Cannot the example of successful integration in Europe be imitated? Could not the techniques of international and supranational cooperation developed in Luxembourg, Paris, and Brussels be put to use in Accra, Bangkok, and Cairo, as well as on the East River in New York? Or, in a different perspective, will not the progress of unity in Europe inevitably have its integrating repercussions in other regions and at the level of the United Nations even without efforts at conscious imitation?

Such a development would be most satisfying. Presumably it would contribute to world peace by creating ever-expanding islands of practical cooperation, eventually spilling over into the controversy-laden fields

---

This chapter originally appeared in the Summer 1961 issue of International Organization.

which threaten us directly with thermonuclear destruction. The functionalist theory of international peace might be put to work by a generalization of the European mode of post-1945 international cooperation. Further, those who hope to contribute to the peaceful solution of conflict could take much solace from such a development, for the post-1945 European mode of resolving conflicts among states has demonstrated that "there often comes a moment when there is a simultaneous revolution of interests on both sides and unity precipitates itself," to quote Mary Follett.[1]

Before abandoning ourselves to such pleasant speculation, however, we would do well to state systematically what we have learned about the causes of European integration and then to investigate where else these causes might be operative. This effort calls for some definitions.

We are interested in tracing progress toward a terminal condition called *political community*. Successful nation-states constitute such communities and subsequent amalgamations of several such states may also form communities. A variety of constitutional and structural factors are compatible with this notion; political community exists when there is likelihood of internal peaceful change in a setting of contending groups with mutually antagonistic claims. The process of attaining this condition among nation-states we call *integration*, the process whereby political actors in several distinct national settings are persuaded to shift their loyalties, expectations, and political activities toward a new and larger center, whose institutions possess or demand jurisdiction over the pre-existing national states. It should be noted that the objective economic, social, and communications "factors" often identified with "integration," in my scheme, are conditions typical of an ongoing political community. At best they may serve as indicators to help us assess the progress of integration.

This focus precludes attention to what may be called the "immanent myth" of European unity, which owes its inspiration to cultural-historical antecedents considered equally relevant to the contemporary process of integration. It appears to me that European unity under the Roman, Frankish, and medieval Roman-German imperial realms has no more analytical importance than the unity of all Islam in the eighth century, the domains of the Ming Empire in the fifteenth or the Guptas in the fifth. The mere fact that specific regions were unified politically and culturally at one time seems not to prevent them from subsequently dividing into warring nations denying in their conduct the cultural unity

---

[1] As cited in Metcalf and Urwick, eds., *Dynamic Administration*, Harper & Brothers, New York, 1940, p. 40.

the historian wishes to impute to them: they do not then constitute any kind of political community. If this is so, we cannot use some previous historical experience that involved the notion of community as an argument for assuming the natural and inevitable re-emergence of this happy state of affairs. It may indeed emerge, but in response to the factors we shall discuss. Naturally, in the political advocacy of integration by some specific movement, the "memory" of a historical community may play its part in the construction of a myth; but this does not make the past an active causative agent. On the other hand, a series of traumatic events vividly remembered by a generation subjected to integration may launch and then spur the process. The role of two world wars of unprecedented destructiveness and the threat of the victory of a revolutionary totalitarian movement at the end of the second of these wars were undoubtedly primary among the specific stimuli that, in western Europe, made people receptive to the historical-cultural arguments of the mythmakers. This combination of circumstances does not easily permit repetition elsewhere.

Conflict resolution is a particularly interesting indicator for judging progress along the path of integration. A close study of negotiating processes in international relations suggests the prevalence of three types of compromise, each indicative of a certain measure of integration.

(1) The least demanding we may call accommodation on the basis of the minimum common denominator. Equal bargaining partners gradually reduce their antagonistic demands by exchanging concessions of roughly equal value. Gains and losses are easily identified, but the impact of the transaction never goes beyond what the *least* cooperative bargaining partner wishes to concede. This mode of compromise is typical of classic diplomatic negotiations.

(2) Accommodation by "splitting the difference" carries us a little farther along the path of integration. As before, demands are reduced and concessions of roughly equal value are exchanged among autonomous bargain-units. But in this mode of compromise the mediatory services of a secretary general or *ad hoc* international expert study group may be admitted by the parties. Conflict is resolved, not on the basis of the will of the least cooperative, but somewhere between the final bargaining positions. This type of negotiation is prevalent in international economic organizations and in other dealings permitting financial identification of gains or losses, such as the formulation of a scale of assessments for Members of the United Nations.

(3) Finally, accommodation on the basis of deliberately or inadvertently upgrading the common interests of the parties takes us closest to the peaceful change procedures typical of a political community with

its full legislative and judicial jurisdictions, lacking in international relations. To confuse matters further, this mode of conflict resolution is often identified as "integration," as by Mary Follett, who wrote that it, unlike mere compromise, signified "that a solution has been found in which both desires have found a place, that neither side has had to sacrifice anything." [2] If this is so it must mean that the parties succeeded in redefining their conflict so as to work out a solution at a higher level, which almost invariably implies the expansion of the mandate or task of an international or national governmental agency. In terms of results, this mode of accommodation maximizes what I have elsewhere called the "spill-over" effect of international decisions: policies made pursuant to an initial task and grant of power can be made real only if the task itself is expanded, as reflected in the compromises among the states interested in the task. In terms of method, the upgrading of the parties' common interests relies heavily on the services of an institutionalized mediator, whether a single person or a board of experts, with an autonomous range of powers. It thus combines intergovernmental negotiation with the participation of independent experts and spokesmen for interest groups, parliaments, and political parties. It is this combination of interests and institutions that we shall identify as "supranational." The initial creation of such an agency, of course, demands a creative compromise among the states parties to the effort, based on the realization that certain common interests cannot be attained in any other way. This in turn presupposes that identical and converging policy aims, rather than antagonistic ones, predominated at the moment when the supranational organization was set up.

Each of these modes of accommodation, in addition to specifying a type of outcome relating to intensities of integration, also is typified by appropriate institutional mechanisms. There exists, moreover, a fourth prominent procedural device—parliamentary diplomacy—that is capable of producing any of the three outcomes. Parliamentary diplomacy, as Dean Rusk defined it, implies the existence of a continuing organization with a broad frame of reference, public debate, rules of procedure governing the debate, and the statement of conclusions in a formal resolution arrived at by some kind of majority vote.[3] When bodies like the United Nations or the Council of Europe define a conflict situation by filtering discussion through this machinery they may also be setting the limits within which eventual settlement comes about, though parlia-

---

[2] *Ibid.*, p. 32.
[3] Dean Rusk, "Parliamentary Diplomacy—Debate vs. Negotiation," *World Affairs Interpreter*, Summer 1955, Vol. 26, No. 2, pp. 121–122.

mentary diplomacy rarely defines the actual terms of the settlement. Instead it mobilizes political mediatory forces—the uncommitted states, parties, groups, or persons—whose voice in the settlement process is given volume by the reluctance of the parties to the dispute to annoy the mediating forces. Since the institutional context in which parliamentary diplomacy can be practiced maximizes the representation of a variety of interests emanating from the same nation, it opens up areas of maneuver that are foreclosed in negotiations exclusively conducted by carefully instructed single agents of foreign ministries. To that extent it facilitates a greater amount of integration even though it does not necessarily produce outcomes which upgrade common interests.

Where can these modes of accommodation be identified in the history and institutions of European integration?

THE LESSON OF EUROPEAN INTEGRATION

Clearly all these modes of accommodation are part of the European pattern of international adjustment. While they do not provide the only indicators of degrees of integration, they appear to be particularly strategic ones in that they focus on decision-making, thereby acting as a summary of, and an abstraction upon, other factors that could also be used as indicators. Broadly speaking, international institutions maximizing decision-making by means of the second and third modes yield the greatest amount of progress toward the goal of political community.

Parliamentary diplomacy is the chief contribution to European unity which can be credited to the various parliamentary assemblies. They have not meaningfully controlled their various executives nor have they legislated in any real sense, though they have attempted and partially exercised powers in both these fields. But they have acted as a spur to the formation of new voluntary elite groups across national boundaries— the European political groups—and the inter-play among these has produced a type of diplomatic problem-solving that takes its inspiration from parliamentary resolutions and is able to upgrade common interests. As examples we may cite the work of the Council of Europe in relation to the Saar, in refugee relief and resettlement, and in the relaxation of frontier formalities. We may add the work of the Nordic Council in the negotiation of the now superseded Nordic Common Market Agreement. But let it be admitted at the same time that the total contribution of parliamentary diplomacy is not very great. It found no institutional outlet at all in the Organization for European Economic Cooperation (OEEC); yet that organization's contribution to integration was sub-

Summary of Integration Experience of European Organizations

Organization	Institutions	Mode of Accommodation and Functions		Ideological-Social Environment
OEEC–EPU Age: 12 years	Inter-governmental; weak secretariat; strong autonomous expert bodies	Upgrading common interests: Splitting difference: Minimum common denominator:	Remove trade barriers; Divide U.S. aid; emergency distribution of goods; Planning for long-range economic growth	Mixed ideologically, economically, social structure
Council of Europe Age: 12 years	Inter-governmental; inter-parliamentary; weak secretariat; rudimentary judicial institution	Minimum common denominator; Minimum common denominator plus parliamentary diplomacy: Splitting difference and parliamentary diplomacy:	European integration in general; European legislation; Solution of specific short-range problems	Mixed ideologically, economically, social structure, though united on democracy
NATO Age: 13 years	Inter-governmental; inter-parliamentary; strong secretariat; strong autonomous expert bodies	Minimum common denominator: Splitting difference:	Integrated defense policy; Coordinated foreign policy; joint defense economics;	Mixed ideologically, economically, social structure, and in military power

Nordic Council Age: 8 years	Inter-governmental; inter-parliamentary	Upgrading common interests: Parliamentary diplomacy plus minimum common denominator	Planning for new weapons and strategy; Economic integration; legal standardization; social security harmonization	Homogeneous ideologically, but mixed in social structure and economic development
Benelux Age: 17 years	Inter-governmental; inter-parliamentary	Minimum common denominator:	Economic integration	Homogeneous on all counts, except role of agriculture
EEC, ECSC, Euratom Age: 9 and 4 years	Supranational	Upgrading common interests: Splitting difference: Minimum common denominator:	Economic integration in long run; Solution of short-run economic problems; Labor mobility; nuclear planning	Homogeneous on all counts (except in southern Italy)
Western European Union Age: 6 years	Inter-governmental; inter-parliamentary; weak secretariat; strong autonomous expert bodies	Parliamentary diplomacy plus minimum common denominator: Upgrading common interests:	Foreign policy coordination; Arms control	Homogeneous on all counts except separate UK ideological position and special German military position
EFTA Age: 3 years	Inter-governmental; weak secretariat	Splitting difference:	Remove trade barriers	Mixed on all counts

stantial even though it operated primarily on the level of accommodation by "splitting the difference."

The most successful institutions in Europe are the "Communities" of the Six, constitutional hybrids that once caused nightmares to the public lawyer. They facilitate the resolution of conflict by virtue of all three modes, but the upgrading of common interests is their true contribution to the art of political integration. All fundamental decisions are made by the Councils of Ministers. But they are decisions based on continuous compromise, constantly informed by generally respected expert bodies with constitutional powers of their own and in constant contact with supranational voluntary associations and interest groups. The character of decision-making stimulates interest groups to make themselves heard; it spurs political parties in Strasbourg and Luxembourg to work out common positions; it creates an enormous pressure on high national civil servants to get to know and establish rapport with their opposite numbers; and it sharpens the sensitivities of the legal profession to European norms and political processes in preparation for the inevitable flood of litigation before the Court of Justice. In short, many of the decisions are integrative in their immediate economic consequences as well as in the new expectations and political processes which they imply. It is this indirect result that is maximized by the mixture of institutions that usually achieves accommodation at a higher level of agreement as compared to the initial bargaining positions of the parties. Earlier decisions, including the ones constituting the Communities, spill over into new functional contexts, involve more and more people, call for more and more interbureaucratic contact and consultation, thereby creating their own logic in favor of later decisions, meeting, in a community direction, the new problems that grow out of the earlier compromises.

Intergovernmental institutions of the classic variety, even when assisted by respected international civil servants and advisory boards, have not been able to match this performance. The North Atlantic Treaty Organization (NATO) and OEEC, for reasons to be explored, have continued to make their contribution to integration by means of compromises based on techniques found also in the United Nations. They have transcended these only in relation to certain tasks hinging on the direct implications of the welfare state.

This brings us face to face with the key question of which organizational *functions,* or tasks, have contributed most to the process of integration in Europe. The superficial answer clearly points to the field of economics; but by no means all organizations with an economic competence have performed equally well and few of them solve their problems on the basis of upgrading common interests. Parliamentary diplomacy has apparently been of importance in advancing economic integration only in the Nordic Council; OEEC functioned on the basis of "splitting the difference" or compromising on the level of the minimum common denominator in all areas except those relating to currency convertibility and the removal of quotas (in which common interests were indeed upgraded). The European Free Trade Association (EFTA) has not taken strides comparable to those of the European Economic Community (EEC) and the European Coal and Steel Community (ECSC).

Not merely economic tasks, therefore, but the degree of functional specificity of the economic task is causally related to the intensity of integration. The more specific the task, the more likely important progress toward political community. It is not enough to be concerned with the reduction of trade barriers or the forecasting of industrial productivity. Specificity of task is essential, with respect to such assignments as creating a common market for narrowly defined products, unifying railway rates, removing restrictive practices in certain branches of industry, removing import quotas by fixed percentage points during fixed periods, and the like. Functional specificity, however, may be so trivial as to remain outside the stream of human expectations and actions vital for integration. This would seem to be the case with the standardization of railway rolling stock, for example, or the installation of uniform road signs. The task, in short, must be both specific and economically important in the sense of containing the potential for spilling over from one vital area of welfare policy into others.

Non-economic tasks have shown themselves much more barren than economic tasks. The cultural activities of the Council of Europe lack a focus on intensely experienced human wants. Its emergency aid measures have been short-range and its contributions to the solution of political tensions non-repetitive. The "European review" function is much too vague to yield observable results. The standardization efforts of the Nordic Council lack the stimulus of controversy and debate; they are so deeply rooted in the Scandinavian setting that one suspects integration of proceeding even without the Council. Continuous contact among civil servants and ministers is capable of contributing to integration in narrowly defined areas even without the participation of parliamentarians. The only functionally specific assignment of the Western European Union (WEU) is the supervision of the arms aspects of the Paris and London Agreements (1954). This function is being carried out in a supranational manner, but the reason is in the non-controversial and non-recurrent aspect of German rearmament, at least at the intergovernmental level. The other activities of WEU are unlikely to be remembered by history.

What about the field of European conventions? Surely these are specific in content and many of them relate to economics and welfare policy. The fact remains, however, that their very content reflects merely the minimum common denominator among the existing practices and policies of the member states, and that the Council had to resort to the device of "partial agreements" to get beyond this level. Conventions that depart from this denominator tend not to be ratified by the country whose standards are below the norms fixed in Strasbourg.[4] Integration, therefore, is advanced by the European conventions only to the extent that their content calls for a new—a supranational— political process that can generate new expectations and policies. This, probably, is the case only with reference to the field of human rights, a very significant field indeed. Moreover, there recently evolved in the Council the practice, among the members of the Committee of Ministers, of reporting annually on the willingness and speed of ratifying conventions. While this practice falls short of supranationality it nevertheless exposes the reporting country to the possibility of criticism and pressure.

Military and defense questions have not displayed a close affinity to integration unless the issue involves the related question of saving and allocating resources for welfare measures. NATO's experience in the financing of infrastructure programs, weapons research, integration of air warning systems, and the switch to centrally controlled nuclear deterrents indicates that the upgrading of common interests does take place—not without obstacles and delays—when the economic burdens of defense for small countries are considered incompatible with their welfare commitments. But the other activities of the Atlantic Alliance make plain that more primitive modes of accommodation continue to flourish and that integration is more pronounced on paper than in the command post, the procurement center, and the council chamber.

This survey of the functional lessons of European integration leads to the inevitable conclusion that functional contexts are autonomous. Integrative forces that flow from one kind of activity do not necessarily infect other activities, even if carried out by the same organization. OEEC could not repeat in the field of tariff bargaining the results it

---

[4] The conventions dealing with the equivalence of university degrees and the movement of persons are exceptions to this generalization. Both of them involved some measure of upgrading common interests.

obtained on questions of convertibility. NATO cannot transfer its success in planning strategy for new weapons systems to the standardization of the enlistment period; and ECSC has shown itself more adept in negotiating cumulative compromises on the creation of a common market than on short-run solutions for the coal crisis. Decisions made by identical officials, in organizations with a stable membership, in a non-revolutionary socio-ideological setting with similar institutional characteristics nevertheless vary sharply in their integrative impact, depending on the functional context. If this is true even in the European setting, how much more true it is likely to be in the United Nations. But the converse proposition is equally important: the autonomy of functional contexts means that disintegration in one range of relations among certain states does not necessarily imply parallel disintegration in other relations among the same states. Thus the breakdown of the Free Trade Area negotiations did not entail a retreat from monetary convertibility; NATO's work on unifying air raid warning systems was not interrupted by the split between the Six of EEC and the Seven of EFTA.

The attempt to compare the European experience with efforts elsewhere compels attention to the environment in which the process of integration is taking place, which some scholars call the "background" factors. This investigation will show that while "Europe"—in the largest sense of the nineteen countries west of the Iron Curtain—possesses no completely common factor at all, significant islands of almost identical environmental factors exist among certain of them.

Social structure provides one set of factors. With the exception of Greece, Turkey, Portugal, parts of Spain, and southern Italy, the western European social scene is dominated by pluralism. Articulate voluntary groups, led by bureaucratized but accessible elites, compete with each other more-or-less rationally for political power and social status. The population is mobilized and participates in this process through affiliation with mass organizations. In the countries mentioned, however, affective and functionally diffuse social relations prevail.

Economic and industrial development furnishes a second set of factors. With the exception of the same countries as above plus Ireland, we are dealing with a very high level of economic development—including that of the countries in which the dominant products are agricultural—in productivity, investment, and consumption. Significantly correlated with industrialization we find the usual high degree of urbanization and ever-growing demands for government services and durable consumer goods. We also find increasing demands on limited natural resources and greater dependence on foreign (or regional) trade. But note some partial exceptions: Norway's industrial weakness compared to that of Sweden, Belgium's agricultural inefficiency compared to that of the Netherlands.

Ideological patterns provide the final set of factors. Since policies of integration are, in the first instance, advanced or blocked by the activities of political parties and their ministers, parties may be used as an index of ideological homogeneity. A given cluster of countries is ideologically "homogeneous" if the divisions among the political parties are, very roughly, the same among all the countries in the cluster, when the principles professed and the concrete socio-economic interests represented by the parties are roughly analogous on both sides of a frontier. Given this definition, the Scandinavian countries emerge as ideologically homogeneous among themselves (with the partial exception of Iceland) but quite dissimilar from the rest of Europe. The Benelux countries, West Germany, Switzerland, and Austria seem to be homogeneous and seem to have considerable affinity with Italy and France. But a disturbing element is introduced here by the large anti-parliamentary minorities in France and Italy. Portugal, Greece, Spain, and Turkey lack the typical European socio-economic structure and therefore the appropriate party systems; they do not fit into any neat ideological package. The British and Irish parties show some affinity for their continental colleagues, especially the socialists, but the patterns of interest aggregation and political style differ sufficiently to prevent the positing of a homogeneous pattern. We therefore have two large ideological clusters: (1) Scandinavia, and (2) the Six (plus Switzerland and Austria), as well as a number of single national systems whose characteristics seem *sui generis*.

Let us relate these environmental patterns to the integration process. Integration proceeds most rapidly and drastically when it responds to socio-economic demands emanating from an industrial-urban environment, when it is an adaptation to cries for increasing welfare benefits and security born by the growth of a new type of society. In the words of two European scholars:

For decades industrialism has been revising the workways and consuming habits of people everywhere. It has enabled cities to grow and the urban way of life to spread. Urbanism is the great outreaching dynamic, breaking down isolation and encroaching upon tradition. Modern industrial urbanism is innately inimical to any isolation. It demands access and stimulates mobility. As earlier it resisted being confined to city walls, now it resists being confined to limited political areas. This resistance to confinement is greater than the resistance against the encroachments. In the measure that industrial urbanism has gained in this contest against the rooted barriers—in that measure integration is needed. The effort toward European integration reflects this need of industrial urbanism for wider organization.[5]

I reject the teleological aspects of this statement. In terms of a social process based on rational human perceptions and motives, no mere concept "calls for" or "needs" anything; a discrete set of group motives, converging with motives of cognate groups from across the border, results in a certain pattern of policy; the aims and the policy reflect demands born from the environment, and the latter policies may well change the environment in a wholly unintended fashion. Only in this sense, then, does industrial urbanism favor integration. Because the modern "industrial-political" actor fears that his way of life cannot be safeguarded without structural adaptation, he turns to integration; but by the same token, political actors who are neither industrial, nor urban, nor modern in their outlook usually do not favor this kind of adaptation, for they seek refuge instead in national exclusiveness.

Thus, countries dominated by a nonpluralistic social structure are poor candidates for participation in the integration process. Even if their governments do partake at the official level, the consequences of their participation are unlikely to be felt elsewhere in the social structure. Hence the impact of European integration, in all its aspects, has been minimal in Portugal, Turkey, and Greece. Finally, sufficient ideological homogeneity for value-sharing among important national elite groups is essential for rapid integration. The implications for Europe are obvious as reflected in the differential rates of progress toward political community which have been made within Scandinavia, within the Six, and within Benelux compared to the all-European level represented by OEEC, NATO, and the Council of Europe.

In addition to these environmental considerations, which relate to the internal characteristics of the region undergoing integration, there are often external environmental factors of importance. Fear of a common enemy is an absolutely necessary precondition for integration in military organizations: without the Soviet Union there would have been no NATO. But the "common enemy" may be a more subtle manifestation, such as fear of external groupings of culturally and economically suspect forces: such considerations were not irrelevant to the "third force" argument that entered the integration process among the Six and is apparent in the convergence of interests which resulted in the Organization for Economic Cooperation and Development

---

[5] Jan J. Schokking and Nels Anderson, "Observations on the European Integration Process," *Journal of Conflict Resolution*, December, 1960, Vol. 4, No. 4, p. 409.

(OECD). While external environments produce motives favoring integration, they are never sufficient in themselves to explain the rate and intensity of the process.

Institutions, functions, and environments provide useful categories for arranging the human data among which our various modes of accommodation made themselves felt; but they do not exhaust the list of crucial given factors of which we are all aware and without which the process of integration simply cannot be discussed. Variations in national policy, for instance, are fundamental to the life of international organizations, especially in agencies that do not possess the institutional power to influence significantly the policy aims of their member states.

The importance of this lesson must be illustrated from the experience of one of the more successful European organizations, OEEC, with multilateral accommodation in liberalizing trade and payments—the aspect of OEEC that contributed most to integration in Europe.[6] The typical OEEC procedure included confrontation, collection of detailed information, mediation in closed sessions, and the working out of specific solutions to crises by autonomous bodies of national experts. The procedures were perfected during the period (1948–51) when the chief task of OEEC was the distribution of United States aid, assistance that was conditional on trade and payments liberalization. During the next phase (1952–56) the procedure continued and was remarkably successful in further removing obstacles to intra-regional commerce, despite the cessation of United States aid. Why? Largely because the major national policies continued to be oriented toward liberalization, and the recurrent French and British payments crises could therefore not successfully challenge the multilateral decision-making process; continuing French and British demands for a relaxation of the OEEC Code resulted in successive compromises along the principle of "splitting the difference," but involving the upgrading of common interests in the system of review and accountability which accompanied the relaxation. Since 1956, all this has changed. Further economic integration has become enmeshed in the political issue of the Six against the Seven, with the result that the procedures that had apparently been institutionalized successfully in an earlier phase of OEEC's life have stagnated with disuse. Fundamental changes in national policies provide the crucial explanatory variable.

This process went on in a setting of intergovernmentalism. More than in the supranational setting, an environment of intergovernmentalism permits great freedom to states strongly endowed in a specific func-

---

[6] My discussion of OEEC benefited greatly from the advice and criticism of William Diebold, Jr., and Robert Triffin.

tional context. Let us use monetary cooperation as an example. The history of OEEC suggests—as that of ECSC and EEC does not—that certain types of states can use their special bargaining power more readily to get their way. Thus, economically weak countries whose trade is not crucial to the system are readily exempted from the governing norms and play little part in decision-making; but economically strong countries, in terms of total foreign trade *and* credit capacity, possess a *de facto* veto power. Structural creditors whose role in regional trade is secondary, occasionally assert a veto power and delay decisions, but their influence is never dominant. Structural or occasional debtors (France and the United Kingdom) with a very important stake in regional trade are able to exercise a constant blackmail power and to succeed in obtaining exemptions from regional rules, since they are immune to the threat of retaliation and responsive only to the techniques of discreet mediation and confrontation.

The lesson of European integration can be summarized as follows:

1. *Institutionally,* supranational bodies most readily lend themselves to accommodation on the basis of upgrading common interests. This is equally true of intergovernmental bodies that permit certain of their expert commissions the role usually associated with the Communities of the Six, such as the OEEC Steering Board for Trade, the Council of Europe's Commissioner for Refugees, and WEU's Armaments Control Agency. These institutions are least susceptible to the alternation of phases and most likely to develop cumulative decision-making precedents.

2. *Functionally,* specific economic tasks resolving policy differences emerging from previous imperfect compromises on welfare questions, but involving large mass interests, are most intimately related to rapid integration. Conflicts may be resolved by all the usual methods, but upgrading common interests predominates. The tendency toward autonomy of tasks can be overcome only by building into the institutions specific assignments that maximize the spill-over process.

3. *Environmentally,* integration fares best in situations controlled by social groupings representing the rational interests of urban-industrial society, groups seeking to maximize their economic benefits and dividing along regionally homogeneous ideological-political lines. Changing national policy inhibits integration unless compensated by strong central institutions maximizing the spill-over process.

Obviously, integration may take place and has taken place among nations that have few of these characteristics and through international organizations that depart little from the classic intergovernmental pattern. But the pace and intensity of such integration is pallid in such a context as compared to the situation in which all optimal conditions are met. Hence it should come as no surprise that the Communities of the Six represent the most, and the Council of Europe the least, successful organizations in a European spectrum in which all organizations make some contribution to some aspect of the integration process.

THE LESSONS APPLIED TO OTHER REGIONS

Before proceeding to a projection of these conclusions at the global level of the United Nations, it might be instructive to see to what extent they can be used to explain progress toward political community in other areas of the world. I have selected three such areas, the European members of the Soviet bloc, the Arab world, and the Western Hemisphere. Each of these possesses more unifying environmental characteristics in certain aspects than does western Europe. The Arab and Latin American worlds are, respectively, relatively homogeneous with reference to language and religion. They share, less uniformly, it is true, economic underdevelopment and dependence on monoculture. They also share certain ideological commitments, at least if we do not probe too deeply below the surface of ringing affirmations and generous platitudes. The Soviet bloc owes its unity less to any of these considerations than to the organizational and ideological ties among the ruling elites—and these may be undergoing disintegration now.

Whatever assurance may be warranted in our discussion of European integration is not readily transferable to other regional contexts. The generalizations offered for the Arab world and for Latin America do not merit firm theoretical assertion. While recent work on the Soviet bloc enables us to speak with considerable confidence, no similar work has yet been done on integration in the other regions.[7] The generalizations here advanced are therefore far more tentative and should be regarded as strong theoretical possibilities derived from firmer propositions culled from the European context and projected on the basis of information available at the moment.

Soviet Bloc

There are no supranational organizations in the bloc now, nor were the relations of a supranational type that dominated during the Stalin

---

[7] See, above all, Zbigniew K. Brzezinski, *The Soviet Bloc*, Harvard University Press, Cambridge, Mass., 1960; and George Modelski, *The Communist International System*, Princeton, Center of International Studies, December 1, 1960, and the literature cited there.

era. On the contrary, the organizations that prevail are intergovern-mental and the party meetings that take place seem almost like diplo-matic conferences. The law of alternating phases seems to apply, as exemplified by the lack of cumulative decision-making and precedent formation. Organizational tasks expand most readily when they are specific; the most continuous type of integrative activity is in the area of joint economic planning with highly detailed objectives. Environ-mentally speaking, this activity goes on in a setting dominated by a resolution to industrialize, with growing urbanization and a deepening socio-economic division of labor in each Communist country, even though totalitarianism precludes the flowering of a pluralist society.

The truly revealing lesson of the Soviet bloc, however, emerges from the organizational context. Actually, integration was *least* successful when the Communist Party of the Soviet Union possessed an organiza-tional monopoly over the process. The Stalin period witnessed a mini-mum of military cooperation, no joint economic planning, no exchange of information apart from the slavish imitation in eastern Europe of Soviet examples, and no successful value-sharing among fellow Com-munists. Integration was a one-way process in which the aims of the European satellites were simply subordinated to those of the Soviet Union. The brittleness of the structure stood exposed in the fall of 1956. Now, with the occasional flowering of "revisionism," there is little central direction, but, paradoxically, a good deal of practical integra-tion. The dismantlement of the central apparatus of coercion and manipulation yields to a process of voluntary integration based on a calculation of economic advantage, accompanied by the proper dosages of ideological compromise negotiated among equals. The modes of accommodation are as varied as elsewhere, with the upgrading of com-mon interests by no means always victorious. However, the more varied the centers of power in the bloc become, with the implied instability of alignments and unpredictability of compromise patterns, the more likely the emergence of some habits of continuous intra-bloc adjustment by techniques not unlike those of Western Europe.

Hence, the essential lessons of the western European integration process seem to hold in the Communist setting, with the pragmatic value-sharing of allied Communist parties taking the place of inter-action among kindred democratic parties. However, the continuation of this process clearly depends on the observation by the satellite rulers of the limits to voluntarism imposed by the Soviets. Imre Nagy demon-strates the non-observance of these limits, while Wladislaw Gomulka exemplifies the principle of limited dissent within a framework of fundamental loyalty to bloc objectives. Unlike other regional systems, voluntary integration in the Soviet bloc depends on the patience of *one* national elite.

Arab States

Institutions in the Arab world contain no trace of supranationality. The Arab League as well as the African organs in which certain Arab states participate are intergovernmental conferences, with either weak secretariats or none at all. While their deliberations are eloquently clothed in the phraseology of Arab Brotherhood and often refer to the lofty aims of the Arab Nation, they result in accommodations based on the minimum common denominator, if they achieve accommodation at all. But this is a symptom of the lack of integration rather than a cause.

Much the same is true of the conclusions which can be drawn from a functional analysis. In principle, Arab institutions have tasks which cover collective security and peaceful settlement of disputes among the members, security against external aggression, economic integration, regional investment, legal harmonization, cultural cooperation, coordination of transport and communication—the list of activities is identical with the European prototype. The only functions successfully carried out, however, are of a purely negative character. While the autonomy of functional contexts is fully intact in the Arab world, none of the tasks show a tendency toward spilling over into new areas of common concern, and many show evidence of periodic atrophy. Nothing of consequence has occurred toward economic and legal integration, though some common transport policy measures have been elaborated. The most striking successes were the defense of the Middle East against Western and Israeli policy. Arab unity has been sustained in keeping up the economic-diplomatic boycott of Israel and in making common policy against Western countries suspected of neo-imperialist designs.

Security and peaceful settlement among members of the Arab League has been less consistently achieved. When the total international environment made it seem that the consequences of inter-Arab strife (as in the Lebanon-Jordan crisis of 1958) would be destructive for all concerned, the phrases of Arab Brotherhood enshrined in League proceedings were translated into reality. But the same machinery proved quite useless in settling the differences between Egypt on the one hand and Jordan and Iraq on the other in connection with the liquidation of the Palestine conflict. Nor did it help to smooth the quarrels between Nasser, Kassim, and Bourguiba. Whenever the Arab League served essentially as a front for Egyptian national policy its activities were doomed to failure; whenever the convergence of interests permitted a different internal alignment successful mediation took place. In no instance did the League acquire the role of an integrating mechanism standing above the separate policies of its members. Success in highly specific security undertakings, lack of success in other pursuits, the prevalence of the minimum common denominator; these are merely more symptoms, not causes, of lack of integration and progress toward an Arab political community.

The explanation, then, may be found in the environment with its deceptive facade of unity. With the exception of the pan-Arab Socialist Renaissance Party (Ba'ath) there are few ideological links of unity among Arab political groups. Each modernizing elite in power, whether an intellectuals' independence movement or the army, acts and thinks only in the context of its state; each traditional-feudal oligarchical elite is intent on preserving its position and rejects cooperation with hostile Arab groups across the border. They "integrate" in meeting jointly experienced threats from outside the region; they cannot meaningfully work together on normally integrative tasks because they experience no common needs. Even in the area of economic development it is the maximization of national resources which motivates elites, not a pooling of resources. In fact, Iraqi nationalist suspicion that Egypt had its eye on Iraq oil may have been a factor in the split among such similarly motivated leaders as Kassim and Nasser. On the other hand, it is possible that a jointly experienced desire in pooling the major Middle Eastern resource—oil—so as to exert greater control over prices and marketing conditions may eventually result in a sufficiently specific convergence of aims to permit the evolution of a vital regional task administered by supranational techniques. This has not yet occurred, but the example of Europe would suggest this as the most likely area of intense integration.

If Europe is to serve as our model, too few of the preconditions for integration exist in the Arab world to make an imitation of the integration process a likelihood in the near future. If neither the economic nor the social environment bears any resemblance to that of the West, the ideologies which prevail are unlikely to conform to that pattern. Forcible integration—conquest—remains the major possibility, but this would hardly be an application of the European modes of accommodation.

The Americas

Though there are no supranational institutions in the Western Hemisphere, the fact remains that the prevailing intergovernmental organizations contain bodies that, on occasion, perform as if they were supranational. This is true of the Inter-American Peace Committee and of occasional subcommittees of the Organization of American States (OAS) Council. It is also possible that certain bodies of the Central American and Latin American common market organizations will develop such modes of behavior. However, ways of accommodation thus far have never gone beyond the minimum common denominator. They have had distinct integrative consequences because the techniques of consultation have created precedents, subsequently applied in similar situations. Still, it may well be that the determining role of historical phases applies here too, preventing the precedents from becoming cumulative.

Precision can here be gained from functional analysis. Within OAS a growing complexity of economic, social, and cultural organs has resulted only in cumulative inaction: the clashing expectations and demands of the United States and of the underdeveloped Latin American countries have thus far checkmated one another. It is possible that the Alliance for Progress will change this picture. The Inter-American Economic and Social Council, in principle, acquired the power to review and criticize the progress of the aid and development programs. But so far it has not carried out this confrontation function as did OEEC. The Nine Wise Men of OAS were to act as the supreme guides for national development programs. But the reforms in the Alliance machinery enacted in 1963 indicate that this function had not been consistently performed. So far, there has been little expansion of the OAS task, let alone a spill-over.

But the same is not true of the maintenance of security and the peaceful solution of disputes among members of OAS. A mixture of quiet mediation, admonition, and the threat of economic and military sanctions has sufficed to stop almost a dozen Western Hemisphere wars since 1945. Why? Essentially because no major ideological issues were at stake. The wars in question involved the mercenary ragamuffins of one oligarchy arrayed against those of another in very minor military skirmishes. It is in these situations that the mediatory prowess of OAS proves itself; here it achieves the institutionalization of precedent. But when this context changes a new picture emerges. Wars involving the issue of outside intervention—whether collective or unilateral—in a civil conflict in which revolutionary forces are arrayed against a traditional oligarchy (Guatemala, the Dominican Republic, Costa Rica, Cuba) cannot be readily settled by OAS conciliation. Costa Rica was saved and the Trujillo regime faced with collective denunciation and sanctions because there was a huge majority in favor of the democratic forces in question. But the Guatemalan and Cuban cases show that OAS intervention to preserve the status quo is considered hostile to modernization and thus cannot easily receive organizational approval. Is it not likely that the very success of OAS in collective security is possible only as long as the issue of interfering with modernization is not involved? If so, we are now living in a new phase in which past precedents will not shape future policy, which may imply a decay in the hitherto successful security function of OAS.

The current preparation by OAS of a convention on human rights and of a document concerning the limits of multilateral intervention on behalf of democracy may prove that common interests, for the first time, can be upgraded in this field. It would imply institutional growth, an involvement in new tasks, a spill-over, and a definite advance toward political community. While this has not yet happened, it could suggest that economics need not be the chief carrier of the integration process. In fact, this begs one of the most puzzling of questions: can only industrialized nations integrate or can the very fact of underdevelopment be a spur to regional unity? When one superdeveloped power confronts twenty disunited nations eager for aid, the answer is no. But would this be true if OAS possessed the power to distribute aid on the scale of OEEC under the Marshall Plan? There are two Latin American common market organizations now in existence, each using as its *raison d'être* the need for development and the creation of large markets as a spur to industrialization.[8] The tasks imposed by their respective treaties are less precise and more permissive than the Treaty of Rome, and they lack the power to hold out and withdraw economic rewards to their members. The picture for integration seems unpromising, but again it may be too soon to judge, especially since defense against the export prowess and possible protectionism of a united Europe is another factor making for unity in Latin America. Regional unity in Europe may yet father regional unity in Latin America even though the process obeys different impulses.

If this reasoning is correct, the fact of underdevelopment and the prevalence of monoculture may turn out to be environmental factors favorable to integration, though they were hostile to it in Europe. At the same time, social and economic underdevelopment creates major regional ideological affinities, especially among radical socialist-nationalist reformist parties of the *Aprista* type. But regimes and parties have

---

[8] See R. F. Mikesell, "The Movement toward Regional Trading Groups in Latin America," in A. O. Hirschmann (ed.), *Latin American Issues*, New York: Twentieth Century Fund, 1961. Victor Urquidi, *Free Trade and Economic Integration in Latin America*, Berkeley: University of California Press, 1962.

TABLE 15. *Regional Coverage* of ILO Conventions, August 1960*

Category of Convention	OAS	EEC	EFTA	NATO	Arab League	All ILO Members
Occupational Hazards (13, 62)	24	67	29	33	19	28
Freedom of Association (11, 87, 98)	48	89	76	75	37	55
Anti-Discrimination (100, 111)	29	33	43	33	25	27
Social Security (2, 3, 12, 17, 18, 19, 24, 25, 35, 36, 37, 38, 39, 40, 42, 44, 48, 102, 103)	21	51	37	33	13	22
Hours and Vacations (1, 4, 14, 20, 30, 41, 47, 52, 67, 89, 101, 106)	24	31	24	22	14	24
Administration of Labor Legislation (26, 34, 63, 81, 94, 95, 99)	29	57	49	41	14	30
Minimum Age and Protection of the Young (5, 6, 10, 33, 59, 60, 77, 78, 79, 90)	25	55	23	29	5	25

Source: International Labour Organization, International Labour Conventions, Chart of Ratifications, 1960. The computations are by the author.
* "Coverage" is the ratio of actual ratifications to possible ratifications for all the members of a given regional organization, expressed in per cent.

a habit of changing rapidly in this area. Even if they remain in power for longer periods, the preoccupation with purely national development has thus far carried the day. The intensification of the national-revolutionary process may still have the same disintegrative consequences here as in the Middle East.

Returning to our initial propositions, then, let us reiterate that intensity of integration is positively correlated with industrialization and

TABLE 16. *Coverage* of Council of Europe Conventions*
(as of March 20, 1959)

Coverage in %

Type of Convention	Total	EEC	EFTA	Nordic Council	United Kingdom	Greece	Turkey	Ireland
Political Integration (nos. 1, 2, 3, 5, 6, 7, 8, 9, 23)	66	61	81	85	67	50	25	50
Economic Integration (nos. 4, 10, 11, 12, 13, 14, 15, 21, 25)	56	75	60	53	75	11	0	75
Cultural Integration and International Understanding (nos. 18, 19, 20, 27)	62	63	70	56	100	25	50	75
General Convenience (nos. 16, 17, 22, 24, 26)	50	53	64	60	60	20	40	60
Total:	59	63	69	64	76	27	29	65

Source: European Yearbook, Vol. VI, for the information on ratifications. The computations are by the author .
* "Coverage" is the ratio of actual to possible ratifications of each convention in each category. Possible ratifications were so computed as to exclude countries to which specific conventions are not applicable because of
their subject matter.

economic diversification. These conditions, in turn, imply an interest in social legislation at the national level; when a regional integration process is launched, the need for an intra-regional harmonization of social legislation is frequently expressed. That being the case, the degree of existing uniformity of such legislation, prepared often under the auspices of the International Labor Organization (ILO) and subject to its continuing review, provides a useful indicator for judging the existence of commonly experienced needs and interests. Table 15 makes clear that the indicator of international social legislation confirms our earlier reasoning concerning the impact of industrialism on integration. The ILO conventions involved, of course, were drafted on the basis of global considerations; even so the interest shown by regional organizations grouping underdeveloped countries is minimal. Table 16 offers similar computations for the conventions concluded under the auspices of the Council of Europe, showing their coverage for the important regional organizations within Europe and for certain countries relatively aloof from the work of integration. Again, the figures support the proposition that environmentally similar countries, with a common basis in pluralism and industrialism, tend to express the joint interests which flow from this environment in harmonizing national legislation. While the over-all coverage of ILO conventions is about 33 per cent, that of the European conventions is 59 per cent.

THE LESSON APPLIED TO
THE UNITED NATIONS

If the attempt to apply to other areas the categories of analysis developed in the European context must be treated with caution, the same is true to an even greater extent when we shift our focus to the United Nations. Far from being a finished theory of integration at the global level, the generalizations here advanced constitute merely an attempt to subject a variety of international phenomena to the rigor of a unified set of concepts in an effort to narrow the field of analysis to a few central propositions. Hence I continue to apply the ordering concepts of environment, function, and institution, even though they may lead to less satisfactory results.

To impute environmental homogeneity to the United Nations member states would be futile. Any superficial examination on the basis of the indicators we used in the case of Europe will demonstrate the absence of pervasive traits common to all Members. More than half of the Member States are nonindustrial and underdeveloped; two-thirds, perhaps, lack a rational pluralistic social structure and continue to exhibit various degrees of traditionalism; totalitarian, democratic, and oligarchical regimes are represented in about equal numbers. Most important, perhaps, the ideals of member states run the gamut from the advocacy of revolutionary change to the staunch defense of some status quo. The United Nations environment, in short, is volatile and dynamic: it changes with every admission of a new member, with every revolution, almost with every election. The western European environment, in contrast, is the epitome of stability.

The United Nations during the period of deceptive inter-allied unity was one kind of system; it functioned very differently during the subsequent period of United States-NATO supremacy, to give way to still another mode of action when neutralism came into its own with the mass admission of new members in 1955. The advent of the African states and the eventual obsolescence of the whole colonial issue is certain to create a new environment again. Environmental instability is much greater than in any regional example here investigated, and the performance of the United Nations system is proportionately uneven.

In fact, the environment was singled out for initial attention here because it imposes on the United Nations an entirely different species of organizational life as contrasted with regional systems. Regional integration responds to certain *common* environmental features, no matter how elusive or temporary; it is based on certain common needs experienced by all participants, often in defense against some outside force. Nothing of the kind is true in the United Nations. The United Nations system represents the institutionalized attack-and-retreat of hostile forces seeking to get the better of each other by peaceful means, but without any intention of deliberately emphasizing what they may share in common. Integrative consequences flowing from this game are wholly unintended, though none the less real when they do occur. Consequently, it is idle to expect stable agreement on the primacy of certain tasks in the United Nations; the volatile environment is responsible for a shifting perception of necessary and common tasks, thus interfering with the functional specificity desirable for integration.

It would be a mistake to conclude from this picture that the institutions of the United Nations may be dismissed as irretrievably impotent. The United Nations institutional structure is so complex and the diversity of tasks so considerable that they extend from pure intergovernmental diplomacy to certain cautious approaches to supranationality. Further, the variety of organs is so great and the conditions under which they function so diffuse that all modes of accommodation can and do flourish under the proper circumstances. Institutionally, then, the system is exceedingly flexible and has shown the most startling constitutional adaptations, often to the chagrin of international lawyers.

But it remains true just the same that the dominant mode of accommodation has been compromise on the basis of the minimum common denominator, though "splitting the difference" is not unknown in the activities of certain specialized agencies. The upgrading of common interests has occasionally been attempted, as indicated in a variety of colonial, economic development, and military proposals, beginning with the Baruch Plan. Yet, the record points to the lesson that *successful* United Nations action or solution of crises has *always* been based on the minimum common denominator, success being judged by the degree of implementation given to United Nations resolutions. Resolutions, by contrast, which emerge through the process of parliamentary diplomacy and represent the view of a majority sharply contested by the defeated minority never achieve full implementation. Bona fide compromise may resolve individual crises (as in Korea, Indochina, Lebanon, and aspects of the Palestine war), but unless the process yields to more community-oriented modes of accommodation, these remain *ad hoc* settlements of no integrative significance.

Now it is true that the efforts of the Secretary General, acting in the name of the United Nations, to deal with certain crises contain a dose of supranationalism and seek to upgrade common interests. By committing the United Nations to a given course of action (as in the Congo) and subsequently requesting ever larger authority from the Security Council or the General Assembly to enable him to carry out tasks assumed earlier, the Secretary General causes the accretion of new powers and responsibilities to the United Nations as a whole. In the European context such efforts often resulted in a permanent growth of community-oriented procedures; in the United Nations this has not occurred. Member states, in deference to changing policy at home and shifting alignments abroad, will acquiesce in such courses of action in New York and then proceed to sabotage them in the field: United Nations authority did not increase in the Congo context, not because Mr. Hammarskjold made mistakes, but because certain crucial member states blocked the execution of his mandate. Much the same is true of the UN operation in Suez. The claim for supranational powers and the desire to upgrade common interests in peaceful change and relative stability—both of which do grow out of crises dealt with by the United Nations—are contrary to the persistence of member states to use the techniques only for the advancement of their own local policy aims, as exemplified by the conduct of Ghana, Guinea, Egypt, and Belgium in the Congo crisis.

The prevalence of environmental changes in an institutionally weak system results in a paucity of cumulative decisions creating integrative precedents. While this was also true in certain European organizations and in the Western Hemisphere, it is much more striking at the global level. The first Charter provisions with respect to collective security and enforcement were changed by the Uniting for Peace Resolution, a change that had fallen into quiet disuse by 1955. Powers given to the Secretary General vary—but do not necessarily grow—from crisis to crisis. Issues which appeared settled reappear a few years later, including major constitutional questions.

But despite all this, one major procedural advance in the direction of political community has shown a tenacious persistence: the role of a *stable* majority in the General Assembly, through the medium of parliamentary diplomacy, to set the limits and define the direction of certain crucial tasks. In the realm of security and enforcement, this has resulted in the enshrinement of the conciliation process, as executed through the agency of uncommitted nations. But a much more stable majority has imposed its stamp on other organizational tasks, which confirms at the global level that functional specificity bears the major responsibility for integration, and that functional contexts tend toward autonomy in New York as in Strasbourg. Chief among these tasks is the expanding work of the United Nations in economic development and technical assistance, followed by the significant accretions of authority in situations involving the peaceful transfer from colonial status to independence. The stable core of the majority responsible for pushing these tasks forward is made up of the bulk of Latin American, Asian, and African nations, joined in certain decolonization ventures by the Soviet bloc.

Environmental heterogeneity and institutional weakness need not prevent global integration around certain tasks which command general interest; but it is the political component of the environment that defines the nature of convergence of national aims. Integration in the United Nations system has occurred, not in the context of purely non-controversial and technical activities that are of equal interest to all Member States, even though of no transcendent importance to any of them, but in areas of convergence due to the major political conflicts of our era. The Cold War, the anti-colonial struggle, and the revolution of rising expectations are responsible for the national policy aims which, by converging at the United Nations, have resulted in new and larger tasks. Furthermore, the dependence of the major powers and their allies in their ideological conflict on the support of nations more interested in anti-colonialism and economic development neatly merges these separate strains into one mélange, infusing the Cold War with the colonial issue, and economic development with the East-West ideological struggle. Thus, the universal military-ideological environment based on conflict begets certain areas of common interest in which organizational tasks have expanded.

In the realm of collective security this has resulted in the erosion of a task and in the decadence of institutions of a quasi-supranational character. But in the functional realm of economics the picture is otherwise. Originally, the United Nations' task was the elaboration of universal economic policy tending toward a common world trade and payments system, coordinated countercyclical policies, and continuous consultation on all issues relating to economic stability, including commodity trade. This task was not successfully carried out in the United Nations, in the International Monetary Fund, or in the Food and Agriculture Organization. Universal economic policy foundered on the ideologically mixed environment that produced irreconcilable demands.

But more specific economic aims resulted in a spectacular expansion of another task: international investment and related activities of technical assistance. The history of the expanded International Bank for Reconstruction and Development responsibilities and operations, the creation of three new United Nations investment agencies since 1955, and the integration of investment with highly focused and centrally controlled technical aid, through the United Nations Special Fund, speaks for itself. Further, each decision to expand the United Nations' task was taken on the basis of majority pressure mobilized by parliamentary diplomacy and followed by detailed compromises among the major contributing powers, involving both an upgrading of common interests and a splitting of the difference. Routinized administrative control by international civil servants may follow eventually, thus submitting national development programs to an integrating process. The upgrading of common interests would then continue to be manifest in the flow of decisions made by such agencies as the Special Fund. While this has not yet happened, it should at least be noted that the controls exercised by the Special Fund are much more rigorous than is the supervision of the Technical Assistance Board.

Anti-colonialism suggests a parallel lesson. The irreconcilable demands implicit in the environment prevented the firm but general colonial policy that is suggested by the UN Charter from developing. General discussions on colonialism included ample invective but no concrete solutions. Peaceful change, as a regular integrative process in United Nations organs, was not in evidence with reference to colonial disputes. But the very Cold War pressures that resulted in progressive compromises among the major powers in the economic development field also brought pressure on the West to yield to the anti-colonial demands mobilized through parliamentary diplomacy. The result was a recurrent pattern of enhanced United Nations responsibility with respect to assuring a peaceful transition to independence in the case of specific territories facing specific problems, through the processes of the trusteeship system. Somewhat more generally, this constellation of forces brought about an institutionalized increase in the procedural powers of the United Nations to hear and deal with complaints. If "peaceful change" means the gradual yielding of one type of policy in the face of the onslaught of another, minimizing violence, and relying on parliamentary diplomatic pressure allied with Cold War overtones, the demise of colonialism under United Nations auspices provides a striking example of task expansion. In contrast to the collective security function, the existence of a stable United Nations majority on the colonial issue has brought about cumulative precedents on procedure that may survive the historical phases that buffet the universal system.

Let us complete this functional survey with a word about universal human rights. I strongly suspect that here the dominance of phases reasserts itself and that the integrative role of this function, which exists at the regional level, will have no global counterpart. The prominence of universal human rights in United Nations discussion is due almost solely to the desire of member states to score propaganda points off one another: initially the West used the issue to embarrass the Soviet Union; now the Afro-Asian, Latin American, and Soviet blocs are tactically united in using the issue to embarrass the West on the colonial and overseas investment issues. The imminent end of colonial rule will destroy this tactical alliance. Then, it is highly doubtful that either the Soviet Union or the underdeveloped countries with totalitarian tendencies will be eager to create a system of universal private rights or a scheme of international accountability. In the European context the protection of individual rights could have integrative results just because the pre-existing environment was already homogeneous, a point much less strikingly applicable in the Western Hemisphere. But no integrative consequences can emerge at the United Nations level if many of the member states are motivated purely by short-run interests that will not survive the current phase.

This analysis suggests further functional areas in which integrative United Nations activities could well be undertaken. True, neither colonialism nor human rights is likely to provide opportunities for converging interests in a few years. But economic development will continue to offer a field of action to such aims as long as the current world tripolarity prevails; in fact, that very condition suggests additional common interests. The peaceful uses of outer space, pooled space research, and United Nations control over extra-terrestrial bodies are obvious candidates. Less obvious but clearly within our framework of analysis is the field of regulated arms reduction and the increasingly international peaceful use of nuclear energy. These activities involve converging interests among conflicting states; they have a very high spill-over potential and require supranational administrative bodies for adequate control. In short, they evoke the upgrading of common interests in the execution of highly specific programs.

But let us guard against the fallacy that *any* non-political program yields greater integrative results than would a concerted political effort to call into life a world political community. Our European survey makes clear that politically infused economic tasks, flowing from an industrial environment with a pluralistic society, yield the greatest amount of integration. Other regional experiences do not clearly support this conclusion, but the United Nations experience conforms, at least, to the economic component in the proposition. Yet the economic work of the United Nations is obviously less integrative than that of Europe for the institutional and environmental reasons stated. The art of manipulating integration consists in isolating functional areas which produce converging interests among moderately hostile states, and in capitalizing upon those "non-political" aims which very soon spill over into the realm of politics when specific programs are envisaged by strong international institutions. The urban-industrial-pluralistic environment is optimal for this purpose, but not unique.

INTEGRATION AS A DISCONTINUOUS PROCESS

Five major conclusions can be drawn from this discussion. Processes which yield optimal progress toward the end of political community at the European level simply cannot be reproduced in other contexts because the necessary preconditions exist to a much lesser degree. Therefore, European integration will proceed at a much more rapid pace than universal integration. Further, other regions with strongly varying environmental factors are unlikely to imitate successfully the European example.

However, it is by no means clear that slightly different functional pursuits, responding to a different set of converging interests, may not

TABLE 17. *Cohesion of Regional Caucus Groups in the United Nations General Assembly, 1945–1958*

Cohesion of Member States

Caucus	Before Creation of Caucus %			After Creation of Caucus %			During the Whole Period %**		
	Iden-tical	Soli-darity	Divided	Iden-tical	Soli-darity	Divided	Iden-tical	Soli-darity	Divided
African*	—	—	—	46.7	33.3	20.0			
Western European	65.0	23.8	11.2	82.4	11.0	6.6			
Asian-African	11.4	36.4	53.9	34.4	42.2	23.4			
Benelux							77.5	17.0	5.5
Scandinavian							68.3	23.9	7.8
Commonwealth							13.0	27.7	59.3
Arab							63.4	27.2	9.4
Latin American							28.8	33.2	38.0
Soviet							96.0	3.9	0.1

Source: Thomas Hovet, Jr., *Bloc Politics in the United Nations*, Center for International Studies, Massachusetts Institute of Technology, 1958, pp. 64–65, 86, 98, 111, 121–122, 131, 172, 187. Hovet's study is based on the counting of an "adjusted gross" number of roll-call votes. For the meaning of this device, see Hovet, pp. 239ff. For an "identical" vote the frequency of members voting the same way, not considering abstention, is counted; for a "solidarity" vote, the frequency of members of a caucusing group abstaining rather than voting against their colleagues is determined; a "divided" vote covers the situations of direct opposition among members of a group.

* The African caucus had functioned for only two sessions at the time these computations were made, thus precluding firm conclusions. Prior to the formation of the caucus there were not enough African Member States to create a meaningful statistical pattern.

** The caucusing groups listed for "the whole period" were formed before or at the time of the first meeting of the General Assembly.

also yield integration. The Soviet and Latin American examples sug gest that this may be the case. But it is also true that if regional integration continues to go forward in these areas, it will obey impulses peculiar to them and thus fail to demonstrate any universal "law of integration" deduced from the European example.

Integration at the universal level obeys still different impulses. It flows from much more intense conflict than the regional process, in deference to the heterogeneity of the environment in which it unrolls. Consequently, the areas of common interest are more difficult to isolate and the proper specific functions harder to define. In view of the prevalence of phases it then becomes very hazardous to forecast any even and consistent pattern of integration.

The United Nations effort suffers from the built-in defect that the

TABLE 18. *Cohesion of Members of Regional Pacts in the United Nations General Assembly, 1945–1958*

	Before Conclusion of Pact		After Conclusion of Pact	
Pact	Identical Votes %	Divided Votes %	Identical Votes %	Divided Votes %
ANZUS	75.8	13.8	78.2	5.4
Central Treaty Organization	39.2	26.2	55.0	15.0
Council of Europe	51.0	21.0	43.0	30.0
NATO	47.4	21.1	55.4	21.3
Organization of Central American States	48.3	24.2	67.5	29.8
Southeast Asia Treaty Organization	37.0	34.8	75.0	10.0
Western European Union	—*	—*	75.0	3.6

Source: Thomas Hovet, Jr., *Bloc Politics in the United Nations,* Center for International Studies, Massachusetts Institute of Technology, 1958, pp. 196–203. This computation is based on certain roll-call votes considered as relating to "significant resolutions" on a variety of issues before the United Nations. A panel of outstanding participants in the debates determined which of the votes during each session merited the label "significant." It is Hovet's conclusion that in all instances votes dealing with matters of collective measures and the peaceful settlement of disputes commanded the greatest cohesion among the members of each regional pact.

* Since Italy did not participate in UN debates prior to 1955, no meaningful figure for the pre-pact period can be given.

very economic development and technical aid activities which at the moment constitute its integrative task may create the kind of national environment in which *less* integration will take place a generation from now. To the extent that the United Nations effort strengthens national economies and administrative structures it actually may *reduce* the final integrative component. Functionally specific economic tasks found to provide progress toward a political community in Europe may thus have the opposite final effect at the world level. Whether, in some future United Nations phase, space and nuclear tasks would produce more integration remains an open question.

The element of discontinuity among the various processes is increased by the continued autonomy of the universal and regional decision-making contexts. As Tables 17 and 18 make clear, there is no overwhelming evidence that the members of a cohesive regional system remain united in the United Nations, nor is there evidence that normally weak and heterogeneous regional systems may not perform cohesively in New York. In short, the contexts remain separate and distinct in the minds of policy-makers, a feature hardly conducive to the elaboration of a unified and global integration process.

A final element of discontinuity must be frankly exposed. Regional integration, because it proceeds more rapidly and responds to a greater number of optimal factors, may eventually slow down universal integration altogether. The regional process may create a relatively small number of integrated political communities, facing each other in the United Nations systems. In fact, the expanded United Nations task looking toward pooled economic development and regional agencies in Africa, Southeast Asia, and elsewhere, may actually contribute to this trend. In that case, the growth of fewer and larger political communities will contribute to regional, but not to universal, peace. The universal system will remain what it now is: the arena for minimizing conflict and maximizing common interest in deference to the minimum common denominator.

Chapter 12

The United Nations as
a Peace-Preserving Force

ARTHUR L. BURNS and NINA HEATHCOTE

The following chapter focuses on the contribution made by the United Nations military force to world stability, from the effective employment of the United Nations Emergency Force (UNEF) in 1957 to the United Nations Force (UNF) operation against the Katangese in January, 1963. We are particularly concerned with the military force employed by the United Nations Operation in the Congo (UNOC). This was the first deployment of UN military power—except for the special case of Korea—where force was actually used. UNF fought two actions in Katanga during 1961; it was used in Orientale to disarm pro-Gizenga gendarmes in 1962, and to end Katangese secession in 1962–1963. The discussion to follow is directed towards answering two basic questions: Have any of these actions shown that military force in United Nations hands is an effective instrument for the preservation of peace? What sorts of precedent will they become for UN forces in the future?

This chapter represents a condensation and revision of materials appearing in a book by the same authors, Peace-Keeping by U.N. Forces: From Suez to the Congo, *Praeger, New York, 1963.*

THE UN AND INTERNATIONAL POLITICS

The United Nations was founded as an organization for making and preserving peace, but it does not follow that that is now its principal function nor that the UN is now the principal maintainer of peace. But one may argue that the UN has become among other things, the institution that *formalizes* and *legitimates* some of the relationships of international politics.

International politics, in our view, is simply politics unregulated by containment within the forms of any single state, though it does not reproduce all the characteristic features of internal politics. External politics goes on outside all institutions and in other institutions beside the United Nations. From this point of view the UN is merely the formalized part of a largely informal and world-wide "conversation."

Once we characterize the United Nations in this manner, and not as an incipient world government, we can fairly concede it an ancillary but independent role in keeping the peace. It does so for the most part not by the exercise of any physical force, but chiefly by virtue of the right, which some of the world public thinks it has, to represent mankind's conscience and respect for law.

This follows because international politics is not carried on by impersonal nation-states, or similar partly mythical collectives, but by representative persons. Few people can sink themselves wholly in the representative role, yet because they cannot, an international organization such as the United Nations has some hope of affecting the conduct of international affairs. The "representative person" is by no means thrust back upon his own personal conscience only. There is a community of persons all over the world, which takes note of his representative acts. Pragmatic and realistic concessions to the "factor of prestige" are in reality concessions to the efficacy of this international community conscience. In this study we assess the sort of showing which the UN has made, particularly in the Congo dispute, during the last six years before the bar of that conscience.

PRECEDENTS TO THE CONGO ACTIONS

The United Nations Emergency Force was despatched to Suez in November 1956, in order to separate the combatants, at the request of Egypt, which was about to be defeated by the joint efforts of invading Anglo-French and Israeli forces. Behind this United Nations enterprise stood all but two or three European countries and the two super-powers, which were prepared to forego their immediate interests in the area in order to avoid a major war. The Suez action was distinguished by a clear distinction between internal and external issues, and by virtual resolution of the armed conflict before the UNEF arrived on the scene. Thus, it was to be merely a "border patrol" policing an already-concluded cease-fire. These important features distinguished the successful Suez operation from the later Congo action.

Lebanon and Jordan also served as precedents for the Congo action. In Lebanon an observer corps of over 500 officers was established by a resolution of the Security Council on June 11, 1958. Its function was to observe the Lebanon-Syrian border, in response to a Lebanese complaint that the U.A.R. authorities had instigated anti-Government riots in Lebanon, and that arms and men were being smuggled for that purpose across the Syrian border. The crisis assumed international proportions when, in response to a successful coup against the Iraqi Government and unrest in Jordan, the United States landed troops in Lebanon. This provoked immediate protests from Russia, who threatened military action. The United States Government alleged that the landing of the troops had in view only protection of Lebanon against intervention from the U.A.R.

The UN observers, however, reported to the United Nations that they had found little evidence of external interference. The crisis was resolved peacefully. On August 21 a resolution sponsored by ten Arab states, including Lebanon and Jordan, was passed by the General Assembly. It called, among other things, for withdrawal of foreign troops from the territories of those two countries. As the government and the rebels in Lebanon settled their dispute, the U.S. troops were withdrawn on November 2, and on November 25 the Lebanese crisis was deleted from the Security Council agenda.

Coincident with the Lebanon crisis, an alleged threat by the U.A.R. against Jordan was reported to the Security Council on July 17—the day on which British troops, responding to the Royal Jordanian government's request, were arriving in Jordan. The Jordanian representative mentioned a sequence of intensifying U.A.R. pressures culminating in troop movements along Jordan's border. The British representative claimed that the United Kingdom deployment was solely to protect Jordan from outside threats, and at two later meetings of the Council acknowledged that Britain was proposing effective UN action in Jordan so that British troops could withdraw. But, as the Council failed to reach decision in Jordan, the issue was referred to the General Assembly's emergency special session of August 13.

Jordan, however, while reiterating her charges against the U.A.R.

and asking for UN help, explicitly opposed receiving UN forces or UN observers. On August 21 the resolution of the ten Arab states (including Lebanon and Jordan) agreed with this objection by omitting reference within their resolution to dispatch of UN forces. The Secretary General's "First Report" of September 29, 1958 also conceded the point by proposing instead the sending of his own special representative with an adequate staff to Jordan (which had acquiesced in this proposal) to uphold the principles of the UN Charter in relation to Jordan. Both Lebanon and the U.A.R. agreed to facilitate communications for this representative, and Ambassador Spinelli was appointed to the post and sent to Amman. But, as in Lebanon, the Jordanian situation stabilized, British forces withdrew by November 2, 1958, and the question was withdrawn from the UN agenda.

Secretary General Hammarskjold hoped to capitalize on the UN's Middle Eastern experience by creating a body of principles and code of operations for future military and observational operations by the Organization. In a "Summary study" (A/3943) of October 9, 1958, he presented to the General Assembly an epitome of UNEF and UNOGIL (United Nations Observation Group in Lebanon) activities, and the principles governing them, which he was to invoke during the Congo action.

In this document, he distinguished the Suez operation—in which it had been possible to interpose a strictly military UN force, without risk of involvement in local politics, between national forces—from the "non-military" UN deployment in Lebanon and the special arrangement in Jordan. Both the latter countries were suffering, in his view, strictly domestic conflicts, for which UN military intervention was inappropriate, even though he recognized that the Lebanon situation could have serious international consequences.

The principles laid down in Hammarskjold's "Summary study" presupposed situations in which the Security Council had *not* invoked enforcement measures. They included the concept of a "status agreement," an understanding "in good faith," between the UN and the host-country, whose consent for the operation would be of course essential. (Such an agreement had been made with Egypt, and far less elaborately with Lebanon.) Permanent Members of the Security Council were to be precluded from supplying units to a UNF. The UN Force was to have freedom of movement within the area of the host-state involved in the agreement, and was to exercise its function neither in cooperation nor in competition with the host government, so as to preserve UN independence. The operation as a whole required a definite mandate from Assembly or Council, and the Secretary General, usually responsible for such operations, was to be confined to the mandate. Because of the presupposition of "non-enforcement measures," the Secretary General would have to see that the Force operated only in self-defense. They must never take a "military initiative." This last principle dominated the early stages of the Congo operation.

In fact, the Assembly never formally adopted Hammarskjold's "Summary study." During the Congo action, however, he himself managed to arrange for the adoption of many of its principles, both in action and in his own reports to the Security Council.

DECISION TO PROVIDE UNITED NATIONS ASSISTANCE TO THE CONGO

Internal disturbances in the Congo made it different from the Suez crisis and set the United Nations a problem with which the Organization was not formally equipped to deal. Article 39 (Chapter VII) and Article 99 (Chapter XV) of the Charter, which are concerned with threats to international peace, seem to presuppose that all the world's populated territories are divided into sovereign nation-states and that any breaches of the peace of which the UN might take cognizance, would occur between such nation-states.

The Congolese Government's request for military assistance from the UN on July 12 and 13, 1960 ignored the internal aspects of the crisis and described it as conflict between two states, Belgium and the Congo, in which Belgium was the aggressor. Had that been the case, the UN probably would not have intervened at all. A positive determination could have led to the adoption of enforcement measures against Belgium under Articles 41 and 42 (Chapter VII) and provoked a Western veto. A negative determination might have compelled the Security Council to refuse all assistance to the Republic of the Congo.

However, the Secretary General, Dag Hammarskjold, asked for a meeting of the Security Council under Article 99 (Chapter XV), which empowers the Secretary General to bring to the attention of the Council "any matter which in his opinion may threaten the maintenance of international peace and order," terms which need not lead immediately to "enforcement measures" under Chapter VII.

Hammarskjold's suggestions to the Council on July 13 circumvented action under Articles 39, 41, or 42 and avoided labelling the crisis an issue between Belgium and the Congo. The UN would provide military assistance for the Congo Government to help restore order and thus to create conditions in which Belgian troops could be withdrawn. The implied aim was to prevent foreign intervention that might have ranged

Belgium and other Colonial Powers against some of the new African states. Neither then nor afterwards did any UN body affirm that there had already been armed aggression by Belgium or any other power against the Republic of the Congo, nor did the Council ever invoke Articles 39, 41, or 42. Instead, the Congo issue was simply brought to the attention of the Security Council by the Secretary General under Article 99, that is, as a threat to international peace. Hammarskjold, by introducing a UN force into an independent state to restore order, had thus made a major innovation in UN practice.

Another of Hammarskjold's innovations was to request deployment of a United Nations force within a Member state and simultaneously because of absence of enforcement measures, to retain the provisions of Article 2(7) (Chapter I) of the Charter, which precludes that force from intervening in the State's internal affairs. In the same spirit was his decision to interpret the mandate by the principles set out in his "Summary study," which in addition prohibited the UNF from "any *initiative* in the use of armed force."

On July 14 the Security Council adopted a Tunisian resolution that, (1) called upon the Government of Belgium to withdraw its troops, and (2) gave the Secretary General the authorization he had asked for on July 13, that is, to restore order in the Congo.

THE UNITED NATIONS IN THE CONGO

The operations of the UNF from mid-July 1960 to mid-February 1961, may be considered as a fair trial of Hammarskjold's hypothesis that a "non-intervening" UNF can maintain sufficient intra-state order to make the host-state viable, and thus to deter international intervention in its conflicts.

By July 26, UNF strength in the Congo was over 8,000, deployed in all provinces but Katanga. Belgian troops had begun to evacuate Leopoldville before July 20. However, on July 17, the Congo Government warned the UN that unless the UN should seem to be able to effect the evacuation of Belgian troops by July 20, they would seek assistance from the Soviet Union. In fact, they had already done so, and Khrushchev had replied sympathetically. This undoubtedly aroused suspicions about Lumumba and his entourage among the Western Powers, and especially in the United States. Soviet representatives continued to stand upon their nation's right to assist the Congo as one sovereign State to another, and at the same time to support the policies of those radical African states that were most insistent upon an all-African UNF in the Congo. The Cold War was already beginning to obtrude itself. A compromise resolution moved by Tunisia and Ceylon was, however, adopted by the Council on July 22. It authorized the Secretary General to take steps for the withdrawal of Belgian troops and requested all states to refrain, (1) from impeding the restoration of law and order in the Congo, and (2) from undermining its territorial integrity and political independence.

At the meeting of July 22, the Russians took care to warn the Council not to consider the Congo resolutions of July 14 and 22 as precedents for the future, and asserted that they did not endow "the United Nations with the right to interfere in the domestic affairs of a State and to assume responsibility for a country's domestic laws and regulations . . ." This meant that the Russians would oppose setting of precedents for growth in the United Nations forces' authority and power to preserve external peace through restoration of internal law and order, and would prevent the Organization from ever becoming a super-state.

Stability in the Congo was threatened from the outset by continued indiscipline of the Force Publique (ANC), and by Katanga's secession, which was announced by Tshombe, the Provincial President, on July 11, 1960. Though his regime never received formal recognition from any state, including Belgium, he had enjoyed the support of Belgian commercial interests and some encouragement from official Belgian sources in his pretensions to independence. Belgium evidently was determined to preserve its vast economic complex in Katanga. Control of Katanga's mineral wealth remains a crucial matter of dispute in the Congo. The ending of Katanga's secession became the first concern of the Central Government, who urged prompt entry of the UNF into Katanga. Dr. Bunche reported on August 5 that the Katangese would probably resist such an entry.

The Security Council met on August 9 and adopted a draft resolution of Ceylon and Tunisia. While invoking Articles 25 and 49 to secure Belgian withdrawal from Katanga, and endorsing UNF entry there, it reaffirmed, ". . . that the United Nations Force in the Congo would not be a party to or in any way intervene in or be used to influence the outcome of any internal conflict, constitutional or otherwise."

In August 1960, the balance of Congolese military power made it likely that such strict non-intervention by the UN would tend inadvertently to assist Tshombe, by providing him time to build up *de facto* authority and power within Katanga. The resolution's non-interventionism thus seemed hard to reconcile in practice with the clauses of the

July mandate, which enjoined a UN relationship to the Congo Government.

On August 12, Hammarskjold led the UNF's entry into Katanga. But at that date he sent to Lumumba and Tshombe a memorandum interpreting Paragraph 4 of the August resolution as forbidding the UNF to assist either the host government or the Katangese. Lumumba challenged this non-interventionist interpretation, later declaring that "the Government and the people of the Congo" had lost their confidence in the Secretary General and that a group of Afro-Asian Observers should be sent to the Congo.

Simultaneously, evacuation of Belgian troops was somewhat delayed, permitting the officers of the Force Publique in Katanga to transfer to the provincial gendarmerie, which later became the core of Tshombe's aggressive forces. Belgium thus continued to be a source of disorder in the Congo, although it is difficult to lay much blame directly at the *official* Belgian door after September, 1960, when her national forces left the Congo.

In Kasai, where Kalonji was leading another breakaway movement, hundreds of tribesmen were reported killed by disorganized units of the Force Publique (ANC) on August 29, 30, and 31. The Secretary General protested to the Russian delegation that 10 Ilyushin-14 aircraft had transported 200 ANC troops from Stanleyville to Bakwanga in Kasai. The Russians in their reply to Hammarskjold of September 10, denied that any Security Council enactment could forbid the rendering of such independent assistance among sovereign powers.

Against such intervention by the U.S.S.R., Hammarskjold could find no absolutely unequivocal or insuperable objections of principle and law, such as enforcement measures might have given him against Belgium. He believed that Lumumba's welcoming of this Soviet military assistance might set off an interventionary war on the Korean or the Spanish model. Nevertheless, Hammarskjold told the Security Council on August 21 that, following the Belgian withdrawal, and given the presence of UNOC, the Congo situation was ceasing to threaten "international peace and security."

On September 5, however, such hopes were dramatically disappointed: the Chief of State, Kasavubu, and Lumumba, the Prime Minister, dismissed each other. Anarchy and civil war ensued in the absence of recognized central authority, which was not restored when on September 14, General Mobutu's military coup set up a near-dictatorship in Leopoldville.

In the face of its host-government's schism there was no precedent on which United Nations Operations in the Congo (UNOC) might act. Under conditions of partial anarchy, it carried on with Hammarskjold's non-interventionary policy. For this the Secretariat was criticized by the Afro-Asians and by the Soviet bloc; for example, in the crisis of September 5, UNOC should have openly supported Lumumba; and his faction should now be helped to overcome the "rebels." These actions would have been a serious departure from the UN's non-intervening principles, and in any case the UNF were too few, even with the pro-Lumumbist section of the ANC, to be sure of overcoming all other armed opposition.

The UN now concentrated upon preservation of life and liberty, citing the best legal grounds available in order to avoid partisan action. Thus, on October 10, it refused to facilitate the ANC's arresting Lumumba, on the ground that the purported warrant flouted his Parliamentary immunity. This antagonized the Leopoldville faction. From then until mid-April of the following year, the UN could count on help from no Congolese party. Nor was any guidance forthcoming from the policy-makers in the UN. The Security Council and the General Assembly sessions in September failed to reach any decision.

At the Security Council meeting of September 16 and 17, the Soviet Union suffered a major reverse. A resolution sponsored by Ceylon and Tunisia condemned "assistance for military purposes" in the Congo "except as part of United Nations action." The Tunisian representative in his speech left no doubt that the movers of the motion had not only Belgium but also the Soviet in mind, and he refused to accept Russian amendments. The question was then referred to the General Assembly emergency special session where a further rebuke was administered to the U.S.S.R. by the Afro-Asians. On September 18, seventeen of the Afro-Asian Powers combined to condemn "direct and indirect provisions of arms or other materials of war and military personnel and other assistance for military purposes in the Congo . . ."

On November 22, the General Assembly approved the seating of the Kasavubu delegation against the wishes of the Soviet bloc. At the end of October, Russia had made it clear that she would not contribute to the cost of maintaining the UNF. Though with the decline of Lumumba's power the Soviets were apt to lose influence in the Congo, the measures that they had taken to advance their position afforded loopholes for intervention exploited later by other Powers.

Afro-Asian support for UNOC, which had survived Lumumba's dismissal, was severely shaken when having freely left the protection afforded him by the UN, he was arrested on December 2, and imprisoned by the Leopoldville authorities. In that situation the UN was not legally empowered, as Hammarskjold later explained, to use force to free him.

In protest against Lumumba's treatment, Ceylon, the U.A.R., Indonesia, Morocco, and Guinea began in December to withdraw their contingents from the Congo force. On December 21, Yugoslavia urgently required the recall of its technical personnel. India also threatened to withdraw support, and Prime Minister Nehru strongly criticized the UNOC on December 12, for having taken a passive role in the Congo. Such actions indicate that the contributing nations' ability to withdraw military assistance is in fact a more effective instrument for limiting the scope of United Nations political action than is finding the money for it. Operations must halt without troops and weapons, or when supporting aircraft cannot get clearance to fly in. The Secretary General's contention was that in such a case, everybody would stand to lose.

This concept of "general loss" perhaps warrants us to refer to a "general purpose" directed toward a common good as a basis for decisions regarding international stabilization, in the same way as we can refer in a guarded way to a "general interest" or "common good" in economic stability. Derivatively, we can talk about member states promoting a United Nations interest, which might incidentally thwart the interests of some individual member or members.

The greatest difficulty in maintaining objects of "general interest" will probably occur whenever a United Nations operation is designed to ease the transfer from colonial status. Those in charge of the operation may be tempted to accept contingents only from those countries likely to be enthusiastic for the United Nations policy in question. If the officials succumb to pressure from particular nations, they will be transforming an apparently impartial operation in the "general interest" into the maneuver of a coalition like the Korean effort. The United Nations began as a wartime coalition, and the Charter empowers the Security Council, by enforcement measures, to undertake operations of the type taken in Korea; and the "Uniting-for-Peace" resolution also enables the Assembly to recommend similar actions, so that not all UN operations need be taken in "the general interest." Hammarskjold, maintaining the character of UNOC despite threats of withdrawal from many sides, sometimes at the cost of immediate effectiveness, preserved the policy of objectivity and impartiality in the Congo which he had begun to establish for the UN at Suez.

Nothing came of the Security Council's December 1960 sessions and the subsequent General Assembly meeting. In mid-January 1961, the

Casablanca Powers issued a joint declaration of withdrawal because the purposes justifying a UNF presence in the Congo were not being realized.

Ceylon, Liberia and the U.A.R. presented to the Security Council a draft resolution that was adopted on February 21. It called for the investigation of Lumumba's assassination which had been reported on February 13, and for proposals for (1) the restoration of parliamentary institutions, (2) the reorganization of the Force Publique (ANC), and (3) measures to prevent civil war. This was due to the outbreaks involving the gendarmerie, particularly in North Katanga. The gendarmerie were distinct from the ANC and became, in effect, the private armies of dissident leaders in the provinces.

Among the strongest arguments for insistence that in any future intranational United Nations operations the UNF be assigned a monopoly of the lawful use of arms, is that founded on the practice common in many unsettled States of maintaining several distinct and independent groups of men-at-arms. While a UNF could not with propriety proclaim martial law, there is a case for requiring that any government which invites the UNF shall agree to put all its forces under UN command, to grant authority to the UNF for apprehending all who unlawfully bear arms, and for seizing unlicensed imports of or stores of weapons. Provided such an agreement were terminable either at a fixed date or by mutual consent of the UN authority and the host government, such practices might not infringe or require the amendment of Charter provisions respecting domestic jurisdiction. The law thus enforced by a UNF would be, normally, that of the host State. More difficult cases would arise in stateless areas or those in which no effective writ was running. The lack of any recognized UN procedure in such situations could well be vexatious for peace-preserving actions in the future.

The above-mentioned three-Power resolution gave no such detailed directions to the Secretary General. It was remarkable in its provision for the use of force to prevent civil war. This was an innovation soon proved open to abuse. Although the second part of the draft expressed a conviction that imposition of any political solution would only "enhance the risk of conflict within the Congo and the threat to international peace and security," three of the operative paragraphs were so ambiguously phrased, particularly when read together, that they could have been interpreted as designing to end Katanga's secession.

Until this resolution was adopted, Hammarskjold had instructed the UNF to use all means *"short of force . . ."* in civil war situations. He had been arguing earlier in the month before the Security Council that if the civil war did break out "in spite of restraining influence of the presence of the United Nations . . . the right thing to do would be for the United Nations Force to withdraw . . ."

In the debate of February 20 and 21, Sir Patrick Dean, the UK representative, had argued that the UNF should not take action by force (except in self-defense) without consultation with the host government, and that even then it should not use its forces to impose a political settlement. Hammarskjold evidently agreed with Sir Patrick's interpretation.

A second three-power resolution was defeated on February 21 by combined abstentions of the Western Powers. Hammarskjold recognized that this second resolution would have made a new departure by authorizing enforcement measures to prevent atrocities, presumably under Article 42. Its defeat meant that the *first* three-power resolution's licensing of the use of force to prevent civil war did not invoke Article 42. Thus, February's Security Council debate had brought no new epoch for UNOC's code of operations.

Yet the three Afro-Asian Powers may have induced the Organization to take the decisive step. They had armed the UNF with a potent phrase—"the use of force"—which, invoked once, was easier to invoke again and which in general may have emboldened the UN officers to resort to force more freely. In this way, the resolution's civil-war clause perhaps spelled the end of Hammarskjold's doctrine of a UNF as a "nonintervening" presence within a member state, and set a precedent for future forcible intervention by the UN.

Had Hammarskjold's doctrine been successful? Certainly, there had been no major civil war in the Congo before February 1961. More importantly, official intervention by other Powers had ceased, or had been prevented. In mid-twentieth century conditions this may have proved of less moment than the unofficial but actual involvement of Western commercial interests, of resurgent African movements, and of Soviet Communist subversives and provocateurs. The Spanish civil war had set a gruesome precedent for informal intervention.

Kasavubu accused the United Nations of declaring war on the Congo, and defied implementation of the new resolution; but patient negotiations by the UNOC with Congolese authorities brought forth better results. On April 17, Kasavubu and the representatives of the Secretary General initialed an agreement that laid the foundation for implementing the February resolution and for cooperation between the United Nations and the future government of the Republic. Later in April a conference of Congolese leaders drafted a constitution and in the third week of July, directly as a result of the UNOC's mediating efforts, paragraph B-1 of the February 21 resolution was implemented by a reconvention of the Congolese Parliament. The new National Government, however, did not command the allegiance of Katanga, whose secession remained a major problem facing the UNOC.

There can be no doubt that it was the Secretary General's policy to bring about Katanga's integration into the Republic of the Congo, though his sole formal mandate for doing so comprised several paragraphs of the General Assembly resolution of September 19, 1961. As far as it went, that was a mandate for integration through persuasion, certainly not through employment of force by the UN.

First UN Armed Action

By September 1961, however, the UNF was engaged in armed action in Katanga. Legal justification of the operation was sought in part from the Security Council's February 21 resolution and in part from Ordinance 70 promulgated by President Kasavubu on August 24. But the Ordinance enjoined only the expulsion of mercenaries from Katanga. With the Congolese Prime Minister's letter requesting UN assistance to implement it, the UNF had a very broad warrant—probably, however, excluding military initiative—to expel the mercenaries, presumably under UNOC's mandate to preserve *law and order*. It did not provide any legal basis for ending Katanga's independence.

The action began on August 28 when the UN moved its troops into Katanga and, as security precautions, seized the airport, the post office, and the telephone and radio station, and raided army headquarters. It then began to arrest foreign personnel and mercenaries. The operation was frustrated, it was alleged, because the Belgian Consul in Katanga, who had promised to be responsible for evacuation of foreign personnel, appeared not to carry out his part of the agreement. After some days of mounting tension in Elisabethville, the UNF attempted on September 13 to resume the action of August 28. When the Katangese resisted, the UN responded with force, beginning an eight-day war.

Why did UNOC take this warlike action at Elisabethville? Neither its mandate nor the Secretary General's Katanga policy nor general principles evidently extended to so extreme a course. The UN sources offered conflicting explanations. The Chief of UN operations in Katanga, Dr. Conor Cruise O'Brien told a news conference on September 13 that Katanga's secession had ended and that, "the action had been taken to prevent civil war between Katangese and Central Government troops who planned an invasion." He was thus implying that the operation was mandated by paragraph A-1 of the February 21 resolution. This clause did allow the use of force to "prevent civil war," but only as a last resort. It did not warrant the ending of Katanga's secession by force even in order to forestall an invasion by the Government.

It seems, in fact, that some UN officials had tried to implement the resolution adopted at a secret session of the Congolese Parliament on September 8, as though that had been part of the Security Council mandate. Tshombe told a news conference on September 9 that the National Parliament had called for suspension of the Katangese Government, arrest of its Ministers including Tshombe, arrival of a special Leopoldville envoy to take control of Katanga, removal of the Katangese Assembly, and disarming of Katanga's army by UN troops.

This plan resembled closely Dr. O'Brien's account of instructions given him by another UN official, Mr. Khiari, on September 10. Many of these instructions were in fact carried out during the following days, though it appears, on Dr. O'Brien's own showing, that no one outside Elisabethville, including Hammarskjold, knew of them. The Secretary General is reported to have wanted only the radio station and the post office in Elisabethville to be occupied and authorized the action in the belief that those points could be taken over with little if any bloodshed.

A different explanation was given by Dr. Linner in the official UN report of September 14 (S 4940), which claimed that the Katanga operation was undertaken in order to evacuate the mercenaries in compliance with the February 21 resolution and that force had been used in self-defense, the UN firing back only after being fired on.

Even this report indicated that the UNF had orders to occupy not only the post office and radio station, but also the headquarters of the Katangese gendarmerie, which could have been gained only by UNF's taking a "military initiative" for which there was no precedent short of the Korean War. On a strict view of the Charter, an enforcement measure from the Security Council would have been needed.

In this way the inconclusive action of September 13, followed as it was by the death of Dag Hammarskjold, an exacting and scrupulous observer of legalities, may prove to have ended the restriction of non-involvement with which he had bound United Nations forces. The "active" policy in September suggests the following inferences: the breakdown in the chain of command seems to show that the UN had no adequate control over its military forces; the unmandated and unauthorized operation that resulted could be fatal as a precedent.

While the press has exaggerated if not indeed invented the "defeat" of the UNF at Elisabethville, the results of the operation were at best inconclusive. Much of the UN's discomfiture could be blamed on the vagueness of the mandate. There was no directive from the Security Council as to how much and in what way the UN troops could use "force" as prescribed in paragraph A-1 of the February 21 resolution. The troops were still under restriction to fire only in self-defense, and were limited to defensive weapons. The UNF's military initiative was further handicapped by having to weigh humanitarian principles against its military advantage.

Britain and France objected to the UN's using force in Katanga as soon as the UNF went into action in September. Britain in particular was blamed for refusal at a crucial time of the fighting to permit three Ethiopian jet fighters on their way to the United Nations forces in Katanga to land and refuel in Uganda, and for her active agitation for a cease-fire; but it is likely that Hammarskjold decided independently to end the fighting, in order to stop bloodshed.

The provisional cease-fire was negotiated on September 20, 1961, after the Secretary General's death, to take effect from 12:01 A.M. on September 21st. Largely due to his holding the UN's Irish garrison captured at Jadotville, Tshombe was able to exact, on October 13, a protocol implementation of the cease-fire agreement which required the United Nations to give up all the points it had occupied during the fighting. Tshombe proclaimed that he had won a victory over the United Nations.

The mandate had not been abandoned, but the United Nations had no immediate opportunity to regain prestige. It was not till after U Thant had been elected Acting Secretary General on November 3 that the Congo question came under review before the Security Council meeting on the 13th.

It is now pertinent to ask, since Katanga was the major threat to stability in the Congo, how the United Nations should have dealt with that problem. It seems that Hammarskjold's policy of non-forcible diplomacy had not succeeded. But the military initiative of September 13 had neither eliminated mercenaries nor ended Katanga's secession. The principal difficulty, the UNF having to fight with "a hand tied behind its back," is inherent in the nature of UN forces. A more determined bid for victory might have been made, but there are many types of military action which if used by a UN force would cause mass withdrawals from the Organization and possibly counter-measures against it. In general, the difficulty in getting the UN Security Council members to agree to clear-cut mandates involving the use of force, and particularly to vote "enforcement measures," underlines the limitations imposed on the UN as a stabilizing factor in situations such as the Congo.

On November 13, Ceylon, Liberia, and the U.A.R. presented a draft resolution which the Security Council adopted after amendment. Its key clauses showed that the Afro-Asians believed that UNOC's mandate to deal with the mercenaries needed strengthening, and that an explicit mandate was needed to end Katanga's secession.

Britain feared the consequences both of a further empowering of UNF to use force, and opposed UNOC's receiving a mandate to conduct a patently political intervention. In this she differed from the United States whose concern was chiefly to eliminate the pro-Communist movement (as Washington regarded it) of Lumumbists in Orientale, and who therefore proposed amendments to deal with the "secession of Orientale and Kivu." On November 21 Sir Patrick Dean found himself opposed to two of the clauses of the November 13 resolution, in the one case because it did not remove the objectionable reference to "use of force," and in the other because it proposed to authorize the Secretary General to "remove or prevent the use for military purposes" of aircraft and other weapons of war, an action which Dean thought would provoke the Katangese. Yet he announced that if all United States amendments were adopted (three were defeated) he would vote for the resolution. As they were not, Britain and France, who later criticized its implementation, did not veto the resolution but merely abstained. The Council thus issued on November 24 a resolution which was certainly ill-drafted, probably *ultra vires* of the Charter, and was not invoked in the actions undertaken by the UN in the following months. For the December 1961 operation in Katanga was undertaken in the name of self-defense and the January 1962 operation against Gizenga in Orientale was taken under a pre-November mandate. Nevertheless, U Thant, in his first address to the Security Council on November 24, endorsed forcible intervention against secession and in support of the Central government on the basis of the February "civil war" clause. So was buried the "non-intervening" policy of Dag Hammarskjold and with it perhaps his scruples about compliance with the Charter. For though the Security Council never invoked the "enforcement measures" of Articles 39, 41, or 42, U Thant's remarks might be taken to establish a precedent for UN military action, under the Security Council but without invocation of the "enforcement" Articles, in aid of *de jure* governments bothered by possibly peaceable secessionists.

Second UN Armed Action

In Katanga, the situation after the September fiasco had steadily deteriorated, and on the afternoon of December 5, the Katangese and the UN forces clashed once again. The immediate occasion was the setting up of road blocks in Elisabethville by the Katangese gendarmerie, according to a plan drawn up by the mercenary officers to "strangle" the UN in and around Elisabethville. The second Katanga operation was fought by the United Nations in thirteen days to a successful conclusion.

As in September, the outbreak of fighting provoked an outcry from some governments and newspapers of Western Europe against the use of force by the United Nations. In order to justify the operation, which he intended to pursue to victory, U Thant fell back on the one undisputed right of the UN troops to employ force, the right of self-defense. In Katanga, this was no mere pretext, and U Thant went out of his way to deny that the action had in view political ends of any sort. But under the guise of self-defense the Secretary General or the UN Command may misuse force in a way not intended by the Security Council or implied by the mandate.

When the UN renewed an earlier request to Britain for twenty-four 1,000 pound bombs to be used in Katanga, rebellion in the Tory ranks caused the UK Government to reverse its decision and to suspend the delivery, and on December 13 to lodge with the UN a formal note requesting an immediate cease-fire. U Thant rejected this request, thanks to U.S. military and political support which, in view of British reservations, proved indispensable. The U.S. also gave the United Nations, after the fighting started, 21 Globemaster transport planes which airlifted thousands of UN troops and large quantities of equipment into the fighting zone in Katanga from other parts of the Congo and from overseas. However, neither America nor Britain insisted upon expulsion of the mercenaries.

During the fighting, the U.S. consulted with U Thant, and assisted in the negotiating of a settlement between Tshombe and Adoula. As a result, an eight-point declaration was signed by Tshombe on December 21, at the Kitona base. The prominent American role in the Kitona negotiations raises the question whether the UN and its servants should ever accept the mediatory assistance of Great Powers in the implementing of mandates which have been laid upon the Secretary General. The answer seems to be that sometimes there is nothing else for it. The

United Nations is not a sovereign Power. In Congo-like situations the Secretary General has no authority to accept a surrender, dictate a peace treaty, or take over administration of a defeated state. But one possible alternative might have been to invite the Congolese Central Government to send in troops and take over the administration.

Did the United States intervention improperly influence the decisions of the Acting Secretary General and his subordinates? Just after the hostilities began, the *New York Times* reported that U Thant was preparing a plan to implement the November resolution involving a house-to-house search by UN troops to seize and thus prevent Katangese soldiers and mercenaries from re-entering Katanga service. Furthermore, the Central Government had signed an agreement with the UN on November 27 which among other provisions enabled the UNOC to hand over for trial to the Congolese authorities any mercenaries apprehended. Some commentators were to be found who suggested following the hold-fire instructions given by the Secretary General on December 18 that he had been persuaded by the U.S. against a more thoroughgoing military action.

If in fact the United Nations was sacrificing lives to achieve something that fell short of the mandate because the Western Powers were demanding an operation of "limited" character, then Security Council resolutions appear to be less determinative, and the Secretariat more responsive than the Charter warrants to pressures from Powers acting outside the Council. If, on the other hand, mercenaries were by December 17 already scattering into the Katanga countryside, part of the point of the UN operation was disappearing with them. In that case the Acting Secretary General in bringing the fighting to a halt is not to be arraigned for having acceded to improper pressures.

On his return to Elisabethville, Tshombe tried to invalidate the Kitona agreement, claiming that it was subject to ratification by the Katanga government and the Assembly, and that he had been pressured into signing it. Indeed a large-scale military engagement must involve some political consequences whether intended or incidental. Thus, the December action and its results may have indicated how in future a United Nations force while engaging in defensive operations may also become an instrument for enforcing political solutions, which may or may not be consistent with peace-keeping and the other provisions of the Charter.

U Thant told the Advisory Council on January 9 that even after the Katangese resistance collapsed, the UN forces were tied down in Elisabethville in an effort to eliminate sniping and to restore normal life to the city, and could not undertake a new major operation against mercenaries who had departed to other parts of Katanga. Moreover, he argued that had the United Nations persisted with military action in order to pursue the mercenaries, the Kitona talks would not have taken place; and that to resume the fighting might cause Tshombe to disavow the Kitona declaration.

Only the Soviet Union was bent on pressing the Secretariat to use force to carry out this part of the mandate. Russia called a Security Council meeting that convened against the wishes of the Congolese Government on January 30. A motion to adjourn the Council *sine die* was opposed only by Russia and her satellite Romania, while Ghana and the U.A.R., the two radical African powers, abstained. Meanwhile the United Nations was seeking, on the one hand to improve relations with the Katanga authorities, and on the other to cut off foreign political and military support for Tshombe which was said to come from Rhodesia and the Belgian controlled mining company, Union Miniere.

To stop the alleged flow of men and materials across Katanga's border, U Thant suggested to the UK and Portugal on December 29 and 30, respectively, that United Nations observers be stationed at a few selected airports and roads leading from Rhodesia and Angola into Katanga. However, both Governments refused. The Secretary General stressed that no charges attached to Angola, but he refused to accept the Rhodesian denial.

It had been alleged by the Afro-Asians present at the November Security Council meeting that the Union Miniere not only financed the Tshombe regime but also manufactured equipment and provided personnel from among its employees to fight the United Nations. This was confirmed in the December UN reports of the fighting. To prevent directly such enterprises from supporting Tshombe would have exceeded the UN's authority since it had not resolved upon enforcement measures even had some of their activities fallen under the anti-civil war ban of paragraph A-1 of the February resolution.

The U.S. therefore undertook the task of persuading the Union Miniere directors to change their company's policy toward the Central Government. Withdrawal of the Union Miniere support from Tshombe might have been sufficient to end the secession of Katanga. The problem of Union Miniere like that of the mercenaries and the illegal traffickers in armaments points to serious weaknesses in the UN as a peacekeeper in ex-colonial situations.

Antoine Gizenga, Lumumbist leader of Orientale, and one of two Vice-Premiers in the Central Government, held no office in the provincial administration, but had spent most of the time since his election in

Stanleyville ignoring frequent summonses to return to his post. It was feared in the West that he was planning a secession or attempting a left-wing takeover of the Central Government, possibly with Soviet assistance, and using the Katanga issue as a lever.

Third UN Armed Action

On January 13, 1962 fighting broke out between Gizenga's gendarmes and the Central Government troops, and the Government called for UN assistance. The Secretary General ruled that the UN would assist the Central Government under the mandate directing the UN to maintain law and order and under paragraph A-1 of the February 21 resolution empowering the UN to use force to prevent civil war in the Congo, thus making UNF participation a clearly political action. This may have had no very startling effect on the future of the Congo. Only one platoon of UN forces took part and did not fire a single shot throughout the operation. But the Secretary General's ruling had for the first time involved the UN in a joint operation with Government against rebels. Whereas Hammarskjold seems to have maintained to the end that the use of force by the UN could and should be restricted to prevention of conflict and should not tilt the balance against any particular faction, U Thant had contended on November 24 that the UN's mandate to "avert civil war," if necessary by force, entailed a "sympathetic attitude" toward the Central Government's efforts at suppression of secessionist activity.

The curious thing is that U Thant invoked this mandate against Gizenga but not against Tshombe. Yet he did not have in reserve against Gizenga the explicit direction to end secession which the November 24 resolution had given him against Tshombe. On the contrary, the United States' attempt to authorize UN action against Gizenga as secessionist had been defeated by the Security Council in November.

Gizenga who, on January 15, 1962, was deposed from his Vice-Premiership by a motion of censure adopted in the Congolese Parliament, requested that UN troops replace the ANC guards outside his residence. However, it seems possible that the UN, in guarding him, went beyond the arrangements necessary for his safety. At the request of the Congolese authorities he was flown into Leopoldville on a UN plane where he was put under UN protection, officially as a "guest" but actually under heavy guard. When he requested on January 22 that this protection be lifted, he did not become a free agent, but in the words of the UN report the protection ". . . is now therefore, left to the Central Government." The London *Observer* described the situation as "protective custody."

It is not clear by what right the UN extended "protection" on behalf of and with the consent of the host government. It certainly has no right, except when taking "enforcement measures" never employed in the Congo, to imprison on its own behalf the dissident political leaders of a member state. The Acting Secretary General's assistance to the Central Government in Orientale certainly stood in sharp contrast with the UN's relationship to the Government during the Katanga operation of December 1961, and during earlier actions of Hammarskjold's regime.

Fourth UN Armed Action

On December 28, 1962, in reply to fire from Katangese gendarmerie in Elisabethville, the United Nations Force took a fourth military action. There are reasons to suppose that the UN had for some time contemplated use of force as a last resort. A UN plan for unifying Katanga with the rest of the Congo drawn up by U Thant in September 1962 failed to gain the necessary support among the interested Powers in spite of the U.S. lobbying in its favor. In October and November a UN military plan, to be used against Katanga was said to be in preparation should the U.S. fail in its efforts.

The nature of the military plan was disclosed by Dr. Ralph J. Bunche in a report on quite a different matter:

A plan of operations to achieve freedom of movement for UNOC throughout Katanga in the event of a continued denial of this freedom by Katangese authorities, which would also ensure the elimination of mercenaries and assist national unity, was devised in the course of consultations involving Mr. Gardiner, the Force Commander, General Prem Chand and myself during my visit to Leopoldville in October of last year. That plan was subsequently approved by you for ultimate execution, if all non-military efforts finally failed.

The first phase of that plan had unexpectedly been activated on 28 December . . .

By late November, Tshombe had evidently managed to avoid participation in the Thant plan. The Adoula Government, in danger of being overthrown by the pro-Gizengist opposition and under pressure to adopt more drastic policies against Katanga, joined the U.S. in supporting the more stringent provisions of the Thant plan, notably to boycott Katangese exports of copper and cobalt should the Tshombe regime refuse to settle with the Adoula Government. Britain and

France remained opposed to this provision, but early in autumn Belgium agreed conditionally on a boycott with the U.S. and West Germany.

Late in October Washington's policy had shifted, in view of the Western Allies' reservations, to the line associated with McGhee, Under-Secretary of State for Political Affairs. There were reports of a McGhee-Spaak plan to allow Katanga better than the 50:50 division of Union Miniere revenue formerly proposed, and greater autonomy than that offered in the constitution projected in the Thant plan. A proposal to modify the latter and to send a UN mission to the Congo was made by McGhee to Thant on November 28th. Officially the U.S. still supported the Thant plan, but was now reported to doubt the wisdom of its program of sanctions against Katanga. Yet the McGhee line risked undermining Adoula's Administration. In October it was said the Russian government had offered Congolese politicians transport and fighter support, should they reject UNOC as a failure. McGhee's views were reported to be "getting small visible acceptance in the Secretariat of the UN and the Congo advisory group."

The policy was officially reversed when a UN spokesman on December 1 dismissed consideration of the McGhee plan and on December 3 the U.S. began assisting a UN military build-up and resumed its airlift, carrying equipment and personnel into the Congo and from Leopoldville to Elisabethville. One week later Robert Gardiner in a letter to Tshombe announced that phases II–IV of the Thant plan, including the economic provisions, would be applied against the Katangese secessionists: although the UNF was a "peace force which was at war with no one and would take no offensive military action," it "would vigorously use its weapons if attacked, and would henceforth take such protective measures as it might deem necessary to prevent recurrence of attacks." By December 14 U Thant had supported Adoula's previous approach to 17 interested Governments asking them to forbid Katangese imports of copper and cobalt. This enterprise failed after a Conservative backbenchers' motion in the Commons had called for prevention by a Security Council initiative of the coercing of Katanga. Belgium and France were also opposed to sanctions. The Nassau communique of December 21, and President Kennedy's remarks about the Congo at his press conference on New Year's Eve, evinced a conflict between Washington's intention to help the UN and the Adoula Government by terminating Katanga's secession, and other Western Allies' mistrust of sanctions and of UN military action. By mid-December U Thant seems to have been building up the UNF with wholehearted U.S. assistance, for a test of strength against Katanga.

President Kennedy, on December 18, directed a U.S. military team—the Truman mission to the Congo—to investigate how much additional military equipment should be supplied to the UN. U Thant did not favor the mission. Russian bloc delegates maintained that the U.S. was interfering as a Great Power in the Congo, thus violating Security Council resolutions. The Congolese Parliamentary Opposition interpreted it as setting up a U.S. base in the Congo, which would soon become active outside the UN. However, the most that can fairly be said against the mission is that its checking of UN requirements on the spot implied a tactless mistrust of the UN's own assessments.

How should we judge the UN's posture on the eve of the final military conflict in Katanga? The Bunche military plan itself could be regarded merely as a sensible contingency precaution. But its declared objectives were hardly in keeping with the spirit of the mandate, at least as formerly understood by Hammarskjold and by others who shared his scruples. One objective was to achieve "freedom of movement for UNOC throughout Katanga." Though Hammarskjold's report of July 18, 1960 mentions "freedom of movement" as a necessary requirement for the deployment of a UNF, U Thant and his staff were obviously giving the phrase a much wider connotation. Secondly, the Security Council resolutions of February 21, 1961 and November 24, 1961 did not authorize the use of force for ending secession, yet the Bunche plan of operations specified that it "would also ensure the elimination of mercenaries and assist national unity . . . if all non-military efforts finally failed." The UN military build-up during December; the evident anxiety of the Secretary General and the U.S. Administration to see an end of Katanga's secession; and the Bunche plan of military operations make the reiterated claims of the Secretariat that no military or political intervention was intended seem quite disingenuous.

No member of the Security Council took the trouble to convoke it on the matter of the UNF's latest military initiative. However, Washington because of its positive support for U Thant's policy, bears more responsibility than the others. The build-up of late 1962 and the subsequent operations of December and January did nothing to restore the UN's name for impartial arbitration, scrupulous adherence to the principles of the Charter or respect for mandates; but it may instead have gained some reputation as an effective preserver of international order in post-colonial situations particularly if supported by a major power such as the United States.

The fighting that began around Elisabethville on Christmas Eve caused few casualties, and had ceased by December 29—elsewhere in

Katanga, except toward Jadotville—by New Year's Eve. UN ground-force action seems, at least after the onset, to have been unexception-able: they had been heavily attacked, and their riposte could have been regarded as a mandated action in self-defense. But the accom-panying air-strikes (on the 29th against the Kolwezi-Kengere airfield, and on the 30th at Kamatanda airfield close to Jadotville) obliterated the Katangese airforce and thus may be criticized as having taken the UN beyond strict requirements of self-defense.

A near-contradiction between two instructions, both telegraphed from UN Headquarters on December 30, allowed Indian troops to occupy Jadotville unopposed on January 3, after a brilliant operation at the Lufira river on the Jadotville road. The Secretary General had issued a statement on New Year's Eve from UN Headquarters in New York alleging that fighting had ceased, that UN forces had acted only "in self-defense . . . to protect their security and their freedom of move-ment." Three days before, however, he had informed President Tshombe that UNOC presences in Jadotville, Kolwezi, and Kipushi would have to be established. The GOC Katanga and the officers of the victorious Indian regiment evidently interpreted their instruction as ordering implementation of the Second Phase of the pre-arranged military plan. They could not have been expected to anticipate the UN's emerging political reasons for deciding, about New Year's Day, to hold back from the capture of Jadotville. British and Belgian authorities had been seeking assurance of a cease-fire and safe conduct for Tshombe. U Thant was determined not to have this final operation interpreted as "intervention in political affairs" or a military victory. Immediately after the occupation of Jadotville he sent Dr. Bunche to Leopoldville to investigate the "serious breakdown in effective com-munication between the United Nations Headquarters and the Leo-poldville Office." Dr. Bunche, reporting on January 10, recommended clarification of military initiatives requiring prior clearance by UN civilian officers; improved and more frequent field reports, preferably by officers specially detached from UNOC Headquarters; and the assignment of a high-level liaison officer to assist the civilian UN Officer-in-Charge. These recommendations, though sound and already called for in 1962, did not touch upon the problem of political control of UN Headquarters itself, nor upon the desirability of an effective policing agreement with the host country, as recommended in the conclusions of the present chapter.

After the capture of Jadotville even the Powers comparatively sympa-thetic to Katanga, such as Belgium and Britain, were working in various ways for an assurance from the Katangese Government that the scorched earth policy threatened by Tshombe would be abandoned and Katanga peacefully integrated into the Congo. Above all Union Miniere on January 8 took fright and appealed to all responsible parties to cooperate in measures to prevent sabotage in Kolwezi. With this collapse of his support Tshombe finally agreed to respect UN freedom of movement and on January 15, in a letter to Adoula and U Thant, announced his readiness to proclaim the end of Katanga's secession and his willingness to direct the means of applying the Thant plan. On January 21 the UN occupied the last stronghold of the gendarmerie—Kolwezi.

LESSONS OF THE CONGO EXPERIENCE

How far has the UN effort in the Congo succeeded in bringing peace and stability? By January 1963, the UN had implemented only in part the very first mandate of July 14, 1960, that is, to enable "the national security forces . . . to meet fully their task." The principal reasons for this delay were political, regional, and tribal conflicts in the Congo itself.

Chief of these disruptive movements was secession, particularly in Katanga. The United Nations leadership considered that until the Republic of the Congo was made politically viable by solving this and all other divisive conflicts, there would be continued danger of foreign intervention.

Afro-Asian Powers have tried throughout the Congo crisis to make the Charter's concern for "political independence and territorial integrity" serve not only against any kind of foreign intervention but also against Katanga's secession. In the Security Council even more effectively than in the Assembly, they promoted the debate about the scope of UNOC; for the Charter narrowly restricts the UN's rights of intervention in internal politics. Should the United Nations concern itself with the problems of secession? Should force be used if secession were judged undesirable? Hammarskjold and U Thant, the two Secretary Generals who held office during the Congo crisis, differed in answering these two main questions. U Thant seems to hold that all secessionist movements are deplorable, and that the UNF may properly take armed action against them. However, neither Secretary General had explicitly ordered the use of force to end Katanga's secession, although they agreed that its continuance was inadvisable.

In November 1961, the Afro-Asians succeeded in getting through the Council a resolution that, while not authorizing the UN to use force against Tshombe, formally condemned Katanga's secession. Did its substance violate domestic jurisdiction provisions of Article 2 (7) of the Charter? As the resolution did not mention Articles 39, 41, or 42 and was therefore not an "enforcement measure," Article 2 (7) was not overridden. Did then clauses 1, 3, and 8 of the resolution, which variously deplore or prohibit the secession of Katanga, amount to violation of Article 2 (7)? In other words, is it proper for the UN and in particular for the Security Council, in the absence of "enforcement measures," to take any formal cognizance of secessionist activity?

If the secession were being supported by the intervention of a foreign *state*, the Security Council could have acted under Articles 39, 41, and 42. But the objects of any such UN action should be to prevent foreign intervention and not to suppress the secession per se.

In Katanga, by November 1961, *individuals* and *groups*, but not states were intervening. Since no aggression had been determined by the Security Council, nor "enforcement measures" adopted, the frequent allegations of foreign intervention in support of Katanga's secession could not justify the UN's proceeding against it. The same argument would apply to the anti-civil war clause of the resolution of February 21. Both the Soviet Union and some Afro-Asians wished to construe it as a mandate for the UNF to subdue Katanga. But the UN, short of adopting "enforcement measures," could not with propriety implement a mandate for suppression of civil war between secessionist and anti-secessionist forces, to suppress the secessionist party. Nor did paragraph A-1 of the February 21 resolution enjoin or suggest such a procedure.

However, no resolution went so far as to authorize employment of force to unify the country. Yet force was used four times by the UNF in the Congo. How was it authorized? Did it achieve its several objectives?

The Katanga operation of September 1961 seems to have been a result of a mistake or a misappropriation of authority. In December of that year a second Katanga action was conducted in terms of self-defense; the January 1962 action in Stanleyville was justified principally as an anti-civil-war measure; and the final Katanga operation of December 1962–January 1963, fought in the name of "freedom of movement" for the UN, ended the secession of that province. The first Katanga operation ended in a stalemate. The political results of the other three actions resembled more closely those envisaged in the U.S. proposals that had been overridden than the spirit of the resolutions passed at the November meeting of the council. In repressing the secessions of both Stanleyville and Katanga, the UNOC which had set out to prevent foreign intervention in the Congo's internal conflicts, ended by itself forcibly intervening in them.

It may be that any intranational operation by the UN will have some propensity to follow the same course. Unless UN forces can seal the national borders, they must act against the intervening foreigner at that point within the nation where his intervention is taking effect, that is, against the movement which he is supporting. But once the UN has become involved in struggle against internal forces it may have to see the internal conflict through, even though external intervention is no longer a threat. This problem illustrates among other things the difficulties of conducting an intranational operation without infringing the Charter's reservations about domestic jurisdiction. Could a mechanism be devised to counter this tendency for a UN action against foreign intervention turning into intervention by the UN and the Powers supporting it? Hammarskjold had tried in his "Summary Study" of 1958 to devise from precedent, UNF experience, and the philosophy of the Charter, a set of principles and policy that could be embodied in Agreements with the host state. It may be possible to devise a type of agreement in which the host country would temporarily authorize the UN to take responsibility for the host's entire security both internal and external, while abstaining from even diplomatic participation in its non-violent political conflicts.

Unlike Hammarskjold, U Thant seems to favor UN military initiatives that have *political* objectives. The events of December 1962–January 1963 suggest that military action can be effective if the UN has predominance of force. This impression is correct only in part. While it is certain the UN's victory was much hastened by the determined air strike that eliminated the Katangese air force, the ground operations of the UN were not particularly overwhelming in numbers of troops employed. What seems to have been decisive was the influx of first-class means of military transport, which made it evident that UN forces could actually achieve the province-wide "freedom of movement" that they were seeking. This kind of equipment would be indispensable also in a purely policing UN action.

The last Katanga operation showed that the UN found no major difficulties in terminating operations conducted for political ends, although it seems to have made no prior arrangements anywhere in Katanga (despite its phased plan for occupation of towns) either for the legal surrender of towns or for the taking of prisoners except in the case of mercenaries. In the earlier diplomatic phase of the Thant plan, however, the absence of a termination procedure for UNOC as a whole enabled Tshombe to temporize.

In the last three military operations in the Congo, it seems that much initiative was exercised by the Secretary General. Since November 1961 the U.S. and the Western Powers seem to have acquiesced in U Thant's avoidance of any further recourse to the Security Council. This development has much affected the control of UN forces that have been entirely at the disposal of the Secretary General—a contrast with Hammarskjold's deference, even while he was enlarging the scope and responsibilities of the Secretary Generalship, to the authority and consensus of the Security Council. The Secretariat has acted in increasing freedom from the mandates, as well as from Security Council consensus since September 1961, when much trouble was taken after the event to make the action appear to accord with Security Council and General Assembly resolutions. In December 1961 it was thought sufficient to invoke the right of self-defense. But in December 1962 no mandate or resolution was specifically invoked. This kind of tendency may be unavoidable in the later stages of the United Nations operation whose presiding officer, the Secretary General, cannot readily be called to account by UN members.

Should the Central Government without further outside assistance succeed in maintaining the unity of the Congo, the proponents of forceful UN action may be able to salvage a victory of prestige for the organization: it may appear to be an ideal instrument for transforming post-colonial situations to the shape desired by the Afro-Asian Powers. This approximates one of Hammarskjold's objectives—a vindication of the Organization as the peculiar guardian and servant of the newer and smaller nations. But Hammarskjold would not allow it to be merely an instrument of power politics for any groups of nations, nor to contravene the Charter's provisions or the principles and the precedents he had worked to establish. By his Congo venture of July–September 1960, he had attempted a consistent *extension* of those precedents to intranational situations, but the logic of events in the Congo has meanwhile rendered that extension inconsistent at least with the principles laid down in Hammarskjold's "Summary Study" of the Suez, Lebanese, and Jordanian affairs.

In our view, something like a new "Summary study" is called for, by which the Secretariat should demonstrate how UN forces could be used effectively in future intranational operations while maintaining Hammarskjold's standards of impartiality and objectivity.

Above all, it will be essential for the Secretariat to insist that UN Members, party to such agreements as those concerning West New Guinea and Cuba, adhere strictly to the commitments they make under United Nations aegis. Permanent Members of the Security Council also would be well advised to help restore the Organization's reputation for consistency, and resist temptations to exploit it for short-term national advantage.

On the credit side, a combination of UN presence, protest from the Secretary General, and firm but polite opposition from Afro-Asians on the Security Council and the General Assembly, brought to an end intervention by countries of the Soviet bloc, and secured the withdrawal of official Belgian forces in three months—a record favorably comparable with the withdrawal of British, French, and Israeli forces after Suez.

Though the UNF was unable to prevent a number of tribal massacres and some civil war in the Congo, and though in the end it had to take military initiatives itself, the number of lives lost in the course of establishing a newly independent nation of fourteen million people does not compare badly with lives lost in other ex-colonial situations, for example, India and Pakistan.

The final outcome is still uncertain: whether the UN presence will help to establish a stable and viable Congo.

Index

291